A Devil of a Whipping

A Devil of a Whipping
The Battle of Cowpens
Lawrence E. Babits

The University of North Carolina Press

Chapel Hill & London

© 1998

The University of North Carolina Press

All rights reserved

Manufactured in the United States of America

The paper in this book meets the guidelines for
permanence and durability of the Committee on
Production Guidelines for Book Longevity of the
Council on Library Resources.

Library of Congress
Cataloging-in-Publication Data

Babits, Lawrence Edward.

A devil of a whipping: the Battle of Cowpens /
Lawrence E. Babits.

   p.   cm.

Includes bibliographical references (p.   ) and index.

ISBN 978-0-8078-2434-4 (cloth : alk. paper)

ISBN 978-0-8078-4926-2 (pbk. : alk. paper)

1. Cowpens, Battle of, 1781. I. Title.

E241.C9B33   1998

973.3'37—dc21   98-13059

   CIP

To

Ernest W. Peterkin

historian, teacher, gentleman

1920–1995

Peter Thorbahn

historian, archaeologist, teacher

1946–1987

The private soldiers of the 21st Infantry, U.S. Army,

who died

1963–1973

contents

Maps

Photographs, Tables, and Figures

Preface

Although a very short battle, Cowpens was an important turning point in the Revolutionary War. The engagement was the finest American tactical demonstration of the war. The battle caught the American public's imagination because it came after large-scale victories left the British in nominal control of the Deep South. After Cowpens, Major General Charles, the Earl Cornwallis, was deprived of his light troops. He reduced his baggage to pursue Brigadier General Daniel Morgan's force, and then Major General Nathanael Greene's southern army, only to run his own army into the ground. The impact of Cowpens on the manpower and the psyche of the British army was immense and helped lead to the Yorktown surrender.

Despite its impact at the time, Cowpens is not well known today. This is unfortunate because it is significant as a tactical masterpiece. Compared with Lexington, Concord, and Yorktown, Cowpens receives little attention from historians or the American public. This omission may be due to a concentration on Washington and his campaigns, especially by northern historians, yet Cowpens helped create the Yorktown victory.

Contemporary and historical accounts about the battle vary. In particular, conflicting claims about numbers are a primary clue to a different battle than has traditionally been reported. Both Morgan and Lieutenant Colonel Banastre Tarleton minimized their own numbers and enlarged their opponent's. There was no reason to pursue this until Bobby G. Moss published his compilation of data relating to the battle.[1] A simple matter of addition and a basic knowledge of statistics confirmed glaring discrepancies between official statements and actual American numbers.

Final stimulation to work on Cowpens came from the brilliant work by Douglas Scott and Richard Fox. Assigned to investigate the battlefield at Little Bighorn National Monument, they located artifacts, excavated, and computerized their data. Their work did not change the battle's outcome, but the new details challenged traditional interpretations about how Custer met his end.[2] Cowpens cannot be investigated the same way because eighteenth-century weapons technology was different. At Cowpens, the many written accounts from both sides make its interpretation easier than that of the battle of the Little Bighorn, where only Indians survived to tell what happened.

Cowpens is unusual for an American Revolutionary War battle. A small, quick fight with immense impact, Cowpens is fairly well documented because it was recognized as a turning point in the war. Primary records make it possible to study this engagement using participant observations. Obscure published documents and the long unutilized pension records provide a new opportunity and good reasons for reexamining the battle. The combination of well-known accounts, lesser-known documentary materials, including the pension records, makes reevaluation of Cowpens necessary, especially since the most-used published accounts were often taken out of the battle's chronological and spatial contexts.

The starting point was Bobby G. Moss's *Patriots at the Cowpens*.[3] Utilizing letters, memoirs, official reports, and pension applications, Moss listed more than 950 Americans who served, or probably served, at Cowpens. While some names were later eliminated, nearly thirty Marylanders and forty Delawares were added. Even with deletions, there were more names than Morgan's official strength at Cowpens. Since pension records represent only those who survived the battle and lived an additional forty years, Morgan had far more men than he claimed. Computerizing the pension data allowed examination of details such as the number in each battle line, militia organization, company positions, and individual soldiers' locations. In some cases, casualty types and locations illuminated previously unsuspected battle segments.

Even though Cowpens was documented by contemporaries[4] and following generations, a new study is necessary because most secondary accounts rely heavily on earlier historians and very few participant accounts.[5] Virtually every writer quoted a few first-person accounts, often without citing them. In most cases, however, statements were taken out of chronological order without regard for battlefield location.[6] No author used all published sources or attempted to resolve differences of chronology and tactics. Furthermore, most recent writers tend to present the southern campaign within a broader context, such as overall strategy in the war or Loyalists.[7] Cowpens then becomes only a small segment of a campaign.

Two historians provide alternative ways of reporting combat. S. L. A. Marshall pioneered battle analysis by examining small units during World War II, Korea, and Vietnam. Marshall used post-battle interviews to create a consensus of what happened. He then drew conclusions about improving American combat effectiveness.[8] John Keegan studied war from a detailed chronological perspective, and his first work, *The Face of Battle*, articulated his approach. Keegan reduced battles to increments of time and types of combat. Using participant accounts, he reconstructed and reinterpreted battles using documentary sources to provide information about types of fighting, states of mind, and unit cohesion. His interpretations resulted in a better understanding of medieval, Napoleonic, and World War I combat.[9]

I tried to integrate both the Marshall and Keegan approaches by treating participant accounts as if they were post-battle interviews. Once a computer organized pension information into categories such as arrival time, wounds, and company commanders, patterns involving groups of men were linked to other narrative accounts. Following Keegan's model, I divided Cowpens into chronological elements to provide viewpoints at specific times and places during the battle.

Participants' details often seem to be in conflict with other contemporary and later accounts. This conflict is misleading. A person saw events from his own perspective based on rank, field position, and perception of time. An officer on horseback, for example, saw more than a private standing in ranks. An officer probably had better knowledge of the planned battle and, later, what actually happened. A private usually remembered things that concerned him directly, or that struck him as notable.[10] Once all accounts were ordered into a coherent chronology, and observers were located on the battlefield, most conflicts resolved and actions became comprehensible.

Cowpens documents can be grouped into several categories. They include eyewitness accounts, secondary accounts by people in direct association with participants shortly after the battle, historians who wrote accounts while participants were living and who corresponded with veterans, participants who wrote memoirs sometime after the battle, and, finally, the pensioners.

An eyewitness was limited by what a soldier could see and his knowledge of the fighting. Lieutenant Roderick MacKenzie and others had clear bias and slanted their accounts to suit their own purposes. Knowing MacKenzie hated Banastre Tarleton makes his commentary valuable for details mentioned in passing and unrelated to his attack on Tarleton. Others, including Sergeant Major William Seymour, Lieutenant Thomas Anderson, and Lieutenant Colonel Banastre Tarleton, presented what they knew as accurately as they could. Later, battle recollections were written by Lieutenant Colonel John Eager Howard and Lieutenant James Simons in response to questions about the battle or to support a veteran's pension application.[11]

Some secondary authors wrote about Cowpens with knowledge acquired from participants soon after the fighting occurred. All were military men with good reason to know what happened and why. These writers include George Hanger, Samuel Shaw, Charles Stedman, and Henry Lee. These writers had access to participants, and since they were still engaged in the conflict, they had a need to know from a tactical viewpoint.[12]

Histories written after the war ended, and later participant memoirs, form another group of battle records. Historical accounts written by William Gordon, David Ramsay, John Marshall, William Johnson, and William Moultrie include participants' information. Memoirs by Thomas Young, Joseph McJunkin, Christopher Brandon, and John Shaw include details not found in other accounts. These authors presented battle information, and errors were certain to draw criticism from eyewitnesses.[13]

Finally, there are the pension accounts. A very few, for badly injured and destitute soldiers, were compiled before 1810. More were recorded after the first pension act was enacted in 1818. Most, perhaps three-fourths, were drawn up during or after 1832 when the second pension act was passed more than fifty years after the battle. Sworn testimony is not free of bias. Veterans trying to demonstrate Revolutionary War service, often without discharge certificates and muster rolls, provided information about comrades, commanding officers, tours of duty, and battles. The passage of time affected memory, but many veterans carefully stated that their declarations were as best recollected.[14]

Even fifty years after the battle, with faulty recollection about dates and places and a tendency to enhance their own participation, sworn pension applications contain details that did not otherwise survive. Even with misspelled names and the wrong rank or date, most accounts fit into useful patterns and are valuable precisely because the information was not intended for historians. Personal comments had no bearing on whether or not a veteran obtained a pension. These "asides" presented in passing provided important details about Cowpens.

A single individual account is not as reliable as a whole range of statements in which several men identified the same commanding officers, approximate arrival time at Cowpens, and other soldiers in their companies. Recitation of details about commanders and tours of duty by one man is neither very important nor potentially very accurate. However, if a group of men residing in different locales in 1832 repeat virtually the same information, their mutual recollections have great validity for re-creating company and regimental organization that survived in no other form. More obviously accurate are statements that a veteran served as a Continental and not as a militiaman, that he volunteered or served as a substitute for someone who is named, or that it was his first, biggest, or only battle. If a veteran reported being wounded at Cowpens, a certain credibility must be given to his recollection for obvious reasons. Many pension applications include depositions containing additional details from former officers. Other supporting documents include statements by physicians who detailed war wounds and scars.

These crucial battle details are presented in passing to document Revolutionary War service. One man recalled that he saw Tarleton; another remembered Morgan's facial scar; a third noted he fired his rifle five times. Inserted into a battle chronology, the recollections bring the combat into focus and better explain what happened and why. Some accounts provide different versions of an incident, as can be seen by comparing Young's and Simons's descriptions of cavalry movement. While details had no real utility for determining pension eligibility, they enhance our understanding of what happened.

The original question about the number of Morgan's men has been answered. Tracing guns across the landscape was impossible; it could not be done because muskets used paper cartridges and rifle balls were patched with cloth. The patched bullets would not exhibit rifling, and there were no brass shell cases for firing-pin analysis, as with the Little Big Horn artifacts. Forensic information was simply not available even though ball size, buttons, and flint types may indicate battle lines or unreported battle episodes.[15]

Additional questions about what happened at certain times and places during the battle were raised. Where did the North Carolina militia go after the initial skirmishing; why were so many wounded by sabers if British dragoons never reached them? Why did South Carolina militiamen run across the battlefield directly toward dragoons they feared? How did forty British dragoons rout several hundred militiamen? What caused a "mistaken order" on the Continental right flank? What did American cavalry do and where? Did Tarleton's men really plunder his baggage and did he attack them? These questions guided research and resulted in a more accurate view of Cowpens than any study presented before.

Acknowledgments

This work is heavily indebted to Bobby G. Moss, Limestone College, Gaffney, South Carolina. He created the initial database of Cowpens participants. If it were not for his drudge work, this study would not be possible. Douglas Scott, National Park Service Midwest Regional Archaeological Center, and Richard A. Fox, Department of Anthropology, University of South Dakota, provided original stimulation with their work on the Custer battlefield. Doug and Rich freely shared information and provided guidance.

From 1967 to 1984, I was a member of the First Maryland Regiment, a group portraying the Revolutionary War Continental soldier. The experience provided practical information and experience about Revolutionary War soldier life. Regimental members William L. Brown III, Burton K. Kummerow, Ernest W. Peterkin, Ross M. Kimmell, Frederick C. Gaede, Michael Black, Thomas Murray, Luther Sowers, John D. Griffiths, Robert L. Klinger, Denis Reen, Jeremy Reen, and others from the "Swamp Platoon" and the "Musick" gave me insights and resources about the past. Many were veterans, and our exposure to Revolutionary War material culture, tactics, rates of fire, weapons accuracy, and the tedium of standing in ranks taught us more about the Revolutionary War's physical aspects. In the words of another war, we drank from the same canteen.

At Cowpens, National Park Service personnel helped greatly. Peter Givins answered questions and provided materials, maps, and encouragement. Patricia Ruff served as liaison during document research. She orchestrated logistics to copy documents at the Southeastern Regional Branch of the National Archives in Atlanta and provided a steady stream of questions about the battle.

At Armstrong State College in Savannah, Georgia, many people contributed to my research. Norman Crawford wrote a computer program to consolidate Cowpens pension data. The Department of History, especially Roger Warlick and Diane Wagner, provided supplies, communications, and encouragement during initial research. The Military Science Department provided a vehicle for a "staff ride" to Cowpens and encouraged continuing research into eighteenth-century military behavior. I wish to acknowledge William C. McManus, G. D. McAdams, and the cadets. Richard Leech created base maps and raised questions about tactics, landscape, and units at Cowpens.

National Archives personnel in Washington, D.C., and Atlanta provided important assistance. In particular, Michael P. Musick in Washington answered questions about the "other American war." In Atlanta, Gayle Peters and Charles Hughes answered detailed questions about the pension files. The Nathanael Greene Papers at the Rhode Island Historical Society provided many documents during my doctoral and Cowpens research projects. Richard K. Showman, Robert McCarthy, and Dennis Conrad answered questions and pointed out key materials. Dick was very helpful in granting access to the Greene papers, which created a thorough background on the southern campaign.

Three people guided me during my military service. George A. Ferguson, Robert M. Hansten, and David A. Hill taught me to soldier between November 1963 and March 1966. They provided key background for my First Maryland experience and Cowpens research. Today's army is not so different from the Continental Army, but I was probably more militiaman than regular during my tour with B Company, 1st Battalion, 21st Infantry "Gimlets."

Jim Rollins and Lynn Meyer provided housing in Atlanta. They fed me and saw that I was entertained by "their Atlanta" during stays with them. They gave me insights into the questions a knowledgeable lay person would ask of my research. Dr. Ben K. Hubby of Savannah reviewed sections relating to battle injuries and smallpox.

Ernest W. Peterkin read the first draft of this manuscript and made key suggestions about organization and details. At East Carolina University, Carl Swanson read, edited, and proofed my manuscript, then offered important suggestions about the time period, the military, and historical writing. Harry Pecorelli III spent many hours refining computerized maps showing unit position and movement. His precision scaling provided confirmation of field width and specific unit positions during the battle. Other maps were scanned and enhanced by John Babits.

At the University of North Carolina Press, David Perry was my initial contact and provided guidance. Pamela Upton then took on the task of final organization. Suzanne Comer Bell completed the editing. I wish to acknowledge their assistance in the final work. They made my job as author much easier than I had anticipated.

My wife, Nancy, read and corrected the manuscript and kept after me to finish it. Our son, John, showed me the differences between drum beatings for right about face, right wheel, left wheel, forward march, and halt. We walked the front end of the Cowpens battlefield one wet, post-rain dawn. His answers about what he could see were clear and concise, leading to a better understanding of battle timing, light conditions, distances, and positioning in the early stages of the Cowpens fighting. Nancy, John, and I wore wet wool, slept in soldiers' tents, and stood in ranks. Our insights into the eighteenth century were bettered by the experience.

One and all, you have my thanks and can take credit for portions of this work. Any errors are, of course, my own.

A Devil of a Whipping

Introduction

I was desirous to have a stroke at Tarlton . . . & I have Given him a devil of a whiping [sic].
—Daniel Morgan to William Snickers, 26 January 1781

American drummers beating a staccato long roll called infantry into formation in the raw predawn hours of 17 January 1781.[1] The drummers signaled a climax to events that began nine months earlier when the British captured Charleston, South Carolina. Less than an hour away from the wet fields in front of the American camp, Banastre Tarleton's feared British Legion and other battalions were closing in on Daniel Morgan's Americans. An uncertain situation would be resolved within two hours on the gentle slopes at a South Carolina crossroads called the Cowpens. The battle marked a turning point in American fortunes. The road through the American position led symbolically, if not quite literally, to Yorktown and British surrender on 19 October 1781.

Three years earlier, in 1778, the Revolutionary War in the North was at a stalemate. The British were unable to destroy General George Washington's army, isolate New England, or convince the rebels to quit fighting. They lost one army at Saratoga and evacuated Philadelphia. Content to hold their base at New York, the British shifted their emphasis southward.

The British effort was directed at the southern colonies for a number of reasons. Repeated calls for help came from southern Loyalists and British policy was to aid their subjects. The 1778 Carlisle Commission, which attempted, unsuccessfully, to reach a negotiated settlement with the Americans, reported Loyalist support in America. However militant they seemed, northern Loyalists usually turned out only when the British army could support them and then in small numbers.

The southern colonies appeared to be different. For one thing, the British had a base in Florida from which Loyalists raided Georgia. Earlier Loyalist uprisings in the South failed because they lacked British military support. Southern Loyalists in England made their feelings known to Lord George Germain, the secretary of state for the American Department.

Reports written by former colonial governors of Georgia and South Carolina asked for a military expedition to retake those colonies.

Despite lukewarm northern Loyalists, Germain opted to support the southerners. Germain's internal political problems threatened the government, and France entered the war. He could point to the Howes's failure. They were mild Whigs relieved of command for inadequately prosecuting the war in the North.[2]

In New York, the commander in chief of the American theater, Sir Henry Clinton, was in a defensive position due to the French entry into the war and his declining military strength. Clinton's forces were depleted by reinforcements sent to Florida, the West Indies, and Canada. Concerned about Washington's army in front of New York, French sea power, and British strategic plans, Clinton issued vague orders to Lieutenant Colonel Archibald Campbell about reinforcing the garrison in Saint Augustine, Florida.

Instead of sailing directly for Florida, Campbell landed in Georgia where his "reinforcements" easily captured Savannah in December 1778. They expanded their hold on Georgia by taking Augusta and Sunbury. After an aborted attack on Charleston, South Carolina, the British bloodily repulsed a French-American attempt to recapture Savannah in October 1779.[3]

The next spring, Clinton directed a major effort against Charleston, which capitulated in May 1780. The British moved quickly to solidify control over South Carolina. While two columns moved into South Carolina's interior, Major General Charles, the Earl Cornwallis, commanded a third force moving toward North Carolina. He sent Lieutenant Colonel Banastre Tarleton, a ruthless cavalry leader, after the last Continentals who were already retreating. Tarleton's rapid movements enabled him to catch the Americans at Waxhaws, just below the North Carolina border. After a brief call for surrender, Tarleton's dragoons attacked, broke American resistance, and then engaged in what infuriated Americans termed a massacre. Waxhaws set the stage for many similar bloody encounters over the next eighteen months. Tarleton's reputation for brutality was established, and his name became a byword for terror and no quarter throughout the South.[4]

While the British successfully waged conventional war against the Continentals and embodied militia, American partisans proved impossible to suppress. After Charleston fell, the British tried to govern South Carolina as a royal colony and reinstituted a Loyalist militia to protect the frontier and maintain order.[5] Even with garrisons across the backcountry, the British colonial government and military could not halt the internecine warfare. British pacification efforts were thwarted by shifting policies, ferocity against rebellious Americans, and Loyalist desires to retaliate against their Whig oppressors. The military's inability to protect paroled Americans and their property alienated inactive Whigs and drove them back into rebellion.[6]

The backcountry erupted after Tory raids, the most notorious led by a New York Loyalist ironically named Christian Huck. Outraged at the murders of neighbors, Whigs wiped out Huck's party in July 1780. In short order, attacks came against British outposts at Hanging Rock, Musgrove's Mill, Rocky Mount, and small foraging parties. The raids served to create further animosity.[7]

In August 1780, an American army under Major General Horatio Gates moved into South Carolina. On 16 August, the Americans were defeated outside Camden. Even though shattered American forces began regrouping in Hillsborough, North Carolina, the British had no regular opposition for the next two months. They also achieved some success against Whig partisans such as General Thomas Sumter.

General Cornwallis was one of the best British field commanders in North America when he succeeded Henry Clinton in command of the southern British forces. He served in America from 1776 until 1778, when he returned to England because his wife was ill. After her death, he returned to America and served until his surrender at Yorktown in 1781. His long experience in America with key roles during the 1776 New York campaign, Brandywine, Monmouth, and Camden demonstrated his abilities. Short and stout, Cornwallis was not a commanding figure, but subordinates respected him. He was fearless in battle, and at a time when other British generals were inclined to be somewhat indecisive and conservative, Cornwallis was a forceful leader.[8]

Cornwallis seized an opportunity presented by the lack of opposition, invaded North Carolina, and occupied Charlotte. He intended to advance against Salisbury, but American resistance stiffened, and militia units attacked British foraging parties. Then a force, composed largely of Tories sent into western North Carolina under Lieutenant Colonel Patrick Ferguson, encountered trouble. Responding to a threat to "lay waste their country," "overmountain" frontiersmen gathered to oppose Ferguson's advance and then moved rapidly against him. Faced with opposition, Ferguson withdrew to Kings Mountain, where he was killed, and his men captured. The Kings Mountain debacle ruined Cornwallis's plans for a further advance because his left-flank screening force was wiped out and Tory support was badly eroded. Cornwallis withdrew from Charlotte and went to Winnsboro, South Carolina, to refit his men.[9]

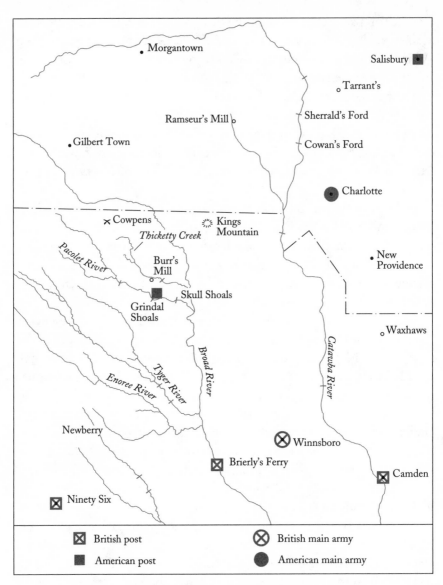

Morgantown

Salisbury ▣

Tarrant's

Ramseur's Mill o

Sherrald's Ford

Cowan's Ford

Gilbert Town

Charlotte ⦿

✕ Cowpens   ☼ Kings Mountain

Thicketty Creek

New Providence

Pacolet River

Burr's Mill o

Skull Shoals

Grindal Shoals ■

Waxhaws o

Catawba River

Enoree River   *Tyger River*   *Broad River*

Newberry

Winnsboro ⊗

Brierly's Ferry ⊠

Camden ⊠

Ninety Six ⊠

⊠ British post   ⊗ British main army

■ American post   ⦿ American main army

MAP I. *Map of the Carolinas Showing Points of Strategic Interest*
Source: *Henry Mouzon, "An Accurate Map of North and South Carolina," 1770.*

    The Kings Mountain victory had several secondary impacts on the war in the South; in particular, the overmountain men's performance both reinforced southern attitudes that militia could win the war and diverted British attention from a "serious deterioration" of control around their bases at Augusta, Ninety Six, and Camden. The British commander at Ninety Six, Colonel John Harris Cruger, failed to win Andrew Pickens to the British side after Loyalist depredations against his family and property, even though Pickens acted as a commissioner to look into treatment of his Tory neighbors captured at Kings Mountain.[10]

For Cornwallis and his troops in South Carolina, the strategic situation in late December 1780 was complex. His men were scattered in a wide arc running across South Carolina from Georgetown, through Camden and Winnsboro to Ninety Six. South of Ninety Six, the line continued to Augusta, Georgia, and a series of small outposts downriver to Savannah. Inside this arc, British or Tory detachments were stationed at Fort Granby (modern Columbia), Fort Watson, Orangeburg, Monck's Corner, and other small posts. The British created these posts to reestablish a Loyalist government, but the small garrisons were vulnerable if a sizable American force moved against them. British troops were stationed between some posts, including Banastre Tarleton's detachment on the Broad River west of Winnsboro.[11]

Cornwallis positioned the main British force in upcountry South Carolina at Winnsboro. Equidistant between Cheraws and Ninety Six, he was about 30 miles from both Friday's Ferry (at Columbia) and Camden. The road net connecting these towns to Winnsboro also fanned north, providing Cornwallis with several options for moving his army. It was an ideal situation to control the upcountry and threaten North Carolina.

The American situation was exceedingly bleak in December 1780. The southern army was located in Charlotte with a detachment at New Providence. At Charlotte, approximately 950 American Continentals and some 1,500 militia were erecting huts for a winter camp. Adding to shortages of food, forage, and other supplies, smallpox broke out in town.[12]

Demoralized American forces received their most important reinforcement when Major General Nathanael Greene rode into Charlotte on 2 December 1780. Greene was a remarkable man. Raised a Quaker, he ran the family ironworks in Coventry, Rhode Island. Excluded from the Quakers when he volunteered for the militia in 1774, he led Rhode Island troops sent to Boston in 1775, and in 1776 was placed in charge of the Long Island, New York, defenses. Appointed quartermaster general of Washington's army in 1778, he performed admirably and organized the department's affairs to ensure a regular supply system. His combat role included participation in every major battle under Washington between 1776 and 1779.

The business skills acquired as an ironworks manager and administrative experience as quartermaster general under Washington prepared Greene for the complex task of keeping the southern army supplied. During his southern campaign of 1780 and 1781, he won no victories but drove the

British into a small enclave between Charleston and Savannah. His major accomplishment was keeping his army in the field. As long as it existed, the army posed a threat to the British and became a rallying point for Whigs. In the meantime, small detachments wiped out isolated British garrisons.

Salisbury, forty-two miles north of Charlotte, was a major transhipment point for supplies collected from the North Carolina piedmont and sent from states farther north. The garrison included craftsmen who manufactured a variety of needed items. Greene instituted clothing production by paying for work with salt. Finally, the town included a jail which held some remaining Kings Mountain prisoners.[13] Hillsborough functioned as the state capital. The North Carolina Board of War resided there, and numerous Continental officers were in town, expediting supply convoys and forwarding troops southward. Supplies gathered from the surrounding area were stockpiled here until wagons were available to transport them to the army.[14]

Greene's conclusions regarding the situation were grim. There were few supplies in Charlotte. Supplies the British did not capture in 1780, the militia plundered or consumed before they could be distributed to the army. Disruptions caused by the war and failed harvests compounded the situation. The Continentals were in a state of poor discipline because they lacked adequate clothing, food, and shelter. Smallpox posed a real problem to the militia but not the Continentals, who had been inoculated. Finally, the British garrison at Winnsboro was a distinct threat, both because of its proximity to Charlotte and the numbers of its reasonably mobile garrison.[15]

When Greene took over the American army, he did not operate in a vacuum. He sent officers to explore river systems north of Charlotte as far as Virginia. Officers were sent south to find a suitable winter campsite. By the time Greene left Charlotte, he had a solid grasp of the strategic potential of the countryside and had reorganized the supply system.[16]

When Greene arrived, a scouting detachment composed of Continental light infantry and militia was at New Providence, fifteen miles below Charlotte. From here they raided south, gathered supplies, encouraged Whigs, and intimidated Loyalists. Just before Greene's arrival, a raiding party from New Providence under William Washington captured the garrison at Rugeley's Mill using a log on wheels to intimidate the Tories.[17]

Faced with a deteriorating situation, Greene had little choice. In mid-December 1780, he issued the orders that set in motion maneuvers culminating in the American victory at Yorktown nine months later. To alleviate supply problems, he reduced the number of men he had to feed in one place. The main army moved back into South Carolina, and Morgan's light infantry were increased and sent into the South Carolina backcountry.[18]

There were several aspects to Greene's plan. First, moving to Hick's Creek, South Carolina, enabled him to supply his main force while threatening British garrisons in eastern South Carolina. By sending Morgan west, British posts in the Carolina backcountry were threatened, and Morgan's detachment could obtain food. American militia operated as a screen in front of both American camps and between British posts, cutting off supplies, foragers, messengers, and small patrols.

Most important, American actions prompted a British reaction. Cornwallis responded by dispatching Tarleton to protect Ninety Six, where he also would be in a position to move against Morgan. Greene divided his army by moving his main force to Hick's Creek (Cheraws), South Carolina. His move back into South Carolina demonstrated that the entire state was not under British control as 1780 ended. Greene wrote both Samuel Huntington, president of the Continental Congress, and George Washington on 28 December 1780 and explained what he had done.[19]

Greene had first-hand knowledge of problems inherent in dividing a force since he had studied tactics and participated in the 1776 New York campaign.[20] Greene weighed economy of force against mass with his own strategic situation in mind.[21] The Americans were not strong enough to fight the British, nor did available food and forage permit an American concentration in sufficient strength. The political situation demanded that Greene exploit momentum acquired by the Kings Mountain victory and keep South Carolina within the revolutionary fold.[22]

Green marched his army from Charlotte on 20 December 1780. They reached the South Carolina campsite on 25 December. Greene partially solved supply problems by shipping food down the Peedee River, but, as he said, Hicks Creek was "no Eden." The men had wornout uniforms and suffered from the weather.[23] The Americans were now positioned far enough to each side of Winnsboro so they could not be surprised by a sudden British movement. Reduced numbers at two locations meant they could better obtain adequate subsistence.

Morgan left Charlotte on 21 December and camped at Grindal Shoals on the Pacolet River.[24] Two separated American units were not the only British problem. Swarms of militia operating over most of the territory Cornwallis nominally controlled terrorized supporters of both sides. One American veteran recalled the time as "almost Fire & Faggot Between Whig & Tory, who were contending for the ascendancy."[25]

The worsening backcountry situation is a difficult aspect of the southern campaign to understand. British plans to maintain royal control behind a military screen were thwarted by Loyalists wanting to settle old scores and men calling themselves militia simply to plunder.[26] Taking advantage of the unrest, Morgan and Greene authorized forays that did little to ease Cornwallis's mind. Lieutenant Colonel Henry Lee and Colonel Francis Marion attacked Georgetown, South Carolina, on 25 January 1781.[27] In the west, Lieutenant Colonel William Washington's Continental dragoons and militia first destroyed a Tory force at Hammond's Store in late December, then moved farther south and burned a fortification a short distance from Ninety Six.[28]

Cornwallis knew of Greene's activity. Spies and scouting parties around Charlotte reported departures with fairly accurate estimates of American numbers.[29] Cornwallis was perplexed because Greene violated a principle dictating consolidation of inferior forces in the face of a superior enemy. Cornwallis felt Morgan could threaten Ninety Six while Greene might move against Camden, Georgetown, or other eastern British posts.

Cornwallis was in difficult straits because the region north of Winnsboro had been subjected to intense foraging by both sides and was virtually stripped of resources. Cornwallis located here partly because the town commanded a backcountry road network and because potentially adequate supplies were available just south of Winnsboro.[30] Greene placed Americans upstream across the rivers most important for supplying British forces at Camden, Georgetown, Fort Granby, and other interior posts, including Winnsboro. While supplies could be floated downstream to American camps, resources the British could not obtain from the interior came from the coast, upstream, or over difficult roads where they were vulnerable to partisan raiders. This crucial logistical aspect of the southern campaign would, in the long run, help ruin Cornwallis and the British southern army.

Greene's innovative response to superior British numbers compounded Cornwallis's dilemma because he wanted to invade North Carolina and march through Charlotte against the American bases at Salisbury and Hillsborough. While Cornwallis gathered supplies, recruited his forces, and made dispositions to defend his rear, he had to deal with Morgan and Ninety Six.[31]

Morgan's threat against Ninety Six so concerned Cornwallis that he wrote Tarleton, "I sent Haldane to you last night, to desire you would pass Broad river, with the legion and the first battalion of the 71st, as soon as possible. If Morgan is still at Williams', or any where within your reach, I should wish you to push him to the utmost: I have not heard, except from M'Arthur, of his having cannon; nor would I believe it, unless he has it from very good authority: It is, however, possible, and Ninety Six is of so much consequence, that no time is to be lost."[32]

Tarleton moved westward and placed his force between Morgan and Ninety Six. Privy to Cornwallis's plans for an invasion of North Carolina, Tarleton was aware of what Cornwallis had in mind. After learning that Ninety Six was not in danger, Tarleton reorganized to "push [Morgan] to the utmost." In addition to acquiring supplies by foraging and impressment, he requested wagons and additional troops because he needed more men to destroy Morgan, and then explained how his movements fit into Cornwallis's plans.[33]

Letters between Cornwallis and Tarleton explain the British response to Morgan. Tarleton would protect Ninety Six, then deal with Morgan. To accomplish the latter, he requested a reinforcement of light troops. Knowing he would move rapidly, he ordered that no women accompany his baggage. If Tarleton pursued Morgan, Ninety Six would be reinforced by the 7th Regiment. At the same time, Cornwallis would invade North Carolina, and by advancing slightly northwest, cut off Morgan. Tarleton clearly saw an opportunity in Greene's division of the Americans. His letter confirmed an understanding of Cornwallis's basic plan and proposed action to destroy a wing of the American forces.[34]

Once it was clear Morgan did not threaten Ninety Six, Cornwallis authorized Tarleton to employ the 7th Regiment and its cannon in the effort to destroy Morgan. Tarleton had about 1,100 men, including local Tories who served as guides. He was now free to drive Morgan out of South Carolina. By advancing, Tarleton's detachment would screen Cornwallis's left flank and protect it from overmountain militia who destroyed Ferguson. British officers with Tarleton later said the force was "designed to penetrate into North Carolina."[35]

Unfortunately for the British, weather interfered with their planned movements. Rains delayed reinforcements marching from the coast under Major General Alexander Leslie, and Cornwallis waited. The rain delayed Tarleton but did not stop his movement against Morgan. While Tarleton had problems gathering basic food to feed his men, his wagons carried some luxurious condiments for the officers.[36]

Aware of coordinated movements against him, Morgan was concerned with feeding his troops.[37] The Flying Army rarely bivouacked together because scattered detachments were positioned where they could obtain food more easily. Given Tory/Patriot animosities, American forces unsurprisingly supplied themselves at Tory expense because they were not required to issue them receipts.[38]

Despite supply problems and the coming and going of militia who claimed enlistments were expiring, Morgan accomplished Greene's strategic aims. He posed a threat to the Carolina backcountry that Cornwallis could not ignore; moreover, he raised American spirits. When Tarleton came after him, however, Morgan withdrew. Over the next week, both commanders prepared for a fight as they moved north. On 17 January 1781, when Tarleton's advance patrol came out of the pine forests and deployed south of the American battle lines, the Americans were ready. Knowing an engagement with Tarleton was inevitable, Morgan chose the ground and his men were rested, ready, and waiting.

What happened was standardized over the years. British infantry drove in Morgan's skirmishers before advancing against American militia. The South Carolinians stood their ground. Every battalion fired at least one close-range volley before retreating around the American left flank with Tarleton's dragoons howling in pursuit. Tarleton's infantry advanced again and engaged the Continentals and Virginia militia in a firefight.

When Tarleton moved to break the main-line deadlock, the American right withdrew. In the crisis, Morgan selected a point where the Continentals would halt, turn, and fire. When they did so, the British infantry collapsed in shock and began a panic-stricken withdrawal. The British fled, and although Tarleton and most of his dragoons eluded pursuit and rejoined Cornwallis, few infantrymen escaped the Americans.

This summation is drawn from popular traditional accounts. Official accounts and later historians related only part of the battle. Participants from the lower ranks provide additional details for incorporation into the battle's history. Morgan, as he described in a letter to his friend William Snickers, *had* given Tarleton "a devil of a whiping [*sic*]."[39] Later, almost nine months to the day, British survivors of Cowpens and ensuing campaigns surrendered at Yorktown, Virginia. How Morgan managed to win with minimal support and a potentially disastrous mix of Continentals, state troops, and militia from six states is the tactical story of Cowpens. How Morgan took a disparate group of men and welded them into a force capable of using traditional European tactics in a new American fashion is the real story of Cowpens, which emerges from new study of published materials and the pension documents.

1 : *Tactics*

The art of disciplining armies, and ranging them into forms . . .
—*George Smith*, An Universal Military Dictionary

Battlefield military operations are called tactics. Tactics are dictated by the weapons and troops available. At Cowpens, the British used infantry, cavalry, and artillery; the Americans, infantry and cavalry. Any soldier, whether infantry, cavalry, or artillery, had specific weapons dictating his employment in battle.[1]

American Continentals and British infantry were armed with smoothbore muskets which also took a bayonet. American militia carried a variety of rifles as well as some muskets, probably with few bayonets. Some Scottish Highlanders in the British army were armed with broadswords at times. Cavalrymen, or dragoons, were armed with short muskets called carbines, but they relied primarily on pistols and sabers. Artillerymen carried muskets in addition to working their cannon. Officers and noncommissioned officers carried swords. Some company-level officers carried short spears called spontoons, which symbolized their rank.

In the eighteenth century, regular, or line, infantry relied on two primary weapons: the musket and the bayonet. During the Revolution, muskets were called firelocks because they generated their own fire, hence the later term *firearm*. A musket was a single-shot smoothbore; the barrel had no grooves on its inside surface.

A musket was fired by a spring-loaded mechanism called the lock. The spring drove the cock holding a piece of flint forward. When the flint struck a piece of metal called the hammer, sparks dropped into the pan and ignited the priming charge. Fire from the priming charge flashed through a hole in the barrel and set off the main charge, forcing the ball out of the barrel toward the target.

A soldier in either army loaded his musket from a paper-wrapped cartridge. The soldier tore the cartridge open and shook a little powder into the pan alongside the barrel. The remaining powder was then poured down the barrel. Next, the ball was placed in the barrel and forced down onto the

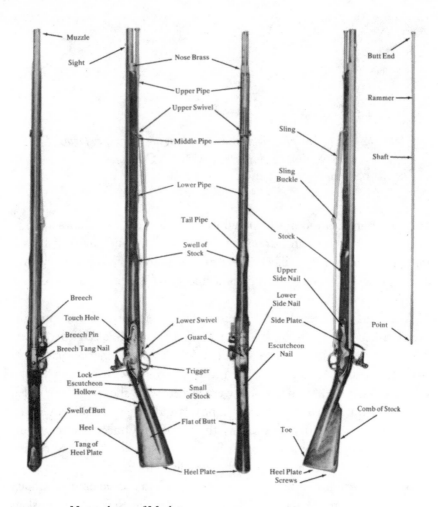

FIGURE I. *Nomenclature of Musket*
Source: *Peterkin,* Exercise of Arms, *47.*

powder by the ramrod. The bullet was smaller than the barrel. The difference in respective diameters created a space between the bullet and the inside of the barrel called windage. The British .75 caliber ball was actually about .70 inch in diameter; the American .69 was about .63 inch.[2] The entire loading process was very structured and designed to eliminate error. The American manual exercise was simpler than the British, largely because Baron Frederick Wilhelm Von Steuben recognized that a reduction in complexity would shorten the time needed to introduce the system into the Continental army.[3]

The standard British musket was the Short Land, New Pattern musket, often called the Brown Bess. It fired a .75 caliber ball about three-quarters of an inch in diameter. Some American militiamen carried British-style muskets, but the American Continentals were armed with French muskets which fired a .69 caliber ball.[4]

Today, muskets have a reputation for being notoriously inaccurate, in part because Tarleton's second in command, Major George Hanger, wrote a critical statement about common soldiers' muskets.[5] Hanger is often cited without clarification, and his observation has become something of a truism. The reputation for inaccuracy is not entirely warranted. In 1781, muskets were state-of-the-art weaponry in large-scale use throughout the Western world. Hanger, in a much less cited observation, pointed out that practice was essential for accuracy.[6]

A well-drilled musketman, given practice and encouraged to shoot rapidly, could deliver fast and accurate fire. Even with undersized bullets it is possible, without ramming, to hit a man-sized target eighty yards away with five out of six shots in one minute.[7] Although special troops called rangers fired this way, regular infantry did not. Since regular infantry rarely practiced firing at targets, the question of musket accuracy should be directed at the shooter rather than the weapon.

Both sides increased musket lethality, if not accuracy, by issuing buck and ball cartridges containing one large ball and at least three smaller (.30 caliber) balls. Washington ordered that "buckshot are to be put into all cartridges which shall hereafter be made" in 1777. One sixty-man Continental company could launch at least 240 projectiles with a single volley. Buckshot could deliver a fatal wound, especially at ranges within fifty yards where volley fire was most commonly used.[8]

American militiamen carried either muskets or rifles. When they had muskets, militiamen commonly used multiple balls and buckshot, but rifles are different in ways that affect loading speed and tactics. Rifle barrels have twisting slanted grooves cut into their interior surface. The grooves cause the bullet to spin in flight and increase accuracy. Evolving firearms technology occurring on the eighteenth-century American frontier resulted in a distinctive American rifle. American rifles were lengthened to allow full burning of the powder charge and to increase accuracy. The bore was reduced to save on ball weight, but by increasing the powder charge, the impact of a heavier ball was maintained. The stock was thinner than European rifles, resulting in the famous "long rifle," "Pennsylvania Rifle," or "Kentucky Rifle."

Rifles used at Cowpens fit a generalized pattern with "a barrel length usually over 40 inches, a bore averaging .40 to .60 caliber (with seven or eight grooves); a long thin stock extending to the muzzle . . . and a patch box."[9] The rifles weighed about six pounds, give or take a few ounces, with balls as "small as thirty-six to the pound, or about" .50 caliber. American rifles used about as much powder as "is contained in a woman's thimble."[10]

Unlike muskets that had a bayonet-locking lug on the front of the barrel by which men might aim, rifles were equipped with front and rear sights. The American rifle had "one rear sight . . . not more than two-sixteenth of an inch in height above the barrel." Tarleton's second in command, George Hanger, later wrote that American riflemen "thought they were generally sure of splitting a man's head at two hundred yards." Hanger "also asked several whether they could hit a man at four hundred yards,—they have replied certainly, or shoot very near him, by only aiming at the top of his head."[11]

Eighteenth-century rifles had several drawbacks. They were, first and foremost, slower to load at a time when speed of fire was paramount. Rifles loaded slower because the powder charge was not premeasured and the ball was "patched." After powder was poured down the barrel, a piece of greased cloth was placed over the muzzle opening. The ball was pressed into the cloth and forced into the barrel. Excess cloth was then cut away before ramming the ball home. The greased cloth surrounding the ball caught the rifling, which made the ball spin and increased accuracy. The patch also acted as a gas seal that created greater muzzle velocity, increasing range and striking power. Experienced riflemen could fire one shot every fifteen seconds on a good day.

American rifles were individual personal weapons with a wide range of bore sizes. The range of bores created problems for supply officers; consequently, they issued riflemen lead bars to make bullets, using molds made for their individual weapons. One-pound lead bars were provided to riflemen marching through Salisbury during the Cowpens campaign.[12]

American riflemen had a fearsome reputation for accuracy. "An expert rifleman . . . can hit the head of a man at 200 yards. I am certain, that, provided an American rifleman were to get a perfect aim at 300 yards at me, standing still, he most undoubtedly would hit me, unless it was a very windy day."[13] This reputation may not be justified in combat. At a skirmish near Weitzell's Mill, North Carolina, American riflemen fired thirty-three shots downhill at a mounted man less than fifty yards away and missed both man and horse.[14]

A lack of accuracy when shooting downhill had implications for the coming battle at Cowpens. Despite constant drill and practical experience, soldiers tended to shoot high when firing downhill. The error was called "over-shooting" in the nineteenth century when Lyman Draper collected veterans' Revolutionary War accounts. "Long experience proves, that marksmen in a valley have the advantage of those on a hill, in firing at each other, which is probably owing to the terrestrial refraction. The forest-hunters, though apprised of this fact, often shoot too high when their object is below them."[15]

At Musgrove's Mill, South Carolina, low American casualties were attributed to the British overshooting Americans down-slope. Richard Thompson "observed the bullet marks on the trees—those of the British and Tories generally indicating aim above the heads of their antagonists, while those of the Whigs were from three to five feet above the ground."[16]

Even on flat ground, some British units often fired high. Before Guilford Courthouse, Henry Lee noted, the British "fire was innocent, overshooting the cavalry entirely; whose caps and accoutrements were all struck with green twigs, cut by the British ball out of the large oaks in the meeting-house yard, under which the cavalry received the volley from the guards."[17] Since the Americans were mounted, the British fire must have been high indeed.

One British unit at Cowpens fired high before the battle. North Carolina militiaman Joseph Graham recalled the British Legion infantry fired, "their balls passing directly through the woods where our line was formed, and skinning saplings and making bark and twigs fly. . . . [T]he firing in Charlotte and beyond had generally passed over their [our] heads, but here it appeared to be horizontal."[18] Henry Lee accounted for differences between American and British accuracy because "we were trained to take aim and fire low, he was not so trained; and from this cause, or from the composition of his cartridge (too much powder for the lead), he always overshot."[19]

Continental soldiers were "completed" to forty rounds and three flints as a standard load of ammunition. The night of 16 January, Morgan, knowing a battle was imminent, ordered militia riflemen to carry at least twenty-four rounds. Thus Morgan had an effective way of judging how much ammunition soldiers had. This was essential knowledge for evaluating a unit's ability to conduct sustained firing.[20]

Eighteenth-century muskets were augmented by using the bayonet, a triangular blade mounted on the musket barrel. Blades ranged from about seventeen inches long for the British Brown Bess to about fifteen inches for French models. American-made bayonets varied.[21] Revolutionary War bayonets had a socket that fit over the barrel and were held in place by a stud two or three inches behind the muzzle.

Bayonets could not be used on Revolutionary War rifles. Since rifles were individually manufactured, they were not standardized as to outside barrel diameter and mass-produced bayonets would not fit them. Many Virginia and Carolina rifle barrels were slightly expanded at the muzzle. This "swamping" made it impossible to mount a socket bayonet. A plug bayonet could not be inserted into the barrel because it would damage the rifling and, once in place, the gun could not be fired. Finally, the rifle's sight was not designed to lock a bayonet in place and would be damaged by the bayonet socket.

Riflemen solved the lack of a bayonet by carrying other blade weapons, the tomahawk and knife. Virginia private Christian Peters was a rifleman, "in all of which service he carried his own Rifle Tomahawk & Butcher knife."[22] There was no universal pattern to the "rifleman's knife," which ranged in blade length from about six inches to a foot. They were mounted with iron, brass, pewter, or silver with a grip of wood, horn, bone, or antler. The tomahawk was a light axe that served a variety of functions.[23]

Finally, another infantry weapon was the spontoon. Basically a spear, in eighteenth-century armies it signified officer rank. British officers carried spontoons into battle at Hobkirk's Hill, South Carolina, 25 May 1781, so it is likely they were used at Cowpens. At least one spontoon was used by a Maryland officer to polevault onto a British cannon.[24]

In the eighteenth century, infantry combat was dictated by the need to best employ muskets and bayonets. When fighting regular infantry, men stood in ranks, standing shoulder to shoulder. Linear formations allowed more men to fire into opposing ranks and to resist a bayonet charge. "By-the-book" linear tactics involved an almost ritual approach as men moved forward in columns, deployed into battle lines, and then advanced to closer range.[25] The linear formations could fire more weapons at one time. The long front allowed massive volley fire but had no depth. A drawback to linear formations was a loss of control as they moved over wooded or rough ground, so attacking forces, at the expense of firepower, might form columns instead to penetrate a line.

The tactical unit during the Revolution was the regiment. Eighteenth-century military personnel used "battalion" and "regiment" interchangeably, especially if a regiment were less than 300 men.[26] A regiment was subdivided into eight companies, each commanded by a captain. A company had two platoons commanded by lieutenants, and was further subdivided into squads or messes. Two companies were combined into a division during firing.

In most cases, an infantry firefight involved one side standing its ground against attackers who sought to drive them away. Volley fire was designed

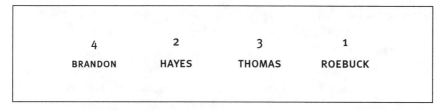

| 4 | 2 | 3 | 1 |
| BRANDON | HAYES | THOMAS | ROEBUCK |

FIGURE 2. *Battalion Firing Sequence According to the Von Steuben Manual*

to kill and for its shock effect to demoralize an enemy before a bayonet charge. No volley was more effective than the first. Tactically, the impact of the first volley cannot be underestimated. In eighteenth-century European armies, it was "a precious resource . . . loaded at leisure before the action began, and it was fired from a clean weapon with a sharp flint. When a volley of such rounds was discharged at short range, it was capable of causing a massacre."[27]

After the initial volley, battalions fired by platoon or division. Firing was almost continuous as platoons or divisions fired in planned sequences to ensure some weapons were always loaded. According to the Von Steuben manual, when more than one battalion was present "they are to do it [volley fire] in succession from right to left; but after the first round, the odd battalions fire so soon as the respective battalions on their left begin to shoulder; and the even battalions fire when the respective battalions on their right begin to shoulder."[28]

In the South, tactical movements evolved away from the slow, steady approach march. By January 1781, both sides deployed rapidly, to close with their opposition as quickly as possible, often with sizable gaps between men. The change in tactics was a response to American rifle fire and British artillery. Rapid deployment meant troops moved from a column as quickly as possible to minimize casualties. "Displaying" took several forms depending on whether or not the movement was to the front, right, or left.

Spacing between infantrymen varied with conditions. American militia usually formed up in loose companies while Continentals stood shoulder to shoulder in two ranks. The British are usually pictured standing shoulder to shoulder, but this is not true for many southern battles where they adopted a wider spacing called open order. The precise meaning of open order is not covered in contemporary manuals. British light infantry in the North employed two forms of open order in 1778 and 1779. "Files by day always loose; usual order 11 inches; open order arm's length; extended order from five yards to fifty." The phrase "always loose" is a close approximation of Tarleton's phrase "loose manner of forming." The extended, or open, order allowed greater distances along a regimental front, reduced chances of damage from musket, rifle, and artillery fire, and made it easier to maintain a linear formation moving through wooded areas. However, it weakened unit cohesion if they were only two-men deep.[29]

Before the British attacked Georgia in December 1778, Lieutenant Colonel Archibald Campbell ordered standard formations for his units including the 71st Regiment. Two formations show one yard per man; the third is 1.6 yards, gaps between men ranged from almost one foot to five feet. At Camden, South Carolina, 16 August 1780, British infantry deployed in a single rank with five feet between men.[30]

Infantry standing on defense could afford to be closely arrayed, but infantry moving through southern woods and overgrown fields needed gaps to pass trees and brush. Attackers could not operate in a column because American riflemen would simply swarm along the flanks and destroy it. The British were forced to use a linear front equal to the length of an American line at their front. Moving forward in open order, the British could compress to provide mutual support or heavier volley fire by platoons or divisions. When officers felt an enemy was sufficiently weakened or disorganized by gunfire, a bayonet charge would drive their opponents off the field.

In Europe, eighteenth-century armies usually deployed in three lines when on defense. Composed of a main battle line, a secondary line some distance to the rear, and a reserve well to the rear of the second line, the arrangement offered support across the battlefront.[31] While Morgan was undoubtedly concerned about his troops' ability to meet the British on equal terms, the British were not unduly concerned about American tactics. They were concerned about the American rifles they knew had greater accuracy and range that made their fire dangerous at a distance. The British devised tactics to minimize the rifle's effectiveness and tried them. When facing "riflemen . . . only. I would treat them the same as my friend Colonel Abercrombie. . . . When Morgan's riflemen came down to Pennsylvania . . . they marched to attack our light infantry. . . . The moment they appeared before him he ordered his troops to charge them with the bayonet; not one man out of four, had time to fire, and those that did had no time given them to load again; the light infantry not only dispersed them instantly but drove them for miles over the country. They never attacked, or even looked at, our light infantry again, without a regular force to support them."[32] Morgan countered these tactics by supporting militia riflemen with Continentals and opting to attack British officers and noncommissioned officers as targets.

Tarleton's infantry component was not as well known as his British Legion dragoons. Mounted troops were an essential part of southern warfare during the Revolution. Their importance was summed up by Major George Hanger, Tarleton's second in command:

> The crackers and militia in those parts of America are all mounted on horse-back, which renders it totally impossible to force them to an engagement with infantry *only*. When they chuse to fight, they dismount, and fasten their horses to the fences and rails; but if not very confident in the superiority of their numbers, they remain on horseback, give their fire, and retreat, which renders it useless to attack them without cavalry: for though you repulse them, and drive them from the field, you never can improve the advantage.[33]

Hanger's comment demonstrates that the British needed cavalry to cope with American militia. Americans rode to battle and then fought on foot for two reasons. First, most were armed with rifles requiring a steady platform for accuracy. Second, they did not have the weapons—carbines, pistols, and, most important, sabers—to engage the British on equal terms. When equipped with pistols and swords, American mounted men did fight on horseback, and Morgan shrewdly separated those who had sabers from those who did not before fighting Tarleton at Cowpens.

Regular cavalry were armed with pistols, sabers, and carbines. The British used a standardized weapon in .65 caliber. Lieutenant Colonel William Washington's Continental Light Dragoons probably carried the standard .67 caliber French carbine at Cowpens.[34] Hand guns carried by cavalrymen and some infantry officers were about nine inches in barrel length, although earlier, longer versions are known. The usual British calibers were .62 or .65 and approximately .69 for the French weapons carried by Americans.[35] The Americans carried a variety of personal weapons including British and French types.

Southern militia dragoons rarely carried carbines, and only about one in four had a pistol. Instead, they used rifles, a weapon they knew intimately. "They carried the muzzle in a small boot, fastened beside the right stirrup leather, and the butt ran through the shot bag belt, so that the lock came directly under the right arm. Those who had a pistol, carried it, swung by a strap, about the size, of a bridle rein, on the left side, over the sword."[36] Some leaders did not feel cavalry gunfire was very useful. In an editorial comment, Robert E. Lee noted "the fire of cavalry is at best innocent, especially in quick action . . . [when] the precision and celerity of the evolution, the adroitness of the rider, . . . and the keen edge of the sabre, with fitness of ground and skill in the leader, constitute their vast power so often decisive in the day of battle."[37]

The basic cavalry weapon was the saber, with a blade about thirty-four inches long.[38] The militia obtained sabers by going "to all the sawmills," wrote Private James Collins, where they would "take all the old whip saws we could find, set three or four smiths to work. . . . [W]e soon had a pretty good supply of swords." The militia "swords and knives, we polished mostly with a grindstone—not a very fine polish to be sure; but they were of a good temper, sharpened to a keen edge."[39] William Washington preferred sabers for combat, describing the sword as the "most destructive and almost the only necessary weapon a Dragoon carries."[40]

Most dragoons wore short jackets and distinctive caplike helmets to provide protection from injury by sabers. The caps often had embellishments such as fur, cloth bands, and unit insignia on them.[41] British dragoons also wore distinctive, regimentally marked headgear.

Cavalry scouted ahead of an advance, covered infantry deployment, provided flank protection, and engaged in direct headlong attacks. Cavalry tactics were predicated on moving rapidly, often in direct, frontal assault. Attacking cavalry could be in column with a narrow front designed to penetrate an enemy line. If they wished to overwhelm a position or sweep through an area with scattered opposition, a broad front with horsemen on line would be used. Against a steady enemy, especially one armed with bayonets, any direct attack would be disastrous, so flanking movements were used. These began in column, but cavalry could deploy rapidly on line. In pursuit of broken infantry, cavalry were at their most effective, and control was loosened as the men simply rode at will, hacking every opponent in sight.

Cavalry were at their best in surprise actions, against men without bayonets, and against retreating, disordered infantry. To counter Tarleton's dragoons, American riflemen were ordered to have "every third man to fire and two to remain in reserve, lest the cavalry should continue to advance after the first fire; or to be used if they wheeled to retire."[42] Morgan promised his militia that bayonet-armed Continental infantry would provide protection from the British dragoons.

Cavalry against cavalry was common, especially when one side had the advantage of numbers or surprise, or when covering disputed ground between armies. Skirmishing occurred frequently in the South, and both sides saw much mounted combat before Cowpens. Generally, a cavalry attack against other mounted men was dictated by the space available, with as many men as possible on line but with some depth on occasion.

Both sides used cavalry as a reserve force to exploit any opportunity.

Because dragoons could move rapidly from point to point, they were ideal for taking advantage of any mistake by the opposing force. They could also move rapidly to cover a breakdown in their own ranks.

Artillery men operated cannon, but individual artillery men were armed with either muskets or carbines. Tarleton's force had two three-pounders, so named because they could fire a single solid shot weighing three pounds. These particular guns were also called grasshoppers because of the style of their carriage.[43]

Artillery tactics were designed to produce a number of results, and the guns were given specialized projectiles for the purpose. For longer-range work, they used solid shot, in Tarleton's case weighing three pounds. For closer work, both grape and case shot were available. These charges consisted of multiple balls, in effect turning the cannon into a giant shotgun to break up enemy formations. Case shot was basically a tin can containing iron balls; grape was stacked on a baseplate and wrapped in canvas and rope.[44]

Initially, cannon fired solid shot at longer ranges. As the distance lessened, gunners switched to grape or case shot. In combat, point-blank artillery fire was understood as the range at which shot would first touch level ground when the gun barrel was level. The three-pounders used at Cowpens had a point-blank range of 180 yards, a little over the distance between the American lines at Cowpens.[45]

British artillerist John Muller recommended ricochet firing because it saved powder and was more dangerous. After the first ricochet, a ball might bounce another 400 yards and still injure men waiting in reserve. Shot was bounced into enemy ranks, because it caused the disorder necessary before ordering a bayonet charge. Ricochet firing might also create panic because the enemy could see the shot coming. Furthermore, the bouncing shot threw up dirt and stones which also caused injuries.[46]

Positioning cannon in a battle line depended on whether an attack or a defense was conducted. Traditionally, Europeans positioned guns with infantry battalions in intervals between companies. In the American campaigns, a gun often would be placed on a battalion flank if it were covered by another unit; or in the battle line where it had the best line of fire. The flank position could fire across an attacker's front. A more central position could fire into the faces of attackers or defenders. In attacks, cannon were generally positioned about 100 yards away from the enemy, but light guns such as three-pounders were used for close support and moved along with the infantry.[47]

Artillery rates of fire varied according to use, but the British had perfected a "quick-fire" drill to speed up firing. Guns such as the grasshopper could fire up to five or six rounds a minute, but this was excessive. Guns moving with infantry would have a much slower rate of fire.[48]

In the employment of fighting forces as an integrated unit, Tarleton would attack with his infantry, cavalry, and artillery, virtually all of them veteran regulars. Tarleton was inclined to use a frontal charge, which worked well at Lenud's Ferry, Monck's Corner, Waxhaws, and Fishing Creek but proved of little success at Charlotte and Blackstock's, a fact not lost on Americans who advised Morgan. In late December, Richard Winn went to Grindal Shoals and discussed Tarleton with Morgan and his staff. Winn noted, "Tarleton never brings on the attack himself. His mode of fighting is surprise. By doing this he sends two or three troops of horse, and, if he can throw the party into confusion, with his reserve he falls on [and] will cut them to pieces."[49]

Morgan planned a defensive stand with infantry, both rifle-armed militia and regulars with muskets, as the main resistance. The American cavalry, composed of militia and regulars, would perform in a supporting role. By defending a position, Morgan minimized chances of disorder inherent in moving men across the landscape and selected the ground over which the British would have to move.

2 : The Opponents

I give this the name of a flying Army.
—Nathanael Greene to Marquis de Lafayette, 29 December 1780

THE AMERICANS

Daniel Morgan's Flying Army grew from company-sized elements in September 1780 into a sizable force by January 1781. Composed of three types of soldier—Continentals, state troops, and militia—the Flying Army was commanded by the one man most likely to achieve success with such a composite force. What, and who, these men were, and how they came to form Morgan's force sheds light on the Revolutionary War in the South.[1]

Daniel Morgan is hardly known as a Revolutionary hero today, but contemporaries considered his experience and talents as legendary. Morgan's veterans remembered him as the "old Waggoner," a nickname earned during the French and Indian War. Described as "stout and active, six feet in height," his manners were plain, an image Morgan encouraged. Invariably portrayed in the hunting frock symbolic of riflemen and his leadership of them, his men identified with him. He "reflected deeply, spoke little, and executed with keen perseverance whatever he undertook." Among intimates, Morgan "expressed his feelings without reserve."[2]

Morgan led through respect and by example. He was a powerful figure who feared no danger and sought the hottest action. During the French and Indian War, he suffered a wound in which the ball entered the back of his neck, passed through his mouth, taking out the left rear teeth, and emerged through his upper left lip. Contemporaries described a livid scar, but illustrations rarely show any indication, although Peale gave him a subdued mark.[3]

While serving as a wagoner during the French and Indian War, Morgan was punished, some say unjustly, for having struck a British officer. One account from a British officer entertained by Morgan after the American victory at Yorktown is typical.

He told us that the British owed him a lash: that he drove one of the waggons which accompanied General Braddock's army. . . . [H]e had, on a certain occasion, knocked down a sentinel; for that offence he had been condemned to receive four hundred lashes, of which only three hundred and ninety-nine were inflicted—"I counted them myself," continued he, laughing, "and am sure that I am right; nay, I convinced the drum-major of his mistake . . . so I am still their creditor to the amount of one lash."[4]

Henry Lee, and other American writers, mention this incident and Morgan obviously relished the story; it is possible he used it to stir up his men before the battle of Cowpens.[5]

When the Revolutionary War broke out, Morgan led riflemen from Frederick County, Virginia, to Boston. Morgan and his men went to Canada with Benedict Arnold in the winter of 1775. In the December assault on Quebec, Morgan took over one column when Arnold was wounded. Captured and then exchanged, Morgan commanded the 11th Virginia Regiment until authorized to raise a rifle corps that played a distinguished role at Saratoga. In 1780 his health failed, and he took a leave of absence and returned to Virginia.[6]

Following the 16 August 1780 Camden debacle, Morgan returned to the army. Congress finally promoted him, and, as a brigadier, he commanded the light troops under Gates, then the Flying Army under Greene. After Cowpens, "sciatica," possibly a slipped disc, hemorrhoids, and rheumatism, left him unfit for service.[7] After the war, Morgan participated in putting down the Whiskey Rebellion and served one term as representative in Congress but did not seek reelection. He retired to his home, Saratoga. The last year of his life he lived in Winchester, Virginia, where he died 6 July 1802.[8]

The requirements of a general described in an eighteenth-century military dictionary show that, except for birth, Morgan was close to the ideal and he obviously impressed his men.[9] "Genl Morgan's personal appearance to be over Six feet high, his metle [sic] to be of much Bodily strength, with a large Scar on his Cheek[. He] wore no marks of distinction as an officer[,] his Sword excepted." The lack of uniform embellishment may have been Morgan's personal preference, or due to a poor supply system.[10]

Morgan's army "family" consisted of staff officers who served in his headquarters. They included a brigade major, a commissary, a quartermaster, a forage master, and various aides. These men were, respectively, responsible for obtaining food, acquiring and maintaining equipment and campsites, and feeding army livestock, especially dragoon and militia horses.[11]

Aides carried orders and assisted in administration. They were more than simple message carriers; they spoke with the authority of Morgan himself. Two aides are known: Major Edward Giles of the Maryland Regiment Extraordinary and the Baron de Glaubec. During the battle, a Maryland surgeon attached to Morgan's staff, Doctor Richard Pindell, helped rally the South Carolina militia before attending to the wounded.[12]

A personal escort for Morgan has never been identified, but it is probable that he had one. Called a "Life Guard," this detachment was typical of an eighteenth-century general's entourage. George Washington had one, and other officers in the South, including militia leaders, did as well. South Carolina militia captain Dennis Tramell, a local resident, with "Genl. Morgan and his life-guard and Aide d camp went out and selected the ground" for the battle.[13]

The core of the American force at Cowpens served under Morgan for more than three months before Cowpens. In addition to Continental light infantry, a Virginia militia battalion under Major Francis Triplett saw extensive service with the Flying Army. North Carolina militiamen under Colonel Joseph McDowell operated as a second militia battalion under Morgan. Finally, cavalry composed largely of the remnants of the Third Continental Dragoons under William Washington completed the components of the Flying Army. This force was first placed under the command of William Smallwood, then Daniel Morgan when he joined the southern army.[14] Drafted militia from Virginia, the Carolinas, and Georgia also served with Morgan as the campaign progressed. In mid-January 1781, local militia from western South Carolina turned out in large numbers for service under Morgan.

Morgan's most reliable soldiers were Continental infantry—Americans with many similarities, especially long service and good discipline, to British regulars. By January 1781, Morgan's Continentals had all served at least one year. Many enlisted men had four or five years' service, and some would serve until 1783. Continental officers were much like their British counterparts and fully as professional. Members of a literate elite, the officers formed the social and economic leadership of their states in later years. Like their men, they had seen extensive service, some dating to 1775.

The five Continental companies formed a battalion commanded by Lieutenant Colonel John Eager Howard of Baltimore, a superb officer. In the northern campaigns, Howard established a solid reputation for leadership and fearlessness in battle. After Cowpens, Howard played a spectacular role at Guilford Courthouse when he led the First Maryland against the British Guards. Howard's reputation for coolness and courage under fire was enhanced at Camden, Hobkirk's Hill, Ninety Six, and Eutaw Springs,

Daniel Morgan; oil painting by Charles Willson Peale
(Independence National Historical Park Collection)

where he was wounded. Nathanael Greene would later write, "Howard, as good an officer as the world affords. He has great ability and the best disposition to promote the service. . . . He deserves a statue of gold."[15]

Serving as Howard's assistant, or brigade major, was Maryland captain Benjamin Brookes. Captain James Somerville served as Howard's adjutant, or his aide. Howard's immediate command consisted of five Continental companies, consolidated from remnants of the old Maryland-Delaware Division plus a Virginia company, "amounting to 300 regular troops."[16]

The Delaware Company commanded by Captain Robert Kirkwood had an incredible reputation by the end of the war. Kirkwood's first biographer was his old comrade in arms, Henry Lee, whose evaluation was based on personal observation.

> That corps . . . was commanded by Captain Kirkwood, who passed through the war with high reputation. . . . Reduced to a captain's command, Kirkwood never could be promoted. . . . Kirkwood retired, upon peace, a captain; and when the army under St. Clair was raised to defend the West from the Indian enemy, this veteran resumed his sword as the eldest captain of the oldest regiment. . . . The gallant Kirkwood fell . . . the thirty-third time he had risked his life for his country; and he died as he had lived, the brave, meritorious, unrewarded, Kirkwood.[17]

Kirkwood was assisted by two other officers, Lieutenant Thomas Anderson and Ensign William Bivins. Kirkwood and Anderson were assigned to the light infantry on 25 September 1780. Bivins, a "nine months regular," joined the army after Camden.[18]

The Delaware Company was composed of about half the Delaware Regiment soldiers who survived the defeat at Camden. Kirkwood's company was given responsibility for difficult tasks during the southern campaign and operated as a special, elite force, often in conjunction with William Washington's dragoons. The unit also had a nickname, "the Delaware Blues."[19] Kirkwood's company is the best-documented Continental unit at Cowpens. Ideally a Continental company numbered eighty men, but sixty was more common later in the war. Since all the men and much of their past service is known, it is possible to break them down into platoons, squads, and messes, on the basis of earlier membership in the old Delaware Regiment. Kirkwood's company had a reported strength of fifty-one privates, three sergeants, three corporals, and an ensign, lieutenant, and captain.[20]

The Delaware Company was not simply a gathering of survivors. A cadre of two sergeants and three corporals was assigned on 16 September 1780. On 20 September, privates were detailed with each company in the old regiment represented by several men and at least one leader. Noncommissioned officers apparently decided with their officers who went to Kirkwood's Company.[21]

The three sixty-man Maryland companies were also created from earlier regiments. Captain Richard Anderson's First Maryland Company was formed with one platoon each from the old 1st and 7th Maryland Regiments. Lieutenant William Adams and Ensign Walter Dyer were placed in this company by brigade orders of 16 December 1780.[22] Captain Henry

Dobson commanded the Second Maryland Company composed of veterans from the 2d, 4th, and 6th Maryland Regiments. He was assisted by Lieutenant James Ewing and Ensign Edward Miles Smith.[23] The Third Maryland Company was made up from the 3rd and 5th Maryland Regiments under the command of Lieutenant Nicholas Mangers. Lieutenant Gassaway Watkins and Ensign Roger Nelson were placed in this company.[24]

Virginia had a history of combining units together as needed. This was particularly true late in the war due to recruiting problems, under-strength units, and various crises in the South. Veterans already in North Carolina, including survivors of the infamous Waxhaws massacre, and new recruits were combined into a Virginia light infantry company and assigned to the Flying Army in October 1780. The commander was initially Captain Peter Bruin, but by January 1781 Bruin was in Virginia, recalled by Jefferson. At Cowpens, Andrew Wallace commanded the Virginia Company. His second-in-command was Captain Conway Oldham.[25]

Intermediate between long-service Continentals and short-term militia were state troops. Men in these units enlisted for six to eighteen months. Pensioners usually mentioned service as state troops, state line, or state regulars rather than militia or Continentals.

A detachment of Virginia State Troops at Portsmouth was commanded by Major Thomas Posey although he, personally, was not at Cowpens. At least one fifty-man company under Captain John Lawson participated in the battle.[26] A very few North Carolina State Troops can be identified by a combination of long-term enlistments and by enlistment in eastern counties. Many seem to have been on duty as artisans at Salisbury when they were sent to join Morgan. At Cowpens, these men were apparently commanded by Captain Henry Connelly.[27]

South Carolina State Troops serving as infantry were commanded by Major Samuel Hammond and Captain Joseph Pickens. These men were raised under Colonel Andrew Pickens and Major James McCall during late 1780, apparently with a core of officers and men from Pickens's Long Cane Regiment. When they joined Morgan, "those who were not so equipped [as cavalry] were armed with Rifles & placed under" Samuel Hammond.[28] Hammond took command of the left wing of skirmishers, so Joseph Pickens, younger brother of Andrew Pickens, took over command of the South Carolina state infantry.[29]

In the absence of a standing, or regular, army, militia were the original colonial defense force. The militia existed from the beginning of colonial settlements and served as an internal peace-keeping force. By 1780, most Americans did not view militia duty as glamorous, rewarding, or desirable.

Continentals openly made fun of the militia. South Carolina's Colonel Francis Marion was "attended by a very few followers, . . . most of them miserably equipped; their appearance was in fact so burlesque, that it was with much difficulty the diversion of the regular soldiery was restrained by the officers; and the general himself was glad of an opportunity of detaching Colonel Marion, at his own instance, toward the interior of South Carolina."[30]

Precise distinctions between regular service and militia duty were made by veterans in their pension statements. They used terms such as Continental, State Line, and Regular to describe long-term service. Militia service was usually short term, and often resulted from an enforced draft, as recalled by Cowpens veteran Virginian Jacob Taylor: "the first time I was enlisted, I considered myself in the regular service. I was in the regular service three years and eight days. The second time I was draughted. The first time I enlisted."[31] Militia service was legally required duty. In an emergency, the age group could expand dramatically.[32]

In the South, militia duty served to identify who supported the patriot or Loyalist sides by noting who reported for duty. Lukewarm British supporters called "pet Tories" turned out with patriot militia but seem to have taken little part. Tories who were more open or obnoxious were singled out for special treatment.[33] Militia responsibilities included collecting supplies. This duty was not simply gathering food, clothing, and leather goods, but included retribution against Loyalists. Patriot militia frequently plundered those who supported the king rather than impress property from those supporting the patriot cause. Loyalist militia operated in the same fashion.[34]

Like the army, the militia was organized into brigades of two or more regiments. A regiment was composed of several companies made up of smaller groups called a "lieutenant's command," a platoon, or a squad, depending on circumstances. Southern militia regiments were organized along county lines with companies drawn from neighborhoods. The county's social and economic elite served as the regiment's leadership while local leaders were company commanders. Musters were usually at the company level with the captain charged with training his men.

Each battalion was commanded by a lieutenant colonel or colonel. It was the custom in South Carolina in 1780 to have two colonels.[35] Pensioners indicated the South Carolina militia followed an alternating system in late 1780 and 1781. In this organizational scheme, some captains served under a certain major and lieutenant colonel to make up a regiment's monthly quota. The next month, the colonel and another major commanded the remainder of the regiment.

The January 1781 situation in backcountry South Carolina was so critical that Whig leaders called for a total manpower commitment regardless of rotation. Duplication of officer positions under the alternating system provided a large number of officers vis-à-vis the number of men. Officers therefore were placed throughout the chain of command where they were needed and often held leadership positions at the squad level where lieutenants commanded groups of four or five.

In North Carolina, officers recruited in accordance with their rank. A captain was expected to raise twenty-five or thirty men, if not more. Ideally, soldiers came from among the neighbors within an officer's home area. In Rowan County, "Lieutenant Elsbury beat up for Volunteers and this declarant with fourteen others joined and entered into the services of the United States." In Lincoln County, a Captain Barber raised "a company of volunteers, about 15 or 20."[36]

In order to alleviate hardship, drafts were usually for a company-sized unit drawn from the entire county. The first call was for volunteers. If enough men were not raised, the county drafted more to fill out the unit. Drafted men were sometimes allowed to obtain substitutes. These replacements were often unmarried, unemployed kin of the drafted man. Other men hired replacements. In any case, volunteers, draftees, and hired replacements were usually men who were not family heads and were often without work. In some cases, those drafted were former Continental soldiers who had come home after a tour of duty and then found their names in the draft pool.[37]

Such was the crisis during late December 1780 that special consideration was given to those who brought their own horses. Rowan County's James Stewart "volunteered his service and furnished his horse and Served a Tour of Six weeks which Service of Self & horse was then considered and agreed to be equated to a Three month Tour on foot." Similar encouragement was given to infantrymen in Surry County, where officers promised Jesse Morris "that if he would volunteer and serve 6 weeks he should receive pay and a discharge for 3 months. He accordingly received a discharge at Burk Courthouse from Captain Hampton for 3 months service but the time he was in actual service on this tour was 6 weeks."[38]

In South Carolina, the crisis was so acute that all available men were called out, and virtually the entire Spartanburg County regiment saw service with Morgan. The battle was fought in Spartanburg District, which provided two battalions, but districts (counties) farther away provided fewer men.[39]

An overview of the militia suggests that, while they may have been undisciplined in a formal military sense, they were not raw troops. Many had considerable combat experience, and virtually all had "smelled powder" in backcountry ambushes or skirmishes. At Cowpens, perhaps one-fifth of the militia had prior Continental service.

Militia strength varied from day to day, depending on the situation, time of service, weather, and a host of other factors, as explained by South Carolina's Aaron Guyton, who later recollected:

> I was under Col Brandon who had a few Brave Men who stood true for the Cause of Liberty in the back part of the State. . . . Some times we had 75 Some Times 150 men, and some times we had 4 or 5 Cols with from 50 to 150 men. Each of them had Command of a Regt at home & some times not more than 5 of his men with him. The Cols were Brandon, Hayes, Robuck, White,—In December 1780 . . . we had no Officer in our Company & only two or three or four men. And the morning before the Battle 17 Jany 1781 we joined Capt John Thompsons Compy.[40]

When field-grade officers, major or above, were mentioned, they rarely led more than 200 men. A militia regiment was actually composed of 100–300 men, organized in companies ranging in size from twenty to forty soldiers. A regiment of ten companies would be a large unit with about 250 men. The term *company*, as defined by the Von Steuben manual, is misleading for militia. Company size is difficult to assess, since few figures exist, but militia captains rarely commanded more than forty men. The immediate impression is that a captain commanded about twenty to thirty men, or half the size of a Continental army company. This helps explain the plethora of captains at Cowpens. A captain's group of twenty or thirty men would be consolidated with another similar "company" to achieve better command and control. In such situations, surplus officers took positions normally filled by sergeants and corporals.

In discussing company size at Cowpens, it is important to realize that the smaller units, and their sizes, were generated from documents. Estimating the size of a company where it is not given is fraught with danger. Pension documents provide clues. Five sixty-man Continental companies, from three states, were examined to show the representativeness of pension data. Five militia companies representing three states provide specific information about unit size that can be compared with pension applications.

The Rockbridge Rifles under Captain James Gilmore claimed 42 enlisted men when they left Lexington, Virginia. Allowing for attrition, they probably had about 38 enlisted men in the battle. Spartanburg captain John Collins raised 24 men the night before Cowpens. Captain Samuel Sexton

TABLE I. *Ratio of Unit Size to Survivors Who Made Pension Application*

Unit	Number	Survivors	Ratio
Continentals			
Delaware Co.	60	10	1:6
1st Maryland Co.	60	16	1:4
2nd Maryland Co.	60	9	1:6.5
3rd Maryland Co.	60	29	1:2
Virginia Co.	60	8[a]	1:8.5
Militia			
Virginia			
Gilmore's Co.	44	6	1:7.3
North Carolina			
M. Clark's Co.	20–30	4	1:5–7.5
South Carolina			
Sexton's Co.	24	1	1:24
Otterson's Co.	30	2	1:15
Collins's Co.	24	3	1:8

[a]Not all Virginia Continentals are included due to difficulty in identification.

of Hayes's Battalion led a newly raised company of 25 men. Another Little River company under Captain John Irby had as many as 70 men.[41]

Continentals are easier to identify because better records were kept and they had longer service commitments than the short militia tours. In comparison with many militia companies, in which only two to six men can be identified, every Delaware soldier at Cowpens is known, and the entire second platoon of the 1st Maryland Company is known as well. While all of Gilmore's Rockbridge County, Virginia, soldiers are known, complete rolls from other militia companies did not survive; their size is known only from pension statements.

Based on an admittedly small sample, for every one person's name in a document, there were about three men who actually were present and fought with the company at Cowpens. For militiamen, the range is much greater, and fewer men apparently survived to claim pensions or identified their company if they did. Militia companies range from a low of one name representing five men to a high of about fifteen. Sexton's company seems aberrant in that no other veteran claimed service with him. A similar case occurred with Irby's seventy-man refugee company in Hayes's Battalion, where only two veterans filed pension applications claiming service under him. Continental numbers are probably more representative because they were easier to identify, not because they survived longer. It is probable that one pensioner represents about four soldiers who served during the Revolutionary War, at least for the limited sample represented by Cowpens pensioners.

Morgan and his subordinates recognized the utility of smaller militia "companies" and shifted them as needed. One Burke County, North Carolina, company was put on the main line's left flank because their captain opted to serve with mounted volunteers augmenting Washington's dragoons.[42] Unit consolidation began even before the men reached Morgan. Some Virginia companies merged in Virginia; North and South Carolina counties did likewise, just as they did before Kings Mountain.[43]

The Virginia militia at Cowpens fit into two major groups. First, there are the four long-service companies from Augusta, Fauquier, and Rockbridge Counties. The other Virginia units were a mix of militia and state troops nominally under the command of Major David Campbell. Major "Frank" Triplett was given command of the Flying Army's Virginia militia at New Providence, North Carolina, in mid-October 1780.[44] In service since October, their three-month enlistments had apparently been extended a month. This battalion is the best-known Cowpens Virginia militia unit.

Three different Fauquier County companies underwent consolidation during the march south. The final result of the mergers and the arrival of additional companies can be seen in the company commanded by Captain John Combs at Cowpens. Combs's Fauquier County Company was originally Triplett's company. When Triplett took command of the Virginia militia, John Combs took over the company. Another captain, James Winn, was a platoon leader whose "company" was a platoon under Combs.[45]

James Tate's Company was one of two raised by draft in Augusta County during October 1780. Some men received their weapons when they arrived in Hillsborough, North Carolina.[46] Captain James Gilmore's Rockbridge County Company was known as the "Rockbridge Rifles" because they carried that weapon.[47] Gilmore's company also included a few men from neighboring Botetourt County. Captain Patrick Buchanan's Company was the second company drafted in Augusta County in the fall of 1780. Except during the battle of Cowpens, Buchanan's company was under Triplett's operational control.[48]

Most Virginia militiamen under Triplett, on the left, and Captain Edmund Tate, on the right, did not claim prior Continental experience. Not mentioning Continental service is an important omission because veterans of the regular army, even today, invariably recall that portion of service as distinctive. Former Continentals would, and did, remember their regular service as different from militia duty.[49]

Fifty-two men from Triplett's Battalion are listed in Moss. The forty-four enlisted men include thirty-six privates and eight sergeants. Twenty-two privates had prior service, seventeen with combat, but only eight (22 percent), all with combat, had Continental experience. The eight sergeants included three Continental combat veterans and three others who had experienced combat as militiamen. Of eight officers, two did not document any combat. Triplett saw combat as a Continental officer. Triplett's men had been together in at least one fight, as most of them mentioned the skirmish at Rugeley's Mill. These numbers hardly warrant suggesting most were "continental veterans," as some historians reported.[50]

Other Virginians claimed service under captains not otherwise known to have served at Cowpens. Patterns emerging from this group make it possible to identify two additional companies, and a third company that arrived as the battle ended. By comparing officers, march routes, arrival times, and experiences during enlistment, two companies from Major David Campbell's Virginia militia regiment can be identified as participants in the battle.[51]

Campbell's Virginia Militia Regiment is mentioned by a number of pensioners and historians. One hundred men under Campbell in Salisbury, North Carolina, were ordered about 8 January to join Morgan. On 16 January, William L. Davidson reported from Charlotte that Campbell was moving to join Morgan by way of Kings Mountain and would be leaving the next day. Pensioners indicate Campbell's Regiment did not travel as an intact unit. At least two of Campbell's companies reached Cowpens in time for the battle as is evidenced by wounds some men received.[52] Since Campbell arrived at Cowpens about noon on 17 January, and one company arrived just as the battle ended, it is most likely he was at Kings Mountain before the 16th. Given the hundred men ordered to Cowpens, the typical number of militia companies, and other units with Campbell, it is likely these companies numbered about twenty-five men each.[53]

The North Carolina militia riflemen are usually described as front-line skirmishers who then withdrew to the militia line. This is true but simplistic. North Carolina unit composition and numbers have been subject to discussion for a long time.[54] The North Carolina militia commander was Colonel Joseph McDowell, whose name was "generally pronounced 'McDoll.'" He lived at Quaker Meadows, and the plantation name served to distinguish him from his nephew of the same name who resided at Pleasant Garden.[55]

McDowell's Battalion had two majors: Charles McDowell, his elder brother, and David McKissick.[56] Each major coordinated two or three companies of skirmishers under Joseph McDowell's overall command. The North Carolina battalion resolved issues of seniority and county affiliation by having majors give orders to captains commanding consolidated companies. This structure enhanced control by creating progressively larger units.

Regardless of county affiliation, all North Carolina militiamen served under McDowell with the exception of twenty-five Burke County men placed under Triplett. McDowell had at least five large, consolidated companies whose men came from Burke, Rowan, Lincoln, Rutherford, Surry, Wilkes, and a group of counties in north-central North Carolina. Each company numbered at least forty men, based on statistical projections from pension records where each man represents at least three and possibly as many as five men. County representation reflects the strategic situation. No North Carolina border county east of Cowpens provided men except one man from Mecklenburg. Border county men were needed to block a British advance through their own counties toward central North Carolina.

Salisbury, North Carolina, was a major production center for clothing, shoes, and accoutrements. The work was performed by artisans who either volunteered for service, were drafted, or were taken out of combat units. As part of their duty, the artisans were sent to Salisbury and utilized their skills as tailors, shoemakers, carpenters, wheelwrights, and leathersmiths, but they could be assigned to other duties. When Tarleton advanced against Morgan, some were formed into a company and sent to Morgan.

If all the militiamen from Guilford, Rockingham, Caswell, Orange, Granville, and Warren Counties, as well as those from the eastern counties, were actually consolidated, as seems likely, they would number about two dozen after deductions were made for known Continentals, state troops, dragoons, and militiamen serving in other units. The twenty-four known men represent a Cowpens company of about sixty to seventy-five men. This composite company was created with men from counties providing squads or individual men. So many Guilford County men claimed service under Rowan County's Captain William Wilson that it is possible he led this "Northern Company" at Cowpens.

The Burke County Company is well known. On first impression, it appears the Cowpens skirmish line, if not North Carolina's total contribution to the battle, were all from Burke County. For one thing, Colonel Joseph McDowell, Major Charles McDowell, and Captain Joseph

McDowell were from Burke County. Burke County men included many with extensive prior service. Some, like David Vance, had been Continentals.[57] The commander of the Burke Company was Captain Joseph "Pleasant Garden Joe" McDowell, nephew of Colonel Joseph "Quaker Meadows Joe" McDowell.[58] A final group of Burke County men served under Triplett on the main line's right flank. This company of twenty to thirty men marched to the field under Captain Mordecai Clark. When Clark volunteered to fight on horseback, his men were posted as infantry on Triplett's left flank.[59]

The Rowan County Company was another large unit. Men from adjacent counties served in this company under some eight named captains. Since veterans likely remembered officers as holding their highest earned rank, there were probably fewer captains. The twenty-five officers and men who served under known Rowan County officers indicate a company strength of about seventy-five men under Captain Abel Armstrong.[60]

Men from Surry and Wilkes Counties served in another company. Eleven Surry County veterans, three pensioners from Stokes County, and nine Wilkes County men claimed service at Cowpens. Surry and Wilkes men served together as a unit under Colonel Benjamin Cleveland at Kings Mountain. This company of about sixty men was commanded by Captain Samuel Hampton.[61]

The Lincoln and Rutherford men were combined into a single unit; these new counties were known as Tryon County until 1779. The men of Rutherford and Lincoln served with Burke County men at Kings Mountain under McDowell. Men from all three counties mentioned serving under officers from each other's counties at different times.[62] Thirteen men claimed service at Cowpens, indicating a company of about forty to fifty men. They probably were under Captain Joseph White, who served under Major Charles McDowell.[63]

South Carolina militia infantry formed the second line as a brigade of four battalions under Colonel Andrew Pickens. Morgan gave Pickens overall command of the militia, but official promotion to general did not occur until after 23 January. As senior colonel at Cowpens, Pickens exercised a general's command.[64] His battalions were commanded by Colonel John Thomas Jr., Lieutenant Colonel Benjamin Roebuck, Lieutenant Colonel Joseph Hayes, and Colonel Thomas Brandon. Thomas's Spartanburg Regiment, from the Cowpens neighborhood, provided two battalions. The militia battalions ranged in size from about 120 to more than 250 men.

Andrew Pickens was born in Paxton Township, Pennsylvania, in 1739. At the time of Cowpens, Pickens lived near Long Cane Creek north of Ninety

TABLE 2.

North Carolina Cowpens Pensioners
by County

Bladen	1
Burke	15
Caswell	2
Dobbs	1
Edgecombe	1
Granville	3
Guilford	9
Jones	1
Lincoln	9
Mecklenburg	1
Montgomery	1
New Hanover	1
Orange	5
Rockingham	3
Rowan	23
Rutherford	4
Surry	11
Stokes	3
Wake	3
Warren	2
Wilkes	9
Total	108

Note: Some men in Table 2 are
Continentals and state dragoons.
Wake County men were either Conti-
nental or state troops. Warren County
had one Continental. Guilford County
included at least two dragoons and one
Continental. Orange County included a
Continental and a dragoon. Granville
County's total included one Continental.

Six. Married, with three sons and six daughters, he was a devout Presbyterian of simple habits.[65] In the months before Cowpens, Pickens and his activities seem mysterious. He served as a commissioner to examine treatment of the Kings Mountain prisoners because many were his neighbors. On parole, Pickens did nothing militant until Tory dragoons under Robert Dunlap terrorized his family and destroyed his plantation. The parole violation was noted in a letter Pickens personally presented to Captain Ker, the British commander at White Hall, outside Ninety Six.[66]

Georgia's Major James Jackson served as brigade major under Pickens. He joined Morgan with three small companies after fighting in South Carolina with Georgia refugees. In 1782, Jackson would lead the Americans into Savannah at the head of his Georgia Legion. After the war, he served in the U.S. Congress and as governor of Georgia.[67]

The four battalions deployed from right to left under Roebuck, Thomas, Hayes, and Brandon, all of whom had extensive experience as combat leaders. Lieutenant Colonel Benjamin Roebuck served as second in command of the Spartanburg Regiment. Born in Orange County, Virginia, circa 1755, his family settled in Spartanburg District, South Carolina, in 1777. Roebuck saw combat at Stono River and Savannah as a lieutenant and was a captain at Kings Mountain. Wounded at Mud Lick in March 1781, he was captured while convalescing and imprisoned at Ninety Six.[68]

Roebuck's Battalion consisted of at least three consolidated companies commanded by Captains George Roebuck, Major Parson, and Dennis Tramell. Captain George Roebuck was a brother of the battalion commander. Captain Major Parson had seen service in the South Carolina Continental Line and was wounded in the assault on Savannah in October 1779. Tramell started his military service in 1777 and, by the time of Cowpens, had seen heavy fighting in the South Carolina backcountry.[69]

Captain Dennis Tramell's Company is very well documented for a militia company because pensioners reported information about officers and located the unit on the battlefield. Since the company demonstrates unit consolidation, a discussion of its composition is appropriate. Sergeant James Harden reported the company was often assisted by volunteers under Captain John Lawson. When Lawson was killed at Cowpens, Jeremiah Dickson (Dixon) took command. One of Dickson's men stated that he was a "Flank Guard" to Thomas's Regiment, thus placing Dickson's platoon on the right of the South Carolina militia line.[70]

Colonel John Thomas Jr. succeeded his father as commander of the Upper Ninety Six militia, which became the Spartanburg Regiment. Thomas's major was Henry White, a courageous man better known for his exploits at Ninety Six and Eutaw Springs than Cowpens.[71] Thomas had at least four companies present at Cowpens, under Captain Thomas Farrow, Captain John Files Sr., Captain Andrew Barry, and Captain John Collins.

Captain John Collins noted that "the night before the Battle of the Cowpens I again joined General Morgan with 24 fresh men. and fought with my Company the next day."[72] Captain Andrew Barry led a company that included his brother, John.[73] Captain John Files Sr. commanded a company that included his sons, John Jr., Jeremiah, and Adam. Wounded at Cowpens, he was murdered in May 1781 by a party of Tories and Indians. Captain Thomas Farrow served since the war's beginning with extensive combat experience before Cowpens.[74]

Lieutenant Colonel Joseph Hayes commanded the Little River Regiment, from what is now Laurens County, positioned between Thomas and Brandon. At Kings Mountain, Hayes took over Williams's Regiment when Williams was killed. Contemporaries described him as bold and incautious. Hayes was hacked to death after surrendering Hayes Station, "Edgehill," to William Cunningham during the "Bloody Scout" of November 1781. Hayes's major was probably Robert Dugan of Newberry District.[75]

The Little River Regiment was composed of five companies under Captains James Ewing, William Harris, James Dugan, Samuel Sexton, and James Irby. Captain James Ewing commanded the right flank company located on the Green River Road.[76] Captain William Harris served under Hayes during the fight at Blackstock's Plantation. Promoted about the time of Cowpens, he attained the rank of major before the end of the war.[77] Captain James Dugan was reported as a major at Cowpens, but his brother Robert appears to have held that rank. James was murdered by Tories the night following Cowpens.[78] Captain John Lindsay commanded a platoon in Dugan's Company.

Two officers raised men on the way to Cowpens. Captain Samuel Sexton, while on "route to the Cowpens . . . succeeded in inducing twenty-five men to join . . . and [I] was chosen their captain. . . . [We] offered our services to the army at the Cowpens, were received and I and my Company were put under the command of Colonel Hays." Captain John Irby noted "many refugees . . . formed a volunteer Company to the amount of Sixty or Seventy and that he was elected Captain of said Company and was commissioned as such by General Pickens of South Carolina. That he served as Captain of said Company in the Battle of the Cowpens."[79]

Union County's Fair Forest Regiment was commanded by Colonel Thomas Brandon. Brandon had a fearsome reputation when it came to dealing with Tories. Born in Pennsylvania, he emigrated to Union County.

Lieutenant Colonel William Farr was second in command of the Fair Forest Regiment. Brandon's brigade major was Joseph McJunkin, the brother-in-law of Colonel John Thomas Jr. Brandon's adjutant was Captain Joshua Palmer.[80]

It is difficult to tell where Fair Forest companies served at Cowpens. Veterans were as likely to list Brandon or Farr as the commander, although Farr actually served as a sharpshooter.[81] Placing the Fair Forest companies on the battle line is done on the basis of seniority, casualties, and residence patterns. The companies were probably aligned from the right flank with Robert Anderson, Robert Montgomery, John Thompson, Joseph Hughes, and William Grant. A volunteer company from Chester County gave John Moffett no seniority in the Fair Forest Regiment, so it is likely his men were on the battalion's left incorporated with a Fairfield County company under James Adair.[82]

William Grant Sr. served in the French and Indian War and was a captain under Brandon at Blackstock's. On the basis of seniority, he ranks lower than Thompson.[83] John Moffett, of Chester County, distinguished himself at Fishing Creek and commanded a company at Kings Mountain.[84] A last Fair Forest company was under Samuel Otterson. This company was scouting when the battle began and did not get back in time, but they played a major role in pursuing Tarleton.[85]

Georgia militia was present in three small companies commanded by Major Cunningham and Captains Richard Heard, George Walton, and Joshua Inman.[86] Captain Joshua Inman appears infrequently in documentary sources relating to the Revolution, on muster or pay rolls. Like Joshua Inman, George Walton is one of the forgotten captains of the Revolution.[87] Captain Richard Heard came from Wilkes County, Georgia. His family plantation was called Heard's Fort, in Wilkes County, Georgia.[88] Many other Georgians fought with refugee and South Carolina companies.[89]

Lieutenant Colonel William Washington commanded the mounted Americans. His nominal command, the 3rd Continental Light Dragoons, was augmented by state troops, militia, and volunteers before the battle. His employment of the mounted arm exemplified the phrase "as opportunity presents," because the American cavalry played a key role in sequentially driving off attacks against both flanks. Despite their numerical inferiority, American horsemen were successful at Cowpens because they were employed en masse at critical times.

Washington was of "stout frame, being six feet in height, broad, strong, and corpulent." Lee described him as a "fit man for the common business of life, amiable and good humored, generous, innocent and agreeable." In describing Washington's military accomplishments, Lee commences with the word "bold," which can be seen in engagements such as Hammond's Store, Cowpens, Guilford Courthouse, Hobkirk's Hill, and Eutaw Springs. He preferred action and was very composed in battle.[90]

When the 1st and 3d Dragoon Regiments were sent south in 1780, Washington was in command of the 3d regiment. The light dragoons were badly handled by the British, first at Monck's Corner and later at Lenud's Ferry. Washington attempted to recruit the regiment in North Carolina but was not very successful.[91]

Included in his Continental cavalry at Cowpens were remnants of the 1st Continental Light Dragoon Regiment, but most First Dragoons were stationed below Cheraws on the Peedee River under Captain Griffin Fauntleroy.[92] Enough 1st Continental veterans claimed they were present at Cowpens to suggest they formed a troop under Washington. These men were identified because they mentioned service in the 1st Regiment, or under Theodoric Bland or Anthony White, and also served at Cowpens.[93] When the dragoons were consolidated under Washington in the fall of 1780, some Continental infantrymen were given the opportunity to join. At least three men from the Delaware Regiment did so.[94]

The Continental light dragoons were seriously undermanned and numbered only eighty-two men at the time of Cowpens. While a regiment had four mounted troops and two dismounted troops, Washington's four understrength troops at Cowpens were all mounted.[95] The troops were commanded by Major Richard Call and Captains William Barrett and William Parsons. A Lieutenant Bell apparently commanded Churchill Jones's troop.

A few Virginia state dragoons were initially under the command of Major John Nelson, then Captain Clement Read (Reid). Although General Greene ordered Read back to Virginia in December, a small group, perhaps less than fifteen men, was present at Cowpens. These men were probably the best equipped of Read's troopers, retained because they were needed.[96]

Some North Carolina state dragoons may not have been so designated at the time of Cowpens. However, a number of North Carolina men swore that they served at Cowpens as horsemen. Their enlistment terms were longer than usual for militia. Some used the term "state dragoon(s)" or "light horse"; others claimed service at Cowpens under Washington. These North Carolinians may have been guides similar to those delegated from Hampton's South Carolina state dragoon regiment.[97]

The South Carolina state dragoons were those South Carolina State Troops already "equipped as cavalry" when they joined Morgan under the command of Major James McCall. McCall "had been promoted to the command of a Regiment of Cavalry authorized to be enrolled for six months. . . . very few arrived with swords & pistols. . . . the few 25 - to 30 that were equipped as Horsemen were placed under Col MCall and attached to Col Washington's Command."[98] McCall's twenty-five or thirty men who "arrived with swords & pistols" apparently served in "troops" led by Captain Samuel Taylor, who lost a leg at Cowpens, and Captain Alexander Luckie.[99] Some mounted Georgians were also with the mounted South Carolina State Troops.[100]

American preparations for dealing with Tarleton's legion included equipping men with swords Morgan earlier ordered from the main army. "Two companies of volunteers were called for. One was raised by Major Jolly of Union District, and the other, I think, by Major McCall. . . . We drew swords that night, and were informed we had authority to press any horse not belonging to a dragoon or an officer, into our service for the day." These volunteers numbered forty-five men, probably the number of swords Morgan had available to issue that night. They included William Venable, who was "in Capt George [sic] Taylors Company of Light horse, in Col. Billy Washington's regiment."[101]

Taken as a whole, the Americans might at first seem to be a motley group. A close inspection of participant accounts and pension records reveals that Morgan's men, if untrained in formal European warfare, were hardly green troops new to battle. More than 70 percent had seen combat, some of it heavy. While this is particularly true of the officers, it is also true of the men.

Whatever their experience, Morgan utilized the men he had very well. The British coming after him already had a reputation for brutally handling Americans who broke and ran, and his men knew it. Several men were at Waxhaws when Tarleton's dragoons got the upper hand. Many of them burned with a desire for retribution stronger than any love of liberty, but they knew their enemy was formidable.

THE BRITISH

The British pursuing Morgan were a combined arms task force under a young, aggressive officer named Tarleton. Banastre Tarleton, third child of John and Jane Parker Tarleton, was born 21 August 1754 at the family estate near Liverpool. His family was involved in shipping and owned plantations in the West Indies.[102]

Tarleton studied to become a lawyer at University College, Oxford. There he was closely associated with Francis Rawdon, who would see American service, some of it in the South. Tarleton's time seems to have

Banastre Tarleton; oil painting by Sir Joshua Reynolds
(National Portrait Gallery, London)

been spent at sporting events, but he must have done well enough academically, as he went to London and studied law at Middle Temple after his father's death, a period that included living the life of a rake and gambler.[103]

He eventually quit studying law and purchased a cornet's commission in the 1st Regiment, Dragoon Guards. In 1775, Tarleton was serving in Norwich. He went overseas on leave before 24 December 1775 and saw service at Charleston in June 1776. He also served with the 16th Light Dragoons during the New York campaign.[104] In the winter of 1776–77, he was in the party that captured General Charles Lee. He participated in the Philadelphia Campaign of 1777 and returned to New York with the army in 1778.

While on the Philadelphia Campaign, Tarleton worked on occasion with American Loyalists serving as scouts under the command of Captain Richard Hovenden, the commander who would make first contact with Americans at Cowpens.[105] During 1778, British officers and American Loyalists raised several companies of Americans for British service. One mounted unit was raised by Captain David Kinlock of Fraser's Highlanders, the 71st Regiment. These companies were combined into the British Legion in June and July 1778. Tarleton was appointed major of the legion on 1 August 1778. Thereafter, the history of the British Legion, or Tarleton's legion, as it came to be known, was the history of Tarleton in America. At the time of Cowpens, Banastre Tarleton was twenty-six years old.[106]

Tarleton deserves credit for his rapid marches, hard, driving attacks, and an approach to warfare that seems more modern than that of some contemporaries. The ability to obtain information ahead of the army, the rapidity with which he pursued and destroyed opposition forces, and achieved maximum efforts, at times, from a rather motley group, reflect favorably on his abilities, even though he was often somewhat impulsive on the battlefield.

His command badly damaged American mounted forces at Monck's Corner and Lenud's Ferry in 1780. His destruction of Buford's command at Waxhaws, South Carolina, and the infamous brutality of his officers and men toward wounded and prisoners there and elsewhere, created an impression of savagery that served both to enhance his operations and rally the opposition. Tarleton routed Colonel Thomas Sumter at Fishing Ford, South Carolina, on 18 August 1780,[107] temporarily ending organized American resistance in South Carolina. American writers have generally portrayed him as "Bloody Tarleton" for destroying patriot military units in the South. To some extent this is unwarranted, but a perception of cruelty and arrogance seems to surround Tarleton and his legion, even though there are examples of humanity to friends and enemies alike.[108]

Tarleton's command in January 1781 included infantry, artillery, and cavalry, making up what would be called a combined arms group today. It combined rapid movement with heavy firepower and included all of Cornwallis's light infantry. Both the British Legion infantry and the 71st Regiment were known for their rapid marching and ferocity in battle.

The 7th Regiment of Foot, the Royal Fusiliers, was rebuilt before coming south. The regiment had been destroyed by capture during the American invasion of Canada in 1775. Prisoners exchanged at New York in December 1776 allowed the regiment to reform. The fusiliers saw service in the northern theater between 1777 and 1779. The 7th was sent to Charleston in December 1779.[109] At Cowpens, the 7th was commanded by Major Timothy Newmarsh, a veteran officer of some distinction. There were nine officers and about 168 men arranged in four companies, with a captain, a lieutenant, and about forty men in each company.[110]

The 71st Regiment of Foot, Fraser's Highlanders, was raised specifically for American service in 1775. So many men turned out that two battalions numbering a total of 2,340 men were initially mustered. The 71st was an elite unit and made an impact as the "hired soldiers" mentioned in the Declaration of Independence. The regiment arrived in New York in July 1776 and saw extensive northern service before transfer to the South in December 1778.[111]

Fraser's Highlanders enhanced their solid reputation in the South, commencing with the initial assault on Savannah in December 1778 and the occupation of Georgia. In the battles at Stono and Briar Creek, the taking of Charleston, and the subsequent occupation of South Carolina, the 71st received high honors for their performance. After routing American militia at Camden, the 71st was heavily involved in the destruction of the Maryland and Delaware Division. Justifiably, the 71st Highlanders were regarded as first-rate troops.[112] At Cowpens, the line companies of the 71st had 249 men and 14 officers. "Out of sixteen officers which they had in the field, nine were killed and wounded," and only Ensign Fraser escaped becoming a prisoner of war.[113]

Each British army regiment had two specialized "flank" companies. One was composed of grenadiers; the other was light infantry—men selected for their agility and endurance. Light companies were usually consolidated into battalions operating in front or on the flanks of a military force.[114] The light infantry at Cowpens formed a battalion of four companies detached from the 16th Regiment (41 men), the First Battalion, 71st Regiment (about 35 men), the Second Battalion, 71st Regiment (about 34 men), and the Prince of Wales American Regiment (25–50 men). The low estimate of the light infantry's total strength is about 135; possibly it had as many as 160 men. The range is due to confusion about the Prince of Wales American Regiment's strength.[115] The light infantry battalion commander is unknown. On seniority, command should have gone to the officer leading the 16th Regiment's light infantry company. There were two officers listed for the 71st, but both were lieutenants and only one officer, Lieutenant Lindsay, was with the Prince of Wales's light infantry company.[116]

The British Legion infantry was the foot component of the British Legion. It was raised in New York during July 1778 from the Caledonian Volunteers, a Philadelphia Tory unit, and three other companies originally armed with a "light musket," or fusil.[117] The legion went to Savannah in December 1778. The unit saw extensive service after the fall of Charleston, and many American prisoners were recruited into it during the fall of 1780. Compared with other Tory units, the legion was considered an elite group.[118]

The British Legion compiled a mixed record during the southern campaigns. The legion is well known because its commanding officer, Banastre Tarleton, wrote an account of its 1780–81 activities.[119] Its actual combat performance varied from superb at Waxhaws to very poor at Charlotte and Cowpens. When well led and in a pursuit situation, the legion was almost unbeatable, but when faced with determined opposition, it might opt out of engaging altogether. The British Legion infantry was usually commanded by Major George Hanger, Lord Colraine, but he was absent sick at the time of Cowpens, so the senior Captain John Rousselet was probably acting as commander. British Legion infantry strength at Cowpens was between 200 and 271 enlisted men.[120]

The mounted troops under Tarleton included two units, the 17th Light Dragoons and the British Legion dragoons. The 17th was commanded at Cowpens by Lieutenant Henry Nettles, who came to America in the initial 17th Light Dragoons deployment from Ireland. His deputy was Cornet Patterson.[121]

Arriving in Boston in May 1775, the 17th served in the northern campaigns until 1778. When Campbell took Savannah in 1778, sixty 17th Light Dragoons accompanying the expedition were attached to the British Legion. The unit was still attached to the British Legion at Waxhaws. Some 17th Light Dragoons returned to New York with Clinton before 16 August 1780, but the remainder continued serving with the British Legion.[122]

The 17th Regiment's southern service included Camden, Fishing Creek, and Blackstock's before Cowpens. December reinforcements sent to Cornwallis included about fifty additional members of the regiment. Tarleton requested these men for his detachment, but only if they had horses. In the battle of Cowpens, the 17th Light Dragoons have traditionally been credited with about fifty men, suggesting some new men were present.[123] After Cowpens, they served at Guilford Courthouse and in Virginia before surrendering twenty-five men at Yorktown. An additional 17th officer, Ensign David Ogilvie, commanded a British Legion troop.[124]

Despite a close association, the 17th Light Dragoons never considered themselves part of the British Legion. "When their old regimental uniform was worn out they were offered the green uniform of the legion, but they would have none of it. They preferred to patch their own ragged and faded scarlet, and be men of the Seventeenth."[125]

The other British cavalry unit at Cowpens was the British Legion dragoons, the mounted men of Tarleton's British Legion. For most people, it *was* Tarleton. Its history was the same as that of the legion infantry. As originally formed, it had six companies of dragoons armed with saber and pistol.[126] The British Legion dragoons at Cowpens had approximately 250 men. As with the infantry, they were a mixed group of Tories and former American soldiers enlisted after Camden.

The British artillery at Cowpens is credited with a solid performance, but little is known about them. Generally speaking, the Fourth Battalion, Royal Artillery, served in America during the Revolutionary War and participated in virtually every battle. A light gun called for eleven men and a noncommissioned officer. When two guns were together, a lieutenant commanded them, but Tarleton's two cannon were originally from different commands, the 7th Regiment and Tarleton's legion, so an officer was probably not assigned and no artillery officer served at Cowpens.[127]

About fifty British Loyalist volunteers served Tarleton as scouts. Alexander Chesney raised a company "with great difficulty" in late 1780 and then acted as a guide to Tarleton in January 1781. Chesney commanded militia at Cowpens. The unit dispersed after the battle, but Chesney ordered them to reassemble later.[128]

The two forces commenced maneuvering against each other in the South Carolina backcountry during early January 1781. How they shifted to achieve advantages, obtain supplies, and bring their opponents to battle sets the stage for 17 January. The movements between 10 and 17 January adversely affected the British while providing advantages for the Americans. They are a key aspect of the Cowpens campaign.

3 : Prebattle Activities

Push him to the utmost.
—*Lord Cornwallis to Banastre Tarleton, 2 January 1781*

Once Greene divided the Americans, Morgan was left to his own resourcefulness. He fed his men, kept his army intact, and posed a threat to western British outposts. The British quickly moved to counter Greene's strategy. Cornwallis directed Tarleton to protect Ninety Six, then get rid of Morgan. The movements of both sides culminated in battle on 17 January. To reach the Cowpens crossroads, each side shifted, seeking positional advantages given their original orders. Morgan worked hard to avoid surprise; Tarleton protected Ninety Six and gathered supplies. Once he was ready, Tarleton went after the Americans with care, knowing Morgan was a dangerous opponent. These preliminary movements provide a key to understanding what happened in the battle of Cowpens.[1]

When Morgan marched from Charlotte, the Flying Army crossed into South Carolina at Biggers Ferry on 22 December, then moved to Grindal Shoals, a well-known Pacolet River crossing. The campsite was secured by Lieutenant Colonel Joseph Hayes's Little River militia the day before Morgan arrived. Continental dragoons arrived the next day.[2]

Grindal Shoals was the main Flying Army base until 14 January 1781. The camp was on militant Tory Alexander Chesney's plantation, on the "east side of the river, on the ridge rising just opposite the island in the river." During their stay, Morgan's men plundered Chesney's property of everything usable, including grain, trees, clothing, and blankets. In his claim to the British government, Chesney swore the Americans took at least 500 bushels of "Indian corn, in store, a quantity of oats and other crops."[3] By camping on a Loyalist's property, Morgan punished Chesney, intimidated other Tories, and lessened his army's impact on local patriots.

Morgan's whole force did not camp at Grindal Shoals. Detachments camped at Burr's Mill on Thicketty Creek; dragoons were often at Wofford's Iron Works on Lawson's Fork to repair equipment and shoe horses. Pickens and his brigade reported, then moved into the Fair Forest drainage.

Around 8 January, militia at Grindal Shoals moved across the Pacolet, partly to delay Tarleton, should he make a sudden attack. Other militia were north of the Broad River obtaining supplies, especially forage.[4]

Tarleton's operations against Morgan began when Cornwallis ordered him to protect Ninety Six on 1 January 1781. Tarleton was at Brierly's Ferry on Broad River with "his corps of cavalry and infantry, of five hundred and fifty men, the first battalion of the 71st, consisting of two hundred, and two three-pounders."[5] Cornwallis confirmed on 2 January that "if Morgan is still at William's, or any where within your reach, I should wish you to push him to the utmost. . . . Ninety-Six is of so much consequence, that no time is to be lost." Tarleton quickly learned Ninety Six was not in danger. On 4 January, twenty miles from Brierley's, he halted at Brooke's Bush River Plantation and requested baggage and additional troops. Just as Morgan supplied his men, Tarleton could not move without sufficient food and forage. The area around Brooke's had forage, and he anticipated gathering "four days's flour for a move."[6]

Tarleton also proposed maneuvers to defeat Morgan or drive him away. He wrote Cornwallis that "when I advance, I must either destroy Morgan's Corps, or push it before me over Broad river, towards King's mountain. The advance of the army should commence (when your lordship orders this corps to move) onwards for King's mountain."[7] After Cornwallis sent baggage, dragoons, and the 7th Regiment, Tarleton's command numbered approximately 1,200 men.[8] Tarleton remained at Brooke's, gathering food and forage, until the baggage and reinforcements arrived. Everything was in place by 11 January; Tarleton had four days' food supply, his reinforcements and baggage.

In the meantime, Lieutenant Colonel William Washington, Colonel Thomas Brandon, and Lieutenant Colonel Joseph Hayes returned to Grindal Shoals about 4 January. On their way to rejoin Morgan after the Hammond's Store raid, they were joined by Colonel Andrew Pickens and his Long Cane Creek men.[9] The South Carolina militia now formed a brigade of four regiments under Pickens. Most of this brigade moved to the Fair Forest drainage near Union. Pickens encamped the South Carolina State Troops around Fair Forest Meeting House on Dinning Creek. Hayes's Little River Regiment moved onto high ground above Tyger River's Adams Ford south of Union crossroads. Brandon's Fair Forest Regiment went to Fair Forest Shoal, where Loyalist Thomas Fletchall had a mill, ensuring a supply of flour.[10] The Spartanburg Regiment had two battalions drawn from the area around Grindal Shoals. Colonel John Thomas's men were already with Morgan; Lieutenant Colonel Benjamin Roebuck's men learned

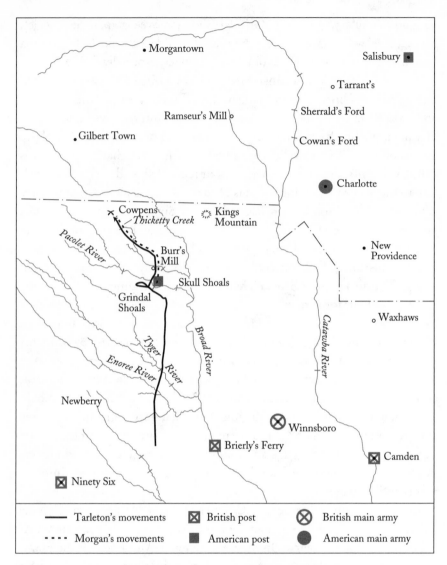

MAP 2. *American and British Movements, 12–16 January 1781*

they were being called up. The Americans were now well placed to exploit the region and oppose the British.

When dragoon replacements and the 7th Regiment reached Tarleton about 8 January, Tarleton was not yet ready to move. By 11 January, Ninety Six was no longer in danger, and Tarleton began operations directly against Morgan. That evening, he camped northwest of Newberry, where he received permission to keep the 7th Regiment. Tarleton continued his advance toward Morgan, crossing Indian and Duncan's Creeks and heading north toward the Enoree River. About this time, he was joined by Captain Alexander Chesney, the Grindal Shoals Tory who came up from Ninety Six to guide Tarleton in the Pacolet River area.[11]

British movements were quickly reported to Morgan, often by several different parties. On 12 January, word came to Pickens that Tarleton was moving rapidly north. Pickens sent the news on to Grindal Shoals, where Morgan issued orders for Washington's cavalry to rejoin the Flying Army. Immediately after sending word, Pickens started his brigade westward.[12] Pickens and his men formed a screen between Morgan and Tarleton while Morgan assembled local militia and shifted units to protect his flanks, the Green River Road escape route, and upper river crossings.

Tarleton continued advancing. On the 14th, he crossed the Enoree River at Kennedy's Ford, only about thirty miles from Grindal Shoals. The British crossed the Tyger River at Adam's Ford, then moved through Union crossroads.[13] North of Union, Tarleton marched northwest to threaten Morgan, Wofford's Iron Works, and any westward retreat Morgan might attempt. Since Chesney was traveling with the British, Tarleton had expert advice about roads and river-crossing points. Tarleton already knew the area because he operated against Sumter during the Blackstock's campaign in November 1780.[14] As Tarleton advanced along the Fair Forest drainage, he drove Pickens's Brigade toward Morgan's concentrating forces. More important, the British entered an area heavily exploited in the fall of 1780 and by Pickens over the last week. The rapid marching also meant British soldiers had no time to forage farther afield as they moved through an area swept clean by both sides.

On the 14th, Morgan moved his militia and Continentals to block the Pacolet fords between Grindal and Troft Shoals.[15] With Tarleton operating along the main road across the upcountry, Morgan could only retreat north to Broad River.[16] Morgan was gradually reinforced by small parties as well as company- and battalion-sized units. The Spartanburg Regiment's second in command, Benjamin Roebuck, was already at Grindal Shoals with some men, calling up his company commanders. Once a decision was made to fight, they would bring in their men.[17]

Not everyone at Grindal Shoals wanted to stay. When their enlistments expired, men wanted to return home. Personal pleas were necessary to keep the army together. Samuel Moore wrote that "Morgan was expecting a reinforcement of fresh troops, who had not yet arrived, and insisted that Capt Whiteside and others, whose time had expired, should not leave him, in his exposed condition, to contend with a handfull of men against a powerful and Victorious enemy. This appeal, which could not be heard with indifference, was not without its effect, and Captain Whiteside and his men remained until after the Battle."[18] Fresh northern reinforcements *were* coming, including state troops and militia from Virginia and North Carolina.

Morgan began moving troops toward the Broad River on 14 January and, on 15 January, his Continentals marched to Burr's Mill, a short distance north of Grindal Shoals. The withdrawal reflected a shrewd strategic assessment. Morgan forced Tarleton to operate where Americans already had taken available provisions, drew him farther from Cornwallis, and moved the Americans closer to supplies and reinforcements. Morgan explained the retreat to the militia and Continentals in terms they would appreciate. Aaron Guyton remembered that Morgan, "hearing of a detachment under Col. Tarlton coming on him and dreading to engage him so near Lord Cornwallis' army, retreated two days up the Country to a place Called the *Cow Pens*." Later, Continental captain Samuel Shaw wrote that Morgan "retreated a considerable distance in order to draw Tarleton from the main body commanded by Cornwallis."[19] The Flying Army grew stronger as detachments came in, but Morgan continued marching northwest, sending units ahead to gather supplies and protect the route.

Tarleton spent 15 January learning details about the Pacolet fords as his troops marched west, bypassing Grindal Shoals and threatening both Wofford's Iron Works and the upper Pacolet fords that allowed access to Morgan's line of retreat. That evening, the British made a show of camping, but they moved immediately after dark.[20] South Carolina militia watching the British and guarding the Pacolet fords were deceived by Tarleton's false night camp. While the Continentals and Virginia militia camped at Burr's Mill above Thicketty Creek, the British moved downstream after dark, found Easterwood Ford unguarded, and crossed at dawn. Tarleton's night countermarch paid off. The British were now within six miles of Morgan, but Tarleton's men lost sleep and put additional miles on their legs.[21]

When Morgan learned of the British crossing, he immediately ordered the Continentals north, without finishing breakfast. McDowell's North Carolina militia remained behind to cover the withdrawal.[22] It was noon before British dragoons completed probing the approaches to Burr's Mill. As British scouts neared the American Burr's Mill camp, "the militia being on horseback started about 12 O'clock," to rejoin Morgan.

Tarleton was wise to conduct a careful reconnaissance. American units were operating between Morgan and the British. South Carolinians James Dillard, Samuel Hammond "and John Greer were sent by General Pickens . . . to reconitre his line of march & to give such notice of the British march as might appear necessary. . . . they . . . run a Tory Colonel near Tarletons line & took a Negroe man & two Horses from him."[23] British dragoons were taken up by the militia as well. South Carolina captain George Gresham reported falling "in with a party of the British advance— we had a skirmish and made two prisoners. We reached the General the evening preceeding the battle of the Cowpens."[24]

The British occupied the American camp late on 16 January. "It yielded a good post, and afforded plenty of provisions, which they had left behind them, half cooked, in every part of their encampment." A food shortage is suggested in Tarleton's comment about the American provisions. The four days already spent pursuing Morgan consumed supplies accumulated earlier at Brooke's Plantation.[25]

While the British camped, Loyalists continued scouting. "Early in the night the patroles reported that General Morgan had struck into byways, tending towards Thickelle creek."[26] Tarleton rested his men a short time but apparently got no sleep himself, since he continued to interview scouts as they came in during the night.

Earlier that afternoon, Morgan went ahead and met with local residents before the Flying Army reached Cowpens. Before deciding to fight, he conducted a reconnaissance the afternoon of 16 January. Captain Dennis Tramell recalled that "the Cowpens . . . being in two and a half miles of [his] residence . . . and he being well acquainted with the local Situation of the ground . . . with Genl. Morgan and his life-guard and Aide d camp went out and selected the ground upon which the Battle was fought."[27]

While Tramell escorted Morgan over the old fields, Americans moved toward Cowpens crossroads from all directions. Continentals and Virginia militia arrived in the late afternoon, accompanied by "Georgia volunteers and South Militia, to the number of between two and three hundred."[28] During the remaining daylight and all through the night, units and individual volunteers came into the American camp. Even Virginians arrived at Cowpens the night before the battle, lending credence to John Eager Howard's recollection "that parties were coming in most of the night, and calling on Morgan for ammunition, and to know the state of affairs. They were all in good spirits, related circumstances of Tarleton's cruelty, and expressed the strongest desire to check his progress."[29]

That afternoon, Morgan had not yet made the decision to fight, but he knew a fight was coming. After completing his reconnaissance, Morgan told Captain Tramell they would fight. Once Morgan decided to fight, he committed totally, and Tramell later recalled the statement "of Genl.

Morgan . . . 'Captain here is Morgan's grave or victory.'" Others recalled a similar statement, such as "on this ground I will defeat the British or lay my bones."[30]

Morgan told the militia a fight was coming, perhaps before making a final decision. South Carolina militiaman Thomas Young noted he and others "arrived at . . . Cowpens about sun-down, and were then told that there we should meet the enemy. . . . [M]any a hearty curse had been vented against Gen. Morgan during that day's march, for retreating, as we thought, to avoid a fight." The militia attitude was crucial to success. If Morgan crossed the Broad River into North Carolina, he would lose South Carolina militiamen composing more than half his force. When the militia learned "we should meet the enemy[,] the news was received with great joy by the army. We were very anxious for battle."[31]

"Morgan did not decide on action until he was joined in the night by Pickens and his followers," but a final decision was forced on him by Tarleton's rapid approach.[32] His reasons for fighting at Cowpens were explained to John Marshall "soon after [Morgan's] return" from the Carolinas. "Morgan had great and just confidence in himself and his troops; he was unwilling to fly from an enemy not so decidedly his superior as to render it madness to fight him; and he also thought that, if he should be overtaken while his men were fatigued and retreating, the probability of success would be much less than if he should exhibit the appearance of fighting from choice."[33]

The decision made, Morgan briefed his officers in a council of war, probably after dark. When Morgan informed subordinates of his decision, Washington allegedly said, "No burning, no flying: but face about and give battle to the enemy, and acquit ourselves like men in defence of their baggage, their lives, and the interests of the Country."[34]

Today, it is called an operations order, but veterans simply recalled an order. Morgan's instructions were first issued to unit commanders on the scene if they had to fight. Later, as other officers arrived, they, too, were briefed about their roles but apparently given only partial views of the whole plan. Each unit "took up Camp all in order for Battle." Only one officer made a record of Morgan's briefing. When Samuel Hammond came in about 8:00 P.M., he was informed of his duties "in case of coming to action."[35] Morgan also issued a password and countersign. "The watchword was . . . 'Who are you?' Answer: 'Fire.' Reply, 'Sword.' So the word was fire and sword. By this we were to know our friends from foes." Unlike other southern battles, no militiamen recalled putting sprigs of green in their hats.[36]

The veteran Continentals had seen battle and had scores to settle for Camden and British treatment of American prisoners. Delaware private Henry Wells was particularly bitter as he recalled, "two of my Cosins fell into the hands of the enemy at Camden, and died from the Severity of their treatment—the other lived to be exchanged, but he returned with a Shattered Constitution."[37] Wallace's Virginia Continentals had no false illusions either. Several were survivors of Waxhaws and bore scars from Tarleton's sabers and bayonets.[38]

The militia needed encouragement. Howard recalled "Morgan was careful to address the officers and men, inspire confidence in them." Militiaman Thomas Young was even more impressed.

> It was upon this occasion I was more perfectly convinced of Gen. Morgans's qualifications to command militia, than I had ever before been. He went among the volunteers, helped them fix their swords, joked with them about their sweet-hearts, told them to keep in good spirits, and the day would be ours. And long after I laid down, he was going about among the soldiers encouraging them, and telling them that the old wagoner would crack his whip over Ben. [Tarlton] in the morning, as sure as they lived. 'Just hold up your heads, boys, three fires,' he would say, 'and you are free, and then when you return to your homes, how the old folks will bless you, and the girls kiss you, for your gallant conduct!' I don't believe he slept a wink that night![39]

Morgan appealed to their bravery and home ties, but kept his demands within practical limits. He mentioned competition between Georgians and Carolinians but asked for only three shots before withdrawing. Once they completed firing, the militia had well-defined routes to the protection of Continental bayonets. Everything was presented in basic terms the men could understand.[40]

Morgan also fed his men. The Americans had food because cattle were driven to the Cowpens earlier that day. Perhaps a battle was not thought so imminent because Reuben Long, one of the drovers, was discharged early on 16 January. Cattle were butchered that night by James Turner and others.[41] Subsistence taken care of, Morgan dealt with another logistical problem. "Orders had been issued to the militia, to have twenty-four rounds of balls prepared and ready for use, before they retired."[42] Continental cartridge boxes generally held about twenty-four rounds, with another sixteen rounds per man in ammunition wagons. The men were issued the extra ammunition when battle was imminent.[43]

By stipulating the number of bullets a man carried, Morgan knew how long a unit could keep firing and when it should be ordered to the rear before running out of ammunition. Envisioning a sequence of linear fire-fights as he drew the British forward and shot them up, Morgan would evaluate British and American fighting capabilities as the battle progressed. Morgan could shift units before they ran out of ammunition. Men could be withdrawn while still possessing ammunition for self-defense and psychological security, reducing chances of a rout.

As men came in, they were formed into more easily controlled units. Smaller "companies" were amalgamated into larger companies within their own battalions. While consolidation improved control, it would not affect men who remained under their original officers. The officers, however, might not be initiating orders, since they were integrated into a larger formation, with additional levels in the chain of command.

As Morgan readied his forces, Tarleton's men at Burr's Mill got what sleep they could. Tarleton continued to collect information and plan for the next day. He used his own Americans well, including Alexander Chesney. "To get intelligence of Morgan's situation he sent me out. . . . I rode to my father's who said Morgan was gone to the Old-fields about an hour before. . . . I immediately returned to Col Tarleton and found he had marched towards the Old fields. I overtook them before 10 oclock . . . on Thickety Creek."[44] Tarleton also interrogated at least one prisoner who claimed to be an American militia colonel. About midnight, scouts brought word "of a corps of mountaineers being upon the march from Green river."[45] Tarleton mulled over intelligence reports and planned his movements. The British had to prevent any junction of Morgan and his reinforcements and attack if the Americans attempted crossing the Broad River. Since the Americans were within five miles of the river, Tarleton would have to move early to catch Morgan at the river crossing about seventeen miles from Burr's Mill.

Around 2:00 A.M., Tarleton roused his men. Lieutenant MacKenzie marched as the light infantry went out first and passed through the pickets when the "pursuit recommenced by two o'clock." At "three o'clock in the morning of the 17th, the pickets being called in, the British troops . . . were directed to follow the route the Americans had taken the preceding evening."[46] It was not difficult to follow the Americans. Large numbers of men, horses, and wagons churned up the rain-soaked dirt roads. Tarleton's comments show the road was only a track or "byway." They didn't take a "main" road until much closer to Cowpens.

The clear trail guided the British, but they had to take care that an American ambush was not sprung on them. The British approach march was slow "on account of the time employed in examining the front and flanks as they proceeded." They marched in a tactical formation allowing rapid deployment to front, rear, or flank. "Three [sic] companies of light infantry, supported by the legion infantry, formed the advance; the 7th regiment, the guns, and the 1st battalion of the 71st, composed the center; and the cavalry and mounted infantry brought up the rear."[47]

Even with artillery, the march was faster than usual because "the baggage and waggons were ordered to remain upon their ground till daybreak, under the protection of a detachment from each corps." Wagons would slow the march because "the ground which the Americans had passed . . . [was] broken, and much intersected by creeks and ravines," and "marshes."[48] Using the torn-up road and getting across ravines, wagons would have slowed Tarleton's advance to a crawl when he most needed speed to catch Morgan.

By all accounts, the British had a difficult time "swimming horses and felling trees for bridges" on this exhausting march to contact. Lieutenant Roderick MacKenzie, traveling with his light infantry company, may have exaggerated, but crossing knee-deep streams in January is hard on mind and body. Natural obstacles were augmented by American militia who, if they did not actively oppose Tarleton, tried to "set the woods on fire in two or three places, which no doubt retarded Tarleton's pursuit each time at least a fourth of an hour."[49]

American scouts saw the British break camp and sent word to Morgan; others observed the march. A detachment was probably on the high ground above three fords crossing Macedonia Creek. Here, most probably because light infantry pointmen heard movements north of the creek, "an advanced guard of cavalry was ordered to the front."[50] Tarleton was prudent in putting mounted men at the front of the column. Dragoons could move more rapidly, scout farther ahead, and report back more quickly.

By the time the dragoons took the lead, Morgan knew Tarleton was closing in. A man on horseback, even moving discreetly in the night, could cover the twelve miles from Burr's Mill in less than an hour. At 3:30 A.M., Morgan knew Tarleton's infantry could not reach the Cowpens before 6:30, even at the killing pace of fifteen minutes per mile.[51] Time and distance gave the Americans at least another two hours of sleep. In the interim between the scouts' first notice of Tarleton's movement and the final warning from outlying videttes, Morgan took his own council and also offered a prayer.[52]

As the British drew nearer, Morgan's scouts continued to report. A last warning by watchers above Macedonia Creek informed Morgan that "One hour before daylight . . . they had advanced within five miles of our camp."[53]

On 17 January sunrise was about 7:36 A.M. in Spartanburg, South Carolina. The weather was cloudy and very humid, so actually viewing the sun was problematical. Since the Americans were in position at sunrise, it must have been approximately 5:30 A.M. when the scout came in. This time agrees with Tarleton's observation that the British crossed Macedonia Creek "before dawn."[54]

The timeframe shows the British took about three hours to cover the first seven miles, an indication of how difficult the marching conditions were. The British vanguard was moving at the rate of a mile every twenty-five minutes. The British still had an hour's marching to cover the last five miles, but now they were marching on higher ground, following drier roads over a more level course without crossing a major stream. They moved even faster because dragoons were checking for ambushes.

Morgan's appreciation of Tarleton's marching speed can be seen in how rapidly his own men moved into position. "Before day Reced Information that Col Tarlton Was Within Five Miles of us With a Strong Body of Horse and Infantry Whereon We got up and put Ourselves in Order of Battle." Rapid movement into battle formation was necessary because "Tarleton came on like a thunder storm. . . . After the tidings of his approach came into camp.—in the night,—we were all awakened, ordered under arms, and formed in order of battle by daybreak."[55]

As Morgan's infantry moved into position, Washington took steps to verify the reports. "Sergeant Everhart . . . [and] ten men, . . . [were] sent to Reconnoitre Lt. Colonel Tarletons Army." The patrol went out from the Cowpens, trotting down the Green River Road to the American forward outpost "stationed three miles in advance." This post was located where several roads came together; the videttes could observe the approaches without moving any appreciable distance.[56]

Captain Joshua Inman of Georgia commanded the videttes. They would provide initial resistance to any British advance and send a last-minute warning of Tarleton's approach. Probably Inman was given this assignment because his company of Georgia Refugees were to be skirmishers.[57] Other videttes were Continental dragoons under Lieutenant Leonard Anderson, and they accompanied Everheart farther down the road. Because they knew the country, two Union County men, Samuel Clowney and Henry W. Deshasure, went with them. After moving approximately a mile, "they came almost in contact with the advanced guard of the British army; they wheeled, and were pursued."[58]

Outnumbered four or five to one, the Americans had no chance in a fight. Their mission was to learn Tarleton's location and bring word back to

Morgan. "Ten men returned, and gave you information of the approach of the Enemy."[59] Two men, "after a severe and bloody contest between the advance of Tarleton and his party" were captured. The Americans were caught because "the advanced Guard . . . were mounted . . . on some of the fleetest race horses . . . in this Country." Everheart's "horse being shot he was captured early in the morning by Quarter Master Wade . . . [and] taken to Col Tarlton." "Our army at this point of time [was] perhaps three miles in the rear."[60]

Immediately after the British dragoons clashed with the American videttes, "two troops of dragoons, under Captain Ogilvie, of the legion, were then ordered to reinforce the advanced guard, and to harass the rear of the enemy." Tarleton proceeded to question the prisoners and "from them information was received that the Americans had halted, and were forming at a place called the Cowpens."[61] A sense of Tarleton's interview survives in Everheart's pension application. "Dismounting from his horse, that officer asked this petitioner after some previous conversation if he expected Mr. Washington & Mr Morgan would fight him that day. Yes if they can keep together only two hundred men was the reply. Then said he it will be another Gates' defeat. I hope to God it will be another Tarlton's defeat said this petitioner. I am Col. Tarlton Sir. And I am Sergeant Everheart."[62]

Very shortly after Tarleton began speaking with Everheart, British dragoons encountered the American skirmish line at Cowpens. They "reported that the American troops were halted and forming."[63] During the interval, Tarleton finished talking with Everheart and moved forward to inspect the American lines.

Morgan's videttes had opposed the advance. Between first contact and British deployment, American resistance stiffened. South Carolina militiaman James Caldwell was

> one of the riflemen thrown forward as sharp-shooters to harrass the enemy on his approach to the Cowpens. They commenced the attack upon Tarleton's columns, two miles in advance of Morgan's line of battle. Large trees . . . were covers for the riflemen against the fire of the advancing columns; but afforded no protection against the charges of the cavalry, who scoured the woods as the infantry advanced. In one of these charges Caldwell was dislodged, and fighting as long as he was able with the butt of his rifle, he was literally cut to pieces by the broadsword of a dragoon. His . . . head, face and hands were covered with scars.[64]

American resistance forced British dragoons to sweep the roadsides for ambush and slowed their advance for the last two miles. With cavalry skirmishing, the infantry moved rapidly. Daylight had not yet occurred when the British arrived at the lower end of the fields around Cowpens.[65]

Not all of Morgan's men went to their fighting positions immediately. Most of "the Army moved in the night about half a miles [sic] from the place they were encamped [to] the place selected for the Battle leaving some men to keep up the fires untill [sic] day light."[66] Maintaining the fires may have been a way to reassure men they could retire to a warm camp if the British did not materialize, or it may have been a ruse to decoy the British should they attack by any route other than the Green River Road.

Morgan's preparations throughout the night were not in vain. His men were fed and resting in line of battle on ground of his own choosing. They knew what was expected. Morgan was "in a popular and forcible style of elocution haranguing them."[67] Other officers did likewise, including "Major Jackson of Georgia who also spoke to the militia." Jackson, as brigade major to the militia, probably spoke only to them. It is likely he also rode down to the skirmish line and spoke with the men under Hammond because they included "his" Georgians.[68]

Both sides were now on the battlefield. Morgan had his men ready and waiting. Tarleton's infantry was coming up and halting in a growing column on the Green River Road while he evaluated the situation and decided how he would engage the Americans. But what of the battlefield and the American positions on it? They would dictate how Tarleton and Morgan would fight their battle.

4 : *The stage is set*

Morgan . . . selected the ground.
—*Dennis Tramell, pensioner, 10 December 1833*

The battle of Cowpens was a chronological series of intense combat episodes as the British encountered different American positions at Cowpens. The Americans were brilliantly posted, placed in progressively stronger lines on land making outstanding use of their skills, and minimizing British advantages. In the week before Cowpens, Morgan created a logistical trap that isolated and weakened Tarleton's force. Now, on the battlefield he had chosen, Morgan laid a tactical trap, taking advantage of Tarleton's aggressiveness and perceptions of how a battle was fought. To understand just what Tarleton's men faced and to present the American order of battle, initial American positions will be discussed in some detail.

American tactical units can be placed on the landscape with reasonable accuracy, but the engagement was a dynamic affair. Initial positions locate a unit when fighting started, but every unit moved during the battle, in many cases, to planned secondary positions. Identifying American positions requires a reader to deal with landscape, tactics, and references to officers, units, and locations.

Just as Morgan inspected the Cowpens road junction, it is necessary to describe the site to understand the physical setting. Modern landscape features may not resemble those impressed into a pensioner's memory on 17 January 1781. Fortunately, several accounts refer to landforms that survive. These generate a framework into which details can be placed by referring to where participants stood. It is possible to create a fairly accurate impression using the existing site, eyewitness accounts, and observations made after the battle.

Morgan's dispositions were dictated by the ground and his assessment of how best to use his men. The 1781 landscape can be reconstructed from contemporary accounts and soil maps. Although agriculture, residential housing, and reforestation altered some perspectives, landmarks are still recognizable. Morgan went to Cowpens because it was a road junction, well known to both American and British forces that assembled there in the past.[1]

The Green River Road intersection is at the north end of the Cowpens battlefield. The intersecting road provided access to other river crossings. Broad River's Island Ford is five miles away to the northeast; Coulter's Ford across the Pacolet River is five miles to the west. The Green River Road went southeast to the Pacolet and north to the Broad River.

Green River Road follows the line of least resistance across the battlefield. In 1781, the road was a dirt track, perhaps fifteen feet wide, running through a heavily wooded landscape.[2] The road was a major thoroughfare following high ground that minimized elevation changes and stream crossings.[3] Today the road follows most of the high ground between the heads of Suck Creek on the east, Cane Creek on the west, and Buck Creek on the northwest. It probably did in the past, too, as these creeks constrict high ground south of the intersection. As one enters Cowpens from the south, the entire field seems to slope slightly down to the right, rising slightly to the front and left.

Captain Dennis Tramell placed the battlefield "between the branch of horse creek and Suck creek." Suck Creek borders the battlefield on the east and northeast. Horse Creek's headwaters are in the angle formed by the Green River Road and Coulter's Ford Road intersection where Little Buck Creek rises.[4] When Benjamin Perry visited Cowpens in the 1830s, he was guided by a veteran of the battle who said "The American Army . . . encamped between the head waters of Suck & a branch of Buck Creek which are not more than two or three hundred yards apart. . . . Morgan drew up his little army on a slight ridge, extending from the head of one of those spring branches to the other."[5] Perry's veteran identified the American campsite, but the traditional camp location, known to South Carolina Cowpens veterans, was a sheltered valley east of the road. This position is shown on the Hammond Map drawn before the battle and shows Pickens's Militia well east of the road.

It is possible the Continentals camped at the actual intersection. The Hammond Map shows Continentals spread across the Green River Road with Triplett's Virginia militia west of the road. Marylander George Wilson was wounded and left behind, "at the head of Bucks Creek," the flat ground at the road junction.[6]

The Flying Army probably covered all approaches to the crossroad, utilizing available water and open, flat ground. The generally level landscape was not missed by participants who called it "Cowpens plains." Richard Winn noted Cowpens was "even enough to make race-paths."[7] If lower ground is included, the vertical profile still varies less than forty-five feet. The landscape has not changed very much since Spartanburg historian J. B. O. Landrum wrote, "What has been described by several writers as eminences on the battle field . . . are nothing more than ridges scarcely noticeable. The main road . . . is in fact so level . . . the only rising ground of any note on the whole field is a little eminence a short distance in rear of the ridge, where the main line was formed. This is of sufficient height to cover a man on horseback placed in the rear of it."[8]

Participants identify landforms using terms including "rivulet," "right ravine," "left ravine," and "the swale." Other features, less prominent and changed since the battle, are a "clump of pines" and the "slope." These terms originating in veterans' recollections and historical usage clarify landscape discussion. "Hayes Rise" and "Morgan Hill" are modern terms used to describe key points on the battlefield.

"Rivulet" was used by local Tory Alexander Chesney to describe the skirmishers' position where "the Americans were posted behind a rivulet."[9] The feature best fitting the context is an intermittent head of Island Creek. This stream eroded the slope, creating a low, flat bottom in front of McDowell's position. After winter rains, this low ground was probably a near bog at the time of the battle.

Militia dragoon Thomas Young reported, "The regulars . . . were formed . . . their right flank resting upon the head of the ravine on the right." The "right ravine" is probably modern-day Maple Swamp, low, boggy ground creating a "peninsula" of higher ground on the main line's right flank.[10]

Young also reported "the militia['s] . . . left flank resting near the head of the ravine on the left."[11] The "left ravine" is the southern head of Suck Creek no. 2. This low ground protected the South Carolina militia line's left flank. The northern head of this creek catches runoff from the swale and covered Triplett's Virginia militia's left flank.

A third ravine, the west ravine, runs south into the bottom drained by the rivulet. This is straight and shallow, suggesting an old property or fence line. If it were present during the battle, trees and brush along its course would have covered the forward American right flank. This ravine does not extend as far as the main line, but it covered the skirmish and militia line right flanks.

At the heads of Suck Creek no. 2 and the rivulet were springs that no longer flow. Three springs forming Suck Creek were still flowing north of the Green River Road in 1898, and the area around the springs was usually a bog.[12] Springs and bogs were also located west of the road where Lit-

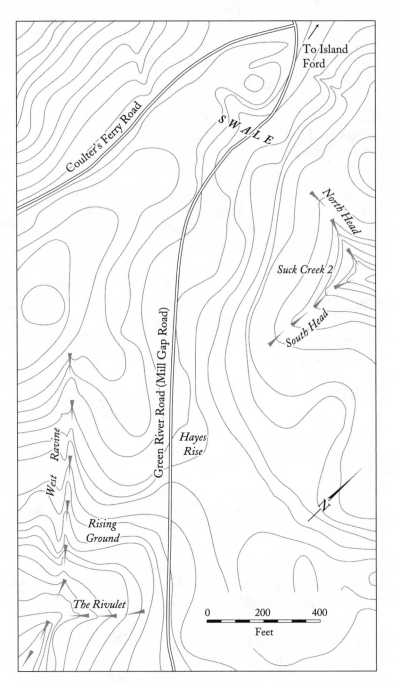

MAP 3. *Topography of the Cowpens Battlefield*

tle Buck, Maple Swamp, and Island Creeks covered the American right flanks. The springs and streams show American flanks *were* covered, if only by boggy ground.[13]

The watercourses were almost certainly covered with stands of cane in 1781. The best-known statement about flank coverage dates to 1898, when a Confederate veteran pointed out that the springs made "a flank movement of cavalry or artillery difficult, if not impossible."[14] Morgan's men were difficult to outflank because of these bogs and springs, especially since it had been raining intermittently for several days before the battle.[15]

"Rising ground" was used by participants to describe slight changes in elevation. The most distinctive change in elevation is north of the rivulet. The change is over twenty vertical feet in less than fifty yards. McDowell placed his skirmishers along a terrace west of the road. This terrace is less distinctive as it curves gently southward east of Green River Road, but this slight elevation still provides a vantage point from which Hammond's Georgia and South Carolina skirmishers directed fire against the British right in the opening phase of the battle.

Militia ridge is a second "rising ground," the "first ridge" mentioned in some accounts. The ridge is highest about seventy-five yards north of the rivulet. As Green River Road proceeds north past the terrace above the rivulet, the land rises about another ten to fifteen feet. The highest point is at the road, where the rise is now emphasized by the old road grade. The northern slope of this ridge is where South Carolina militia battalions were positioned.[16] The high central point at the road is Hayes Rise, a modern term describing the highest point on the ridge.[17] It ends as the ridge slopes east down to more level ground. To the west, the ground rises slightly toward the west ravine.

In a very explicit context, *rising ground* means the edge of militia ridge where the slope rises up from the swale. Howard placed his Continentals on a slight terrace here. Today this terrace above the swale's southern edge is not very pronounced. In the past, before erosion filled the swale, it was significant enough to be shown on one 1781 map.[18]

The "swale" refers to low ground between the main line and Morgan Hill. It is a drainage basin running into Suck Creek no. 2's northern head. Since 1781, erosion has filled in and leveled the swale, which is now slightly higher and dryer. William Johnson described this area in 1822 and pointed out that "the ground, after descending a few yards [the swale], rose into another eminence sufficient in height to cover a man on horseback."[19] The swale was open with scattered pine trees.[20]

"Morgan Hill" is the second "eminence" mentioned by Johnson. From its south slope, the entire battlefield is visible, except for dead space southwest of Hayes Rise. During the militia withdrawal, Morgan may have been on the forward slope of this hill with his aides, guiding the militia into the left rear. Washington and his troopers initially took position on Morgan Hill next to where the Green River Road curves northeast. Behind Morgan Hill is the head of Cudd's (or Little Buck) Creek, a lower area protected from direct fire where the dragoons took refuge from artillery fire early in the battle.

Two other reference points have changed since 1781. The "clump of pines" and the "slope" both relate to an area where militiamen secured their horses.[21] Contemporary accounts suggest a clump of young pines adjacent to a slope, large enough to contain at least 400 horses. The exact site is generally known but not pinpointed. North Carolina captain Connelly remembered, "our horses which was tied about four hundred paces in the rear of the line of Battle."[22]

All sources agree the battlefield was partially open with "not one single *bush* on the field of battle to entangle the troops." Participants suggest certain areas had thicker tree cover than others. Based on their accounts, the skirmish line was located in old fields growing back with pine saplings, but the ground was still relatively open back to the militia line.

The militia took a position before, at, and in a tree line, downslope from the crest of militia ridge. Today this position runs along the scar of an old road perpendicular to the Green River Road. Behind the militia line, tree cover was thicker. Main-line veterans say the fighting was in pine woods, and they generally indicate sunrise somewhat later than men in the two forward lines, another indicator of heavier tree cover.[23]

There are three reasons for a lack of undergrowth. The area may have been burned over to get rid of vermin and to encourage better growth of cattle forage. Animals grazing through the woods would tend to keep brush down as well. Military forces camped here during the Kings Mountain campaign, and many smaller units repeatedly used it as a camping ground. These men would have stripped the brush and trees of limbs for firewood as high as they could reach. Probably all three activities cleared the Cowpens of undergrowth.

Maps show few landscape details but do show approximate unit locations; however, they are confusing and, until recently, only one contemporary map was known. Two additional maps were located in 1992. The newer maps follow Morgan's report of the battle.[24]

The best-known map is by South Carolina captain Samuel Hammond. Hammond shows positions for "troops, *in case of coming to action* [emphasis added]." Hammond prepared it to orient his men on the skirmish line.[25]

John Eager Howard; oil painting by Charles Willson Peale
(Independence National Historical Park Collection)

Hammond's "First View" shows two different American arrangements. The original deployment has a "main guard," or camp, to the north and Triplett's Virginia militia to the west of Howard's Continentals. Pickens is east of Howard. This appears to be the formation in which the Americans camped.[26] He further shows these units with more commanders in positions they were intended to occupy if a fight occurred. These are slightly south of the initial positions involved with camping in order for battle. Since he shows an eastward-running "valley or ravine" in front of the

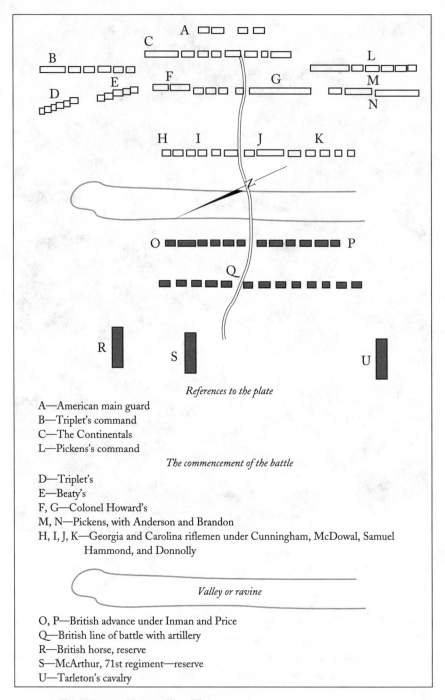

References to the plate

A—American main guard
B—Triplet's command
C—The Continentals
L—Pickens's command

The commencement of the battle

D—Triplet's
E—Beaty's
F, G—Colonel Howard's
M, N—Pickens, with Anderson and Brandon
H, I, J, K—Georgia and Carolina riflemen under Cunningham, McDowal, Samuel
        Hammond, and Donnolly

Valley or ravine

O, P—British advance under Inman and Price
Q—British line of battle with artillery
R—British horse, reserve
S—McArthur, 71st regiment—reserve
U—Tarleton's cavalry

MAP 4. *The Hammond Map—First View*
Source: *Samuel Hammond's "Notes," in Joseph Johnson,*
Traditions and Reminiscences, *529.*

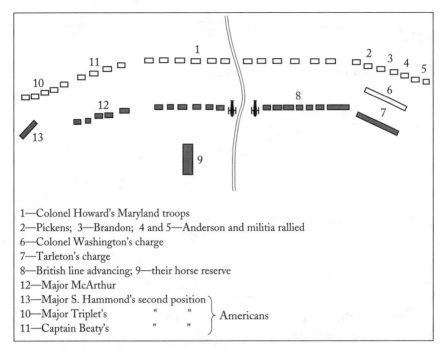

MAP 5. *The Hammond Map—Second View*
Source: *Samuel Hammond's "Notes," in Joseph Johnson,*
Traditions and Reminiscences, *530.*

riflemen, this entire deployment is placed on Morgan Hill overlooking the swale.

Text accompanying Hammond's map is confusing, but the internal problems are the key to understanding Hammond and his map. If the arrow indicates north, Hammond was turned 180 degrees as it actually points to magnetic south. The "valley" running toward the American right cannot be the rivulet and must be the swale. In his written description, Hammond was oriented as if he were facing north, perhaps because he briefed his men so they could face down the Green River Road. The map has the same orientation. Thus, Hammond's "left" is the American military right, or west.

Hammond's "second view" shows American positions after the militia retreated behind the Continentals and, to some extent, after the Continental withdrawal. He has Triplett's Virginians west of Howard in their "second position," suggesting Triplett moved his battalion around behind the Continentals when the bayonet charge took place in the swale. This second view is more a presentation of the units' final positions, as will be seen in coming chapters.

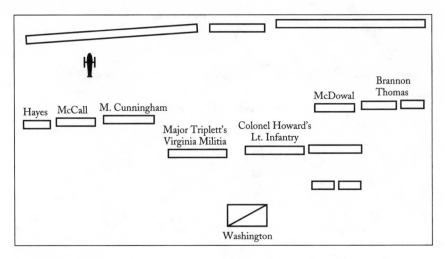

MAP 6. *The "Clove Map"*
Source: *National Archives.*

The two other maps are by the same hand. One, the "Clove Map," reflects a generalized interpretation of Morgan's formal report. It follows Morgan's description of his deployment and agrees in many respects with Hammond's "first view." Again, this is most likely the positioning in case they had to fight.

The "Pigree Map" is more detailed, as it shows unit movements during the battle.[27] The Pigree Map shows later skirmisher positions on the militia-line flanks, but unit locations err in that Hayes is shown on the left flank when he was actually on the Green River Road. Brandon is shown on the right flank when he held the left. McDowell is shown in a central position when he was on the militia-line right flank. This is an adaptation of the Clove Map and Morgan's battle report which the cartographer apparently used to draw these maps, but it reflects unit movements as they occurred as if the starting points were the initial, early evening stations, not their battle positions.

The situation, in terms of men and their tactical disposition, changed between dark on 16 January and dawn, 17 January. Morgan changed his deployment from positions *in case they were attacked* to an alignment for a battle he would fight.[28] The difference is shown by Hammond, who places the same Americans in the two different locations in Map 4. This shift is crucial to understanding the maps and pension accounts. The battle, as fought, reflects Morgan's response to the numbers of men who came in during the night.

Howard later recalled militia coming in all night. One Virginia militia

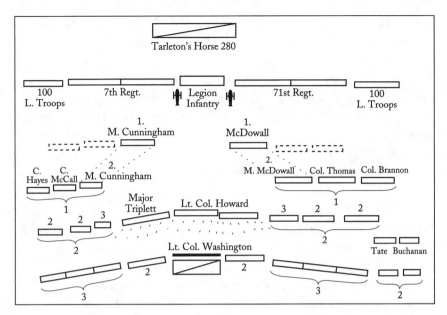

MAP 7. *The "Pigree Map"*
Source: *National Archives.*

company, and possibly some Virginia State Troops, came in the morning before the battle. At least 100 South Carolina militiamen under Irby and Sexton came the night of 16–17 January. Pickens and at least 150 men came in after Morgan had briefed Hammond about 8:00 P.M.[29]

Morgan thought Tarleton would depend on a straightforward charge and initially laid a trap for the British if they should attack him in the night. All three prebattle maps show rifle-armed militia on the wings and slightly forward of the Continentals and Virginians situated across the Green River Road north of the swale. If Tarleton attacked, the British would run a gauntlet that would turn into a double envelopment as they closed with the Continentals blocking the road.

Later that night, Morgan had the manpower to create a defense in depth. Instead of drawing the British into a zone of flanking fire that would both constrict and concentrate them for the Continental volleys, Morgan deployed progressively stronger infantry lines to shoot up the British as they advanced. Damaging the British infantry was a key factor in evening the odds against the Continentals when they engaged Tarleton's infantry.

Initial American positions are derived from analyses of participant and contemporary documents of both sides, Morgan's order, and maps. Pension accounts, in particular, provide keys to understanding how Morgan deployed on 17 January 1781 because they mention landforms. Many positions differ from those enumerated by Morgan and Hammond in the preliminary instructions given early on 16 January. Where these differences occur, endnotes will support changes from Morgan's account and the maps.

Locating larger militia units and Continentals on the landscape is not especially difficult; the same cannot be said for company-level militia organizations. In some cases, officers are incorrectly identified due to misspelled names, assignment to the wrong state, or to a position on the left instead of the right. There are also questions about officer rank held at Cowpens. A final problem exists when two or three men had the same first and last name.

Morgan's plan envisioned a defense in depth, consisting of three linear positions, skirmishers, militia, and Continentals. Ahead of the battle lines, he posted pickets, or videttes. Behind his main-line Continentals, he placed cavalry as a reserve. As soon as Morgan learned Tarleton was nearby, he sent his baggage away up the Island Ford Road.

Outlying American pickets "stationed three miles in advance" were "peculiarly serviceable to you in advertising you of the Enemies approach and skirmishing with their advance." The picket post was composed of both Continental Dragoons under Lieutenant Leonard Anderson and Georgia militia under Captain Joshua Inman.[30]

About three miles behind the videttes, skirmishers deployed across the southern end of the battlefield less than 150 yards in front of Pickens's militia. The right flank was on a commanding rise above the rivulet, protected by soggy ground to its front and a tangle of brush on the right around the ravine. On the left, east of the road, the rise was neither so pronounced nor as well protected. Here, the rise curved forward to create an arena in which the British would deploy.

The skirmishers would force the British to deploy and then fight a delaying action, causing British casualties, as they withdrew. Accounts referring to the militia as the first line indicate many participants recognized the skirmishers as a delaying force, suggesting they were not deployed across the field as significant opposition. It is unlikely the skirmishers lined up in a formal battle line but were, instead, scattered in loose clumps of neighbors under their officers.[31]

Samuel Hammond reported two battalions of skirmishers. "Major McDowal, of the North Carolina Volunteers . . . on the right flank . . . [,] Major Cunningham, of the Georgia Volunteers, on the left." To Cunningham's left was "part of Colonel McCall's regiment of South-Carolina state troops . . . under the command of Major Hammond." These men were all "armed with Rifles."[32]

The North Carolina militia, arranged in five or six companies under county captains, was "orderd out to meet General Tarleton & bring on the action."[33] From right to left, the North Carolina companies were from Burke County, a combined Surry and Wilkes Counties unit, another combined company from Rutherford and Lincoln Counties, a combined northern counties company, and, with their left flank on the road, a Rowan County company.[34]

Sometime in the night, Hammond was given command of the entire left front. The Georgia skirmishers formed three small companies under Major Cunningham. The South Carolina State Troops farther left had about sixty men under Captain Joseph Pickens and Captain Beal.[35]

Private Robert Long described the initial positioning and movement of Hayes's Little River Regiment. While the militia line assembled, the Little River Battalion was "already formed across the road." Hayes then moved "70 or 80 yards in advance; Major McDowell, of North Carolina, in advance of us 70 or 80 yards, and Major Triplet, of Virginia, in our rear." The forward movement was a mistake, as "Hayes' regiment having advanced too far were to retreat and form on our old ground."[36] A mistake it might have been, but the forward movement accomplished two things. First, it created a rallying point for the skirmishers on the military crest of the ridge, halfway between the skirmish line and the militia line. It also created a gap in the militia line through which skirmishers could retreat.

Even if Hayes took his forward position in error, Morgan's plan involved a reverse slope defense,[37] behind the high ground. Morgan, a rifleman himself, was aware of "overshooting." He probably knew the British fired high. A reverse slope defense forced the British to shoot downhill to accentuate the British tendency to shoot high while the lightening sky would silhouette British soldiers against the skyline.

Another possible reason for placing Pickens's militia on the reverse slope relates to flank protection. There is no ravine on either flank of the military crest. There are ravines on both flanks if the militia line ran about seventy yards behind Hayes Rise where Suck Creek no. 2 and Maple Swamp run away from the militia-line position. The boggy ground covered with cane made it difficult for Tarleton's dragoons to operate. Morgan's defensive plan covered both flanks because skirmishers filled gaps between militia and creeks after withdrawing from more forward positions.

When Morgan deployed the militia line, he initially put "Colonels Brannon [sic] and Thomas, of the South Carolina Volunteers, on the right of Major McDowal, and Colonels Hays and McCall of the same corps to the left of Major Cunningham."[38] This was about 8:00 P.M. The plans changed as more men came in and Morgan committed to a fight at Cow-

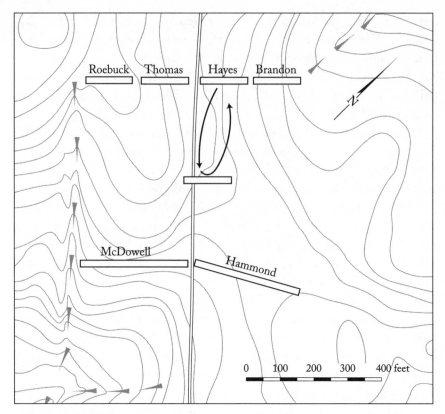

MAP 8. *Hayes's Battalion Movements*

pens. As it worked out, Brandon was east of the road, to Hayes's left; Thomas and Roebuck commanded the Spartanburg Militia west of the road, with Roebuck on the flank.

These four battalions, Roebuck, Thomas, Hayes, and Brandon, formed the militia line's central core, described in most accounts as the first line. They were probably drawn up in a loosely organized linear formation. The left end was anchored on Suck Creek no. 2, where Hammond's skirmishers filled the gap between Brandon's left and the boggy canebrake around the creek's head.[39] On the west, open space between Maple Swamp and the right flank was filled by McDowell's skirmishers.

This battalion placement does not agree with Morgan's battle report or with the three maps. However, if Morgan used his initial plan to organize his report, without incorporating the later changes, the numerous individual accounts would make sense. Morgan was very busy during the night spiriting up the militia and explaining their roles. Participant accounts uniformly place Brandon east of the road and Thomas and Roebuck to the west. Long places Hayes's right company in the road, giving a weight of evidence to a different battle deployment than that drawn up on 16 January.

On the morning of 17 January, the militia aligned on Hayes's Battalion in the road. Then Hammond, Cunningham, and McDowell moved forward and formed the skirmish line. Again, Private Long provides the best account: "[The] infantry marched out in sections, and divided two and two as they got ten paces of Hayes' regiment already formed across the road . . . Cols. Thomas and Roebuck in the extreme right. The left wing was similarly formed of militia." Long amplified this by noting he "was in the centre line on the right wing in Captain Ewing's company."[40]

Hayes's Little River Battalion formed the left center of the militia line on the road. Given Long's statement about Ewing's company on the right flank, and the seniority of other captains under Hayes, a reasonable accounting of company locations can be presented. Ewing, the senior captain, was in the road. In the consolidated units, Dillard's company became the left, or second, platoon under Ewing.[41] Based on seniority, the next company was under William Harris. Finally, the two left companies were commanded by junior captains Sexton and Irby. Thus, the Little River Battalion companies were posted from right to left: Ewing, Harris, Sexton, Irby.[42]

Left of Hayes's Little River Regiment was Colonel Thomas Brandon's Fair Forest Regiment from modern Union County. Brandon was assisted by Lieutenant Colonel William Farr, but it is doubtful if the Fair Forest men deployed in two battalions as the men from Spartanburg did. A subjective arrangement of Brandon's companies is based on seniority and casualties. From right to left, the companies were commanded by Captains Robert Anderson, Robert Montgomery, John Thompson, and William Grant Sr. Lieutenant Joseph Hughes commanded senior captain Benjamin Jolly's company. As a junior officer, Hughes should have been on the left, but as commander of the senior company he was probably on the right. A company of men from Chester and Fairfield districts commanded by John Moffet was placed on the left flank.[43]

To Hayes's right, west of the road, was the Spartanburg Regiment under Colonel John Thomas Jr. Thomas, the regimental colonel, had battalion duty for January. Since the battle was in Spartanburg District, Lieutenant Colonel Benjamin Roebuck's Battalion was called up for the emergency. It was on the right, where Captain Dennis Tramell's company was located on the extreme right flank. To Tramell's left were companies commanded by Captain George Roebuck, Benjamin's brother, and Captain Major Parson.

Thomas placed his battalion with its left flank at the Green River Road. The placement of companies had Captains Andrew Barry, John Collins, Thomas Farrow, and John Files Sr. from right to left.[44]

As the militia infantry settled in, the skirmishers moved forward, and then Hayes advanced his Little River Regiment.[45] Before the British came within range of the militia line's rifles, Hayes moved back and took position between Brandon and Thomas.[46] Morgan's battle plan called for the skirmishers to fall back and reinforce the militia line on both flanks when the British advanced.[47] Between the militia battalions were gaps where some skirmishers would take position. At least two of McDowell's companies took position outside Tramell's Company on the right flank; the Burke County Company and the Surry/Wilkes Company. Hammond's skirmishers took a position between Brandon and the left ravine. Both groups of skirmishers would conduct fighting withdrawals to the main line's flanks.

The main line of American resistance was created with men Morgan had commanded since October. They included five Continental companies, Triplett's Virginia militia, a company of Virginia State Troops, a detachment of North Carolina State Troops, and about twenty-five Burke County militiamen. Many accounts refer to the main line as the second line and its men as light infantry. "The light infantry commanded by Lt.-Col. Howard, and the Virginia Militia under Major Triplett, were formed on a rising ground."[48]

Thomas Young, sitting with the dragoons on Morgan Hill, could see the entire main line. "The regulars, under the command of Col. Howard, a very brave man, were formed in two ranks, their right flank resting upon the head of the ravine on the right."[49] The main line did not extend as far west as the northern head of Maple Swamp, but McDowell's North Carolina skirmishers withdrew into this gap as the battle reached its climax. With the northern head of Suck Creek no. 2 on the left, the main line was covered on both flanks by wet, boggy ground covered with cane, and by skirmishers.

On the right flank, four companies were drawn up as a temporary battalion possibly under the command of Captain Edmund Tate (Tait).[50] From right to left, these companies were the North Carolina State Troops under Captain Henry Connelly,[51] Virginia Continentals under Captain Andrew Wallace, Virginia State Troops under Captain John Lawson, and Augusta County, Virginia, riflemen under Captain Patrick Buchanan.[52]

The center was a solid block of experienced, battle-tested Continentals. Here four, sixty-man Continental companies took up a space 240 feet wide with little or no space between platoons or companies.[53] The companies were under Captain Richard Anderson, Lieutenant Nicholas Mangers, Captain Robert Kirkwood, and Captain Henry Dobson.

To Dobson's left was Major Francis Triplett's Virginia battalion with companies under Captains John Combs, James Tate (Tait),[54] and James Gilmore, as well as a company of Burke County, North Carolina, militia probably commanded by a man named Beatty.[55] Combs's Company's right flank was in the Green River Road because First Sergeant Benjamin Martin stated he "was in the Road all the time of the actions I covered Captain Combs . . . Captain Dobson and Lieutenant Ewen was on the left of the Maryland Troops neare me."[56]

The Continental companies numbered sixty men each. Triplett's left-flank Virginia militia companies were smaller, averaging about forty-five men each. If Buchanan and Lawson were augmented by Campbell's militia just before the battle, their units numbered at least sixty, and probably seventy-five men each. The two flanking North Carolina companies were much smaller. Burke County men with Triplett on the left numbered about twenty-five; the North Carolina State Troops under Connelly probably numbered about the same.

The 600 men in this line covered a front of 200 yards if they were tightly aligned. This is not quite enough to cover the 250 yards between Suck Creek and Maple Swamp, so there was space for the British dragoons to operate. While the flanks were "covered," they were not fully secured until militia skirmishers fell back and filled the gaps between main-line flanks and wet ground.

Morgan's early-evening orders show the main line with gaps between the central core of Continentals and the Virginians to either side of them.[57] While Hammond erred in his use of left and right, he did describe the flank battalions as stepped back, en échelon, to the center. This was an innovative tactical arrangement that allowed gaps through which militia could pass. Morgan was not willing to have his Continentals and Virginians buffeted and disrupted by withdrawing militia.

This unusual and potentially dangerous formation is supported by two British accounts. Scottish historian David Stewart, drawing information from 71st Regiment participants, reported the main line "suddenly faced to the right, and inclined backwards; a manoeuvre by which a space was left for the front line to retreat, without interfering with the ranks." The other account claims the main line "opened to the right and left." One of Combs's Virginians agrees, saying "the rifle men [South Carolina militia] were to fire and pass [through?] breaks in the Centre and fall off to the right and flank of the Musquet Line."[58] This shift let the militia through. Morgan created a buffer behind his main battle line. The *en échelon* Virginians created lanes for the militia to withdraw but also channeled the militia, so Morgan could reform them behind the main line. Morgan probably stationed himself and his aides in the funnel mouth once the militia began to fall back. They helped reorganize those South Carolinians heading for safety. Once the militia passed through, the Virginians moved forward to create a solid line.[59]

Details of Morgan's tactical plan have not been appreciated because most writers omit discussion of his sophisticated, unconventional, main-line deployment, as well as the reverse slope defense.[60] Morgan provided for the main line to withdraw if pressed too hard. "The orders to the second line were, not to be alarmed at the retreat of the militia, to fire low and deliberately, not to break on any account, and if forced to retire, to rally on the eminence in their rear, where they were assured the enemy could not injure them."[61]

Mounted Americans lined up across the Green River Road with "Washington and his men on the wing."[62] "The Third Regiment of Dragoons . . . were so posted in the rear as not to be injured by the enemy's fire, and yet to be able to charge them should an occasion offer." Morgan provided few details about the initial dragoon positions; others were more precise. The cavalry "was formed in the rear of the hollow way [the swale] behind an eminence [Morgan Hill]."[63] Thomas Young, a volunteer dragoon, remembered "the cavalry formed in rear of the center, or rather in rear of the left wing of the regulars."[64] This location placed them behind Kirkwood and Dobson.

The probable arrangement of cavalry units was each troop in column facing south across the swale. This formation allowed rapid deployment to either flank or front. It is likely that Young, in Jolly's Company of forty-five militia volunteers, was on the extreme left. The next unit to the right was a composite troop of Virginia, North Carolina, and South Carolina state dragoons under Major McCall, numbering about fifty men. On the right were eighty-two troopers of the 3rd Continental Light Dragoons under Washington. The three troops of the Third Dragoons were arranged by seniority, from left to right under Captains William Parsons, Churchill Jones, and William Barrett and Major James Call.

When British artillery shot began falling among his troopers, Washington moved them out of the beaten zone.[65] This might be the only direct effect of artillery during the battle. The new cavalry position was a draw northwest of Morgan Hill. It was deep enough to shelter cavalry but close enough to support the infantry.

Morgan initially placed Washington's dragoons as a rallying point, and to counterattack the British. The disposition shows how cleverly Morgan used his cavalry as a reserve and still provided for additional flank coverage. The dragoons served to block fleeing militia, keeping them from running to the rear, but they were close enough to move against any British flanking threat.

The militia horses were tied up east of Morgan Hill. Howard recalled "the militia all rode to the ground and their horses were tied in the woods in the rear of my left flank." The distance was remembered by Henry Connelly, whose horses were "tied about four hundred paces in the rear of the line of Battle."[66]

Morgan sent off his baggage before the battle. The baggage train's location is unknown, but most accounts suggest it was moving up the Island Ford Road. Since the baggage had only thirty minutes to move, it is likely they were less than halfway to the ford, five miles away. One account said the baggage was six miles away, but if the distance is accurate, Morgan's baggage was north of Broad River, and the account probably refers to a time after the battle.[67]

In some ways, Morgan's battle plan was a microcosm of Greene's statement that "We fight, get beat, rise, and fight again."[68] Each American line would fight, withdraw, rally, and fight again as the battle progressed. While proof of Morgan's tactical abilities can be seen in his victory, an assessment rendered by a British military man noted, "The dispositions made by the enemy on this occasion appear to have been judicious."[69]

How judicious they were can be seen by what happened when the British arrived and found the Americans ready for battle. As the Americans waited, some noted weather and other environmental conditions. Participants who mentioned the weather referred to it being a cold and very raw day.[70] Average temperatures from Spartanburg suggest it may have been well below freezing that morning. Initially, the cold may have adversely affected the Americans more than the British. Tarleton's men were warmed up by their exertions; the Americans were standing in wet grass after having moved less than a half mile following a chilling night in the open.

Hugh Allison, a South Carolina militiaman across the Broad River in North Carolina, mentioned seeing two suns in the sky that morning.[71] The atmospheric diffraction resulting in the appearance of two suns is caused by moisture in the air and indicates very high humidity. Not only was it cold, but it was also damp, or, as Captain Connelly reported, "inclined to be rainey." Atmospheric conditions could affect the battle in other ways. Dampness made it difficult for flintlocks to fire or to ignite rapidly, affecting accuracy. Another effect is that vision was different, especially before sunrise. Low clouds or mist affected any assessment of troop dispositions, even after full daylight. Combined with ground cover and elevation, mist may have blocked Tarleton's ability to see the Continentals waiting on the main line, even if he rode to his right to see around Hayes Rise. Moisture in the air could also affect individual soldiers trying to sight on their targets.

High humidity would cause gunsmoke to stay along the battle lines, but participants well to the rear reported being able to see the British advancing and no eyewitness recalled clouds of smoke.[72] Given the high humidity, a lack of references to gunsmoke suggests wind blew it away and also made the cold and damp worse because of wind chill.

Adding to Tarleton's problems with ground cover and the atmosphere, Americans on the first two lines had been told "to ease their joints."[73] This casual order allowed men to get down out of the wind, which further concealed them. It is unlikely Continentals would get such an order, but they were masked by heavier tree cover and the bulk of militia ridge. Trees may have broken the wind, but humidity and rain would keep up a steady dripping and add to the discomfort of men in ranks. It would have been colder under the trees because sunlight would not reach there.

Morgan's preparations throughout the night were not in vain. His men were fed and rested. They were on ground of his choosing, in line of battle, and they knew what was expected. Morgan was "in a popular and forcible style of elocution haranguing them."[74]

5 : The skirmish Line

They intended to eat us up.
—*Daniel Morgan to William Snickers, 23 January 1781*

The first infantry Tarleton encountered were skirmishers, rifle-men from Georgia, North Carolina, and South Carolina. Approximately 150 yards in front of the militia line, they engaged the advancing British, forced their deployment, and started the attriting process.[1] Casualties in-flicted by the skirmishers were probably minor, but they played a key role in wearing down the British in terms of physical stamina and mental desire to win, rather than survive.

British dragoon captain Richard Hovenden probably heard drums, com-mands, and the rattling of accoutrements as men shifted into position long before he saw any Americans in the gray light before sunrise. As "com-manding officer in front [he] reported that the American troops were halted and forming." "We were all awakened, ordered under arms, and formed in order of battle by daybreak. About sunrise . . . the enemy came in full view."[2]

The skirmishers first took positions in the militia line but, as Burke County privates Richard Crabtree and James McDonald said, were then "ordered out to meet General Tarlton, and bring on the action." Few in-structions were given the skirmishers, but they had "orders to feel the enemy as he approached." Most had extensive frontier service and knew generally what to do, but John Baldwin recalled McDowell still "told his men to take aim when they fired."[3] The skirmishers were ordered "not to deliver their fire until the enemy was within fifty yards."[4]

Tarleton lost little time in learning the terrain. Local Tories, including Alexander Chesney, "were immediately consulted relative to the ground which General Morgan then occupied, and the country in his rear. . . . The woods were open and free from swamps; that . . . part of Broad river . . . was about six miles distant."[5] In the gloomy light before daybreak, Tarleton could not see much. Hayes and his men were visible, still positioned on the highest ground behind the skirmishers, but Tarleton could not see the militia line's center or right flank, even if he stood in his stirrups. The militia's left flank would be partially visible as the sun rose but was obscured by scattered trees. Its precise location was masked by Hammond's skirmishers. While he could see militia, he could not see the Continentals deeper in the shadows and behind heavier tree cover well to the rear behind the ridge.[6]

Morgan's trap depended on breaking down the British, and, if Tarleton could not see the American lines, the later appearance of new, stronger lines would come as something of a surprise. The skirmishers huddled in a long, sweeping line of little groups as far as he could see across the front did not look particularly impressive. Hayes's line did not extend far on either side of the road and did not pose any real obstacle either. It might well be these men were only a rear guard to delay the British long enough for the Americans to cross the Broad River.

Private James Collins had a good view from his position on Brandon's left as, "about sunrise . . . the enemy came in full view. The sight, to me at least, seemed somewhat imposing; they halted for a short time. We look'd at each other for a considerable time." Some delay occurred as the British dropped excess equipment and formed a battle line. Delaware's Lieutenant Anderson noted the British "halted and Form'd the Line in Full View as We had no artillery to annoy them."[7]

Tarleton needed more information to precisely evaluate the force opposing him. To learn how the Americans were positioned, Tarleton "ordered the legion dragoons to drive in the militia parties who covered the front, that General Morgan's disposition might be conveniently and distinctly inspected."[8] Secondary accounts report that the British cavalry charged onto the field and drew fire from skirmish-line rifles.[9]

The dragoons assaulted the skirmish line center and left because wet low ground on the American right precluded mounted operations west of the road.[10] Tarleton's cavalry rode forward and then turned right, galloping along the American line in front of the slightly higher ground where the skirmishers were posted. The skirmishers knew how to deal with this threat. "The custom of militia warfare, was to get behind trees where they could shelter their bodies and fire from the side; general Morgan ordered them to adopt this mode, and when charged by the enemy's cavalry, that two should hold their fire in reserve."[11] "The American advanced corps, under Cunningham and M'Dowell, opened their fire and supported it with animation."[12] The bright sparkling flashes from skirmishers' rifles revealed the American left's forward positions from Cunningham's Georgians, around to Joseph Pickens's South Carolina State Troops.

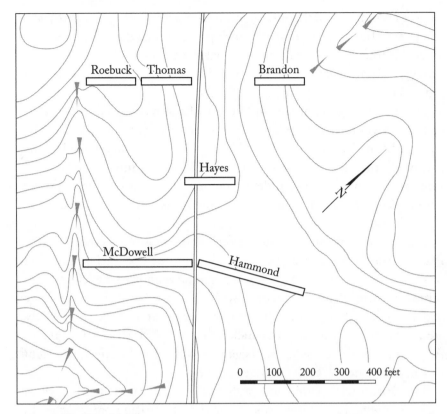

MAP 9. *The Skirmish Line*

The dragoons failed in their mission to drive off the skirmishers so Tarleton could see how the Americans were posted; their failure is an indication of the skirmish line's strength and the determination of those manning it. While some did start drifting to the rear, the skirmishers accomplished two missions by forcing Tarleton to deploy and denying him information. The "parties under Cunningham and M'Dowell prevented his approaching near enough to distinguish satisfactorily the American order of battle."[13]

As Tarleton watched the dragoons, his infantry came up the Green River Road. They halted, took off extra equipment, and caught their breath. After Tarleton evaluated the skirmish line, "the light infantry were then ordered to file to the right till they became equal to the flank of the American front line: The legion infantry were added to their left."[14]

Tarleton knew Morgan was near Broad River and the Americans could not cross it without exposing themselves to disaster if the British caught them during a crossing. Additional British forces east of Broad River were moving north to cut off the Americans. If the men opposing him were just a rear guard, Tarleton had to move quickly to continue the pursuit. A final argument to attack immediately was that American reinforcements were coming.[15] Tarleton had to attack to avoid meeting a stronger American force and get on with the pursuit.

Despite the poor light and visibility, Tarleton made his decision. Predictably, it was to attack; he lost little time in sending his men against the advanced American skirmish line. "Under the fire of a three-pounder, this part of the British troops was instructed to advance within three hundred yards of the enemy."[16] Once Tarleton committed to an attack, the battle was out of his control but he did not know this as his men moved against the skirmish line.

The light infantry and British Legion infantry moved forward east of the road. As the British battle line moved through the open fields, a cannon was trundled forward, firing as it went, aiming slightly to the left to avoid hitting British infantry. Captain Joseph Pickens's South Carolina State Troops were farthest forward because the gentle crest of the ridge curves around to the south and almost parallels the road. As the British advanced, Americans on the extreme left began to withdraw. In effect, the light infantry began to roll back the American line.

The British were within 200 yards of the American militia line when their right wing halted after passing the rivulet. Tarleton ordered the 7th Regiment "to form upon the left of the legion infantry, and the other three-pounder was given to the right division of the 7th: A captain, with fifty dragoons, was placed on each flank of the corps.... The 1st Battalion of the 71st was desired to extend a little to the left of the 7th regiment, and to remain one hundred and fifty yards in the rear. This body of infantry, and near two hundred cavalry, composed the reserve."[17] During the deployment, initial advance, and the 7th Regiment deployment, the British were under constant long-range fire from the skirmishers.

As the 7th Regiment deployed off the road onto low ground in front of McDowell, the 71st Regiment moved to take position on their left flank. George Hanger later noted that when "the 71st were . . . moving up to form in line with the rest of the troops, whether from their not taking ground enough, or from some other circumstance, their right flank *brushed* the left flank of the 7th regiment, and intermixed." Tarleton initially desired the 71st to take position beyond the 7th, but without adequate space to form, the 71st disrupted the 7th and was then detailed as a reserve. The Highlanders extended slightly beyond the 7th's left flank, following about 150 yards behind the line.[18]

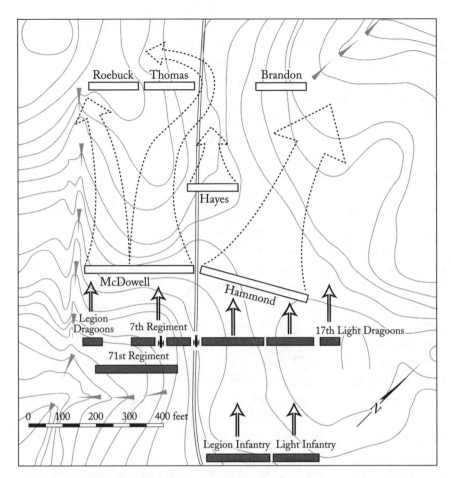

MAP 10. *British Deployment and Skirmish–Line Withdrawal*

The collision of the two units explains why the 7th was late in forming; "Major Newmarsh . . . was *posting* his officers." Newmarsh had to reorder his left flank by showing officers where he wanted them after the 71st marched into them. There was more confusion among the 7th Regiment soldiers because "a scattering fire commenced by some recruits of the 7th. . . . This unsteady behaviour he silenced to the utmost of his power, and then led the line to action."[19] The Green River Road became the axis for the British attack, with legion infantry and 7th Fusileers guiding on the road. Dressing left and right, respectively, and closing up as needed ensured that the infantry line did not drift apart as the attack moved against the Americans.

As the British advanced, American skirmishers on the left conducted a fighting withdrawal and McDowell's men continued a galling oblique fire at the British infantry. Their fire fell initially on the British Legion infantry's left flank, but as the 7th Regiment deployed, they shifted and hit the deploying fusileers. The North Carolinians did not move back until "the bayonet was presented," as the British infantry went forward.[20]

Except for the 7th Regiment's unauthorized, scattering shots, the British did not fire until they engaged the militia line. The 7th Regiment's fire may not have been on command, but it caused McDowell's men to commence withdrawing. As William Lorance noted, he "was in the front line in the beginning of the Action and upon the first fire it fell back upon the second line."[21] The first British firing, aside from the cannon, was the premature shots from the jittery 7th Fusileers.

The British advanced rapidly because Tarleton did not want the Americans to get settled in new positions. Once they were moving, he wanted to keep the pressure on them. The skirmishers continued "to deliver their fire . . . then to retire, covering themselves with trees as occasion offered, loading and firing until they reached and resumed their places in the first line."[22] As they withdrew, McDowell's left-flank skirmishers moved through the gap between Brandon and Thomas created by Hayes's forward movement and took positions wherever they could find gaps to fire through the militia line. McDowell's right, and Hammond's men on the left, moved to the militia's flanks and kept up a long-range fire.

The skirmishers followed orders precisely, forcing a British deployment and firing as they withdrew. "Majors McDowal and Cunningham gave them a heavy and galling fire," "strictly obeyed your orders . . . gradually retreating," and "preserving a desultory well aimed fire." The retrograde movement had been explained to the skirmishers, and "McDowell told his men . . . as they retreated to divide to the right & left & form in the rear."[23]

Immediately after the skirmishers passed their position, the Little River Regiment on Hayes Rise withdrew to complete a solid line across the field. Their withdrawal was hurried; they knew the British were close behind them. Other militiamen could wait, but Hayes had to get his men reformed in a new position before Tarleton's infantry got close enough to charge bayonets.

The British Legion infantry and the light infantry came on quickly, grimly confident, moving steadily at the quick step, more certain of success now that they were going forward. The trap Morgan created was already starting to close on Tarleton's men. The full extent of the South Carolina militia line was revealed only after the British came over the crest of militia ridge. Now, as the last of the skirmishers took their positions, a new, much more deadly phase of the battle began.

6 : The Militia Line

Two-thirds of the British . . . had already fallen.
—Roderick MacKenzie,
Strictures on Lt. Col. Tarleton's History, *1787*

American officers made good use of the interval before the British moved forward, engaged the militia line, and began fighting in earnest.[1] Morgan, the former rifleman, "walked behind and through the ranks everywhere, all the time cracking jokes and encouraging the men, and said, 'Boys, squinney well, and don't touch a trigger until you see the whites of their eyes.'"[2] Morgan, an experienced combat commander, wanted to settle his men and take their minds off the British soldiers' deploying, shifting position, and getting ready to advance.

Tarleton, "relying on the valour of his troops, impatient of delay, and too confident of success, led on in person the first line to the attack." He had good reasons to start the attack quickly. His right was formed and under fire while the fusiliers deployed. The quickest way to end the unequal long-range fight was for the British to get close enough to use their bayonets. Not all the infantry moved forward immediately because "major Newmarsh . . . was posting his officers," then a "fire from some of the recruits of the 7th regiment was suppressed, and the troops moved on in as good a line as troops could move at open files."[3] Stabilizing the line and stopping the fire caused the 7th Fusiliers to lag behind.

Tarleton, aggressive and impatient, urged his men forward without waiting on the 7th Regiment. The fusiliers would just have to catch up. He could not afford to give the Americans time to get ready and certainly did not want his own men to start thinking about what lay just beyond the ridge to their front. The British moved quickly up and through the old skirmish position.

As the infantry moved, both cannon opened up at a range of 200 yards or less, point-blank range for three-pounders. With every shot, the guns recoiled about four feet, were dragged back into position, reloaded, aimed, and fired again. The gunners fired both guns nearly simultaneously as "eight times cannon went off, two at a time."[4] The firing pattern suggests

*William Washington; oil painting by Charles Willson Peale
(Independence National Historical Park Collection)*

the artillerymen were with the battle line. With infantry protection, they had little to fear from militia as they moved forward.

The cannon had little impact on the battle. Few veterans mentioned them, noting only that they signaled the start of fighting or were captured. The American positions complicated observation for the gunners and took American militia out of the direct line of fire. The little guns, even with a light six-ounce charge, threw a three-pound solid shot over 400 yards with just two degrees' elevation. Without raising the tube more than a half degree, and using an eight-ounce charge, shot could fly more than 250 yards before the first bounce, and this placed Washington's dragoons within range.[5] When originally positioned in front of the skirmishers, the guns were elevated to clear the rising ground of militia ridge. The shot fell on the American cavalry, 250 yards behind the militia, and Washington was forced to move his horsemen slightly to the right to avoid the fire.[6]

There was no doubt when the infantry began to move upslope. At sunrise, the British "began the attack by the Discharge of two pieces of Cannon and three Huizzas."[7] By all accounts, the British infantry "was ordered to advance rapidly," with a shout and a steady rush against the militia. Many veterans noted "the moment the british formed their line they shouted and made a great noise to intimidate," "with a loud halloo." At least one American felt the British confidence as they "advanced rapidly, as if certain of victory." Morgan, aware of the psychological impact on his militia, reacted immediately by yelling loud enough for many to hear, "They give us the British halloo, boys, give *them* the Indian halloo, by G——."[8]

Far to the rear, volunteer dragoon Thomas Young saw Morgan ride "down to the rifle men"; he "galloped along the lines, cheering the men, and telling them not to fire until we could see the whites of their eyes." The wind must have been blowing northward because Young could hear, "every officer was crying don't fire! for it was a hard matter for us to keep from it." "Colonel Pickens directed the men under his command, to restrain their fire, till the British were within forty or fifty yards. This order, [was] executed with great firmness."[9]

The British came forward, rapidly moving over the crest toward Pickens's "militia riffle men." Infantrymen were taught to march at eighty steps a minute. In quick time, this increased to a hundred. Every minute they covered 200 to 240 feet. In less than three minutes, they were well within musket range of the rifle-armed militia. Even on line with a rapid pace, they were under control as "the British line advanced at a sort of trot. . . . It was the most beautiful line I ever saw."[10]

The South Carolina battalions waited, a short distance down the rear slope. Tarleton thought "about one thousand militia" were drawn up in his front.[11] The militia were at a tree line, well behind the actual crest and less than 150 yards in front of the Continentals. The South Carolinians had been waiting almost an hour for this moment of truth. They had freshly primed rifles. Those with new flints certainly used them; men with older flints sharpened them and tested the spark before loading and priming. In the damp January weather, fresh charges, fresh priming, and new flints were crucial to good ignition.

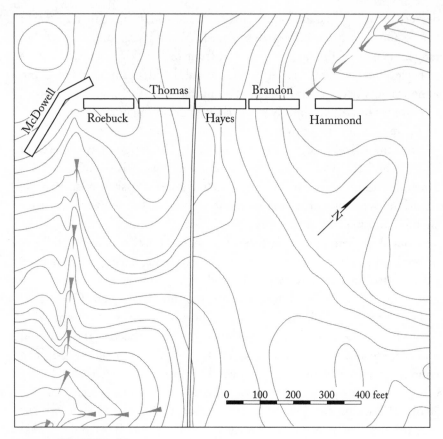

MAP II. *The Militia Line*

The "militia maintained their ground with perfect coolness."[12] The rifle-men knew they would get in a first shot at longer range with greater accuracy than their enemies armed with muskets. The militia were also fresh, if somewhat chilled, and had confidence in their leaders, many of whom they elected or chose to follow. As the British line came on, "small parties of riflemen were detached to skirmish with the enemy."[13] Joseph McJunkin reported, "Morgan had picked out eleven of us who were to fire as a signal for opening the ball, and placed us in front several paces. . . . When they came near enough for us to distinguish plainly their faces, we picked out our man and let fly."[14] The eleven men moved forward of Brandon's line a short distance, perhaps less than twenty feet. Hayes, Roebuck, and Thomas sent out similar detachments.[15]

The Fair Forest battalion's "Col Fair [Farr] . . . believed John Savage fired the first gun . . . he saw Savage fix his eye upon a British officer; he stepped out of the ranks, raised his gun-fired, and he saw the officer fall."

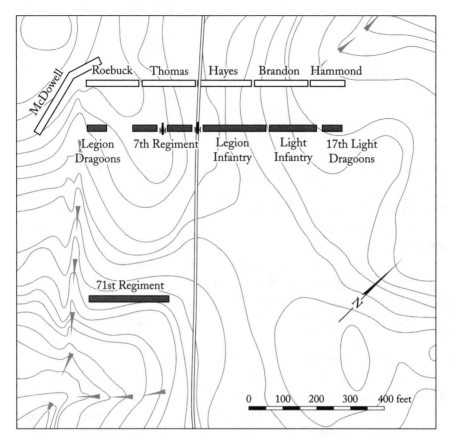

MAP 12. *Militia-Line Firefight*

Savage was east of the road, so the officer was a light infantryman or in the British Legion. Captain John Rousselet, the one British Legion infantry officer killed at Cowpens, was serving as legion commander.[16] He would have been in front, urging his men to keep formation as they advanced.

Savage's shot precipitated other individual firings before an American volley was ordered. The firing began on the American left rather than the right because the light infantry and British Legion were moving ahead of the 7th Regiment and reached the "killing distance" first. The firing was heard by the dragoons, as Thomas Young recalled, "the militia fired first. It was for a time, pop-pop-pop—and then a whole volley."[17]

When the British reached a point "forty or fifty yards" or an even closer—"thirty or forty paces"—the militia commenced volley fire. "General Morgan gave orders for the malitia to fire on the enemy."[18] The difference in range might reflect different British-unit start times and the distance covered during the five to ten seconds after the small parties' fire and

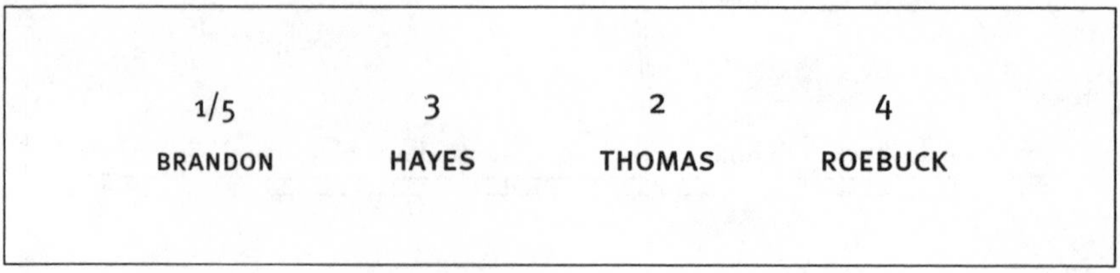

1/5	3	2	4
BRANDON	HAYES	THOMAS	ROEBUCK

FIGURE 3. *South Carolina Militia Battalions Firing Sequence*

the first battalion volley. In that time, the British came another twenty to twenty-five paces nearer, closing the distance from fifty to less than thirty-five yards, before the volley fire started.

The fire was devastating. "The front line . . . poured in a close fire." "The effect of the fire was considerable: it produced something like a recoil, but not to any extent." The impact was magnified because it was aimed rifle fire. The desired effect was achieved because "The fire was returned, but not with vivacity or impression."[19] The light infantry and legion infantry opposite Brandon did not fire but tried to advance as they had been trained to do.

The five volleys reported by Private John Thomas in Combs's Company indicates Roebuck, Thomas, and Hayes each got off one shot while some of Brandon's men fired twice. Brandon's men had little time to reload, but it was enough. The militia were going by the book as "the whole of Col. Pickens' command then kept up a fire by regiments."[20] The volleys took a very short time. From John Savage's first shot until the militia moved off, less than three minutes elapsed.

British infantry was trained to cope with riflemen by attacking them immediately.[21] The light infantry "made two attempts to charge, but were repulsed with loss."[22] Even after the militia opened fire, the British advance was rapid enough to deny most militiamen an opportunity to reload because, as Howard said, there was no "time, especially [for] the riflemen, to fire a second time." They only "gave the enemy one fire," but the four battalions "fired five rounds."[23] Staggered by the first volley and their losses, the light infantry rallied and tried to charge again. Their second effort, less than a minute later, came after the Fair Forest men had reloaded. They fired again and stopped the light infantry a second time.

The American rifle fire was incredibly effective. Lieutenant Roderick MacKenzie, leading a Highland light infantry company and probably also wounded at this time, claimed "Two-thirds of the British infantry officers, had already fallen, and nearly the same proportion of privates." His comment about casualties seems correct for the four to six light infantry officers, as the light infantry received Brandon's two volleys and fire from Hammond's skirmishers. His observations about enlisted men suffering nearly 60 percent casualties gives a clue to the shock effect of the American volleys. Both physically and psychologically, the aimed rifle fire induced "something like a recoil." Far more telling is MacKenzie's admission that many were not shot. The cumulative effect of short rations, lack of sleep, hard marching, cold, wet weather, and the fighting to this point left them unable to continue.[24]

The British Legion was hurt as badly as the light infantry. Four British Legion infantry companies suffered over 90 percent casualties in prisoners and killed. Total British losses on the day would number about 890. About 17 percent were wounded prisoners and nearly 24 percent were dead. For the entire British Legion infantry, this translates to a loss of 19 percent wounded and 26 percent killed, or 45 percent casualties for the whole battle. According to MacKenzie, most dead were in front of the militia line. British militia-line losses impressed Americans. Captain Thomas Farrow, "one of the soldiers who assisted in the burying, observed . . . the dead were found in straight lines across the field, & that it gave them a most singular appearance when seen at a distance."[25]

British return fire was not effective. This is obvious from low American casualties and Joseph McJunkin's 1842 comment, "they shot too high . . . we outshot them."[26] The British usually shot high and now *were* shooting downhill. The combination kept American casualties down, one indication of how judiciously Morgan placed his men on the landscape to achieve an advantage.

Unless an American militiaman specifically noted where, how, or when he was wounded, it is difficult to ascertain losses for the militia line. There were far more militia casualties than Morgan reported, and many were officers. In Roebuck's Battalion, Dennis Tramell's company suffered casualties involving changes in command as well as private soldiers. Private Hugh Warren later reported that when Captain "Lawson was Killed, Jeremiah Dixon took command." Private Henry Pettit reported, "I was Wounded in my thigh which Injured me very much."[27] Farther left in Roebuck's Battalion, Private Samuel Hogg "was *wounded* in the Shoulder." In Thomas's Battalion, Samuel Smith lost "his brother Aaron Smith who was severely wounded . . . he died . . . five days after." In Hayes's Battalion, Captain James Dillard "received a gunshot wound," and at least one man under Irby was wounded in the left thigh by a bayonet.[28]

The British pressed on, despite casualties. "The American militia . . . were unable to resist the assault, and immediately gave way," "moved off precipitately," and were "pursued to the continentals." Even if the British were somewhat slow to charge, the fighting did not last long. "The militia, after a short contest, were dislodged." "The military valour of British troops, when not entirely divested of the powers necessary to its exertion, was not to be resisted by an American militia." The militia "broke in the centre," where the Little River Battalion could not finish reloading before the British charged. Without bayonets, with no time to reload, they can hardly be faulted for fleeing.[29]

The light infantry was the first British unit to charge. They recovered from their initial shock and started forward to give Brandon the bayonet after Hayes fired. Unfortunately for the light infantry, Brandon's men completed reloading before Hayes fired.[30] As the light infantry advanced, the Fair Forest men got off a second volley which stopped the British dead in their tracks.

With the Fair Forest volley, the entire American left was without loaded weapons when the British Legion infantry made their move. The speed with which the Americans fired, the suddenness of the British charge, and the duration of the militia-line fighting seem almost too rapid for twentieth-century comprehension, but the British Legion infantry had been trained by Hanger to cope with riflemen by charging immediately. If they were as quick to charge as the light infantry, they received Hayes's volley, recovered from the shock, delivered their own volley, and then charged. Unlike Brandon's Fair Forest men, the Little River Battalion had not the remotest chance of reloading once the British Legion started forward.

It took British infantry twenty seconds to cover thirty yards at the relatively slow quick step, and many riflemen could reload before the British closed to bayonet distance. At the charge, the British moved much faster, and would close within two or three yards before the militia could complete reloading.[31] The Little River men did not wait to measure distances. On the main line, Lieutenant Colonel Howard saw the British rush "with bayonets upon the militia who had not time, especially the riflemen, to fire a second time."[32] Most casualties occurred among the Fair Forest and Little River Battalions. Sword wounds in these battalions were inflicted slightly later in the battle; gunshot wounds most likely occurred on the militia line before the British "charged us with their bayonets."[33] The only known South Carolina militia bayonet wound occurred in Irby's Company of Hayes's Battalion.[34] If Irby was on Hayes's left flank, the break in the militia line occurred at the junction of the Little River and Fair Forest Regiments.

As the British Legion infantry surged forward, Hayes, his men with unloaded rifles and no bayonets, had no alternative except immediate withdrawal. Once the Little River Battalion moved off, a huge gap appeared in the militia line. Brandon and Thomas followed Hayes rearward. The honor of breaking the militia line should go to the British Legion infantry.

Still, the militia withdrawal was according to plan. It may be that "Pickens ordered a retreat" as the British charge began, if not slightly later when he saw the gap created by the departing Little River men. When "the American militia gave way," "the enemy rent the air with their shouts and quickened their advance," then "pursued to their continentals."[35]

In the British mind, the battle was as good as won.[36] They dispersed the forward skirmishers with ease. The militia proved troublesome, but they were now fleeing the field in disorder. Surely the battle was going well and they could ease their minds about it. Despite casualties, Tarleton's men sensed victory and stepped forward with even more confidence.

The militia's move to safety was not as chaotic as some historians described it.[37] Both Lieutenant Anderson and Sergeant Major Seymour reported orderly movement. "Being overpowered by the superior number of the enemy they retreated, but in very good order, not seeming to be in the least confused." The withdrawing militiamen could see the silent ranks of Delawares, Marylanders, and Virginians waiting for the British. Once they were within forty yards of the Continentals, the militia could quickly withdraw to relative safety after firing another shot. Some Parthian shots were fired as the "riflemen that Was posted in front Who Fought Well Disputing the ground that Was between them and us, Flying from One tree to another."[38] The militia continued their withdrawal.

Traditional accounts state that the militia ran across the front of the main line and escaped beyond the left flank. As they ran, they were charged by British dragoons from Tarleton's left flank.[39] This makes no sense practically, tactically, or historically for either group. Frightened men trying to escape would not expose themselves to British bayonets and sabers by running toward them. Tactically, any militia crossing the Continental front would mask their fire. Morgan never put his main line in jeopardy by obstructing their fire. British dragoons would be equally reluctant to ride along the Continental front exposed to heavy musket fire.

British accounts, coupled with descriptions of original American positioning, explain the militia escape. The main line, "which had as yet taken no share in the action, observing confusion and retrograding in their front, suddenly faced to the right, and inclined backwards; a manoeuvre by which a space was left for the front line to retreat, without interfering with the

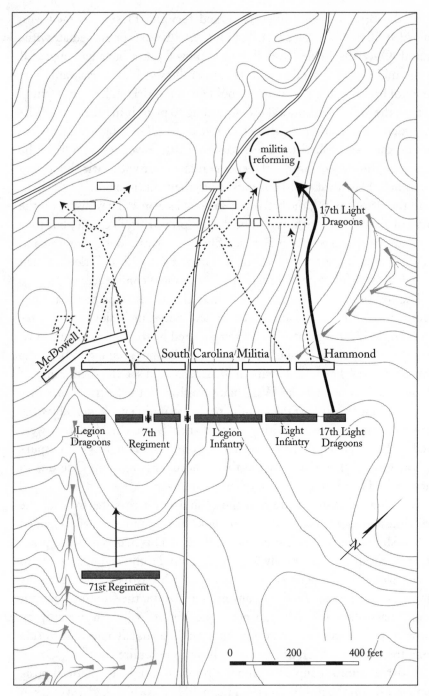

MAP 13. *Militia-Line Withdrawal*

ranks of those who were now to oppose the advance." Another noted, "the second line of the Americans, having opened to the right & left, to afford a passage," the militia went to the rear.[40]

Morgan's tactical plan envisioned South Carolina militiamen withdrawing through the main line and taking a position behind the left flank. The retreat was planned, and "Pickens ordered a retreat to the post assigned to them, on the left of the continental troops." This was accomplished when "the militia fell into our rear."[41] The militia did move rapidly and some did go to their horses. Most, in accordance with orders, went to a position behind Triplett. The withdrawal plan envisioned reforming behind Continental bayonets, and then going back into battle. Morgan and his aides slowed the militia, gathered them into a solid mass, and began reforming them.[42]

The British infantry, having disposed of the militia, continued their advance with vigor. The British pursuit was initially a continuation of the bayonet charge. Seeing the backs of the militia, they surged forward in pursuit, breaking ranks as faster men moved to the front. The "royal troops supposing the victory already gained, ardently pursued, and were thereby thrown into some disorder."[43] When officers sighted the solid regular infantry line, they halted and restored their own line.

As the militia filtered through the main line, "the British approached the continentals. The fire on both sides was well supported, and produced much slaughter." The main battle lines were engaged above the swale. Between Triplett's left flank and the ravine, Hammond's skirmishers, the "volunteers from . . . South Carolina and Georgia . . . were posted to guard the flank." The militia story continues here because once the firefight was under way, Tarleton's "cavalry on the right were directed to charge the enemy's left." The 17th Light Dragoons attacked so suddenly, Hammond's flankers were overwhelmed and simply ridden through.[44]

The lower swale was a riot of confusion. Battalion officers were trying to get companies under control and into formation. Company officers were shouting for their men to reform on them. The men, still excited by their stand, their devastating volley, and the run to the rear, were looking around for their messmates, then for their officers. Some, more poised and pragmatic than most, began reloading. Without any flags, it would have been difficult for anyone to make sense of more than 800 men clustering without formations. Then disaster struck.

"The British broke through the left wing of the Malitia," although Joseph Pickens's South Carolina State Troops offered a brief resistance when Private Charles Holland "was wounded by a sword thrust through the body."[45] As the dragoons galloped down into the swale, the South Carolina militiamen were still milling about and reloading. The 17th changed that.

The militia thought they were safe in the American rear, but any impression of security created by Continental bayonets and their steady musket fire was an illusion. Some idea of the militia's panic can be seen as only forty British dragoons rampaged down upon the disorganized militia and began hacking them about the head and shoulders. Even the usually accurate Robert Long was mentally overwhelmed as surprise magnified British numbers to "200 or 300 cavalry [who came] round in the rear of our left wing." James Collins thought he was about to become a dragoon's trophy. "Now," thought I, "my hide is in the loft."[46]

The 17th "began to cut down the militia very fast." In Brandon's Battalion, John Whelchel received "seven wounds on his head and two on his Shoulders. . . . The wounds in the head opened the skull to the brains." Although his wounds disabled him for only "about forty days," others were horrified. Forty years later, Brandon's adjutant Joshua Palmer recalled John Whelchel "was cut through the skull, to the membrane of the brain . . . [I] did not expect the said John Whelchel would Survive."[47] "As the militia . . . were unable to form . . . they continued to retreat," but others from Brandon's Battalion fought back.

Fair Forest's Lieutenant Joseph Hughes "bears the scars which he received from a Stroke across his right hand from one of Tarlton's Troops." His modest statement does not relate what Private Christopher Brandon saw Hughes do that morning. "He was not only a man of great personal strength, but of remarkable fleetness on foot. As his men, with others, broke at the Cowpens, and fled before Tarleton's cavalry; and though receiving a sabre cut across his right hand, yet with his drawn sword, he would out-run his men, and passing them, face about, and command them to stand, striking right and left to enforce obedience to orders; often repeating with a loud voice: 'You d—d cowards, halt and fight—there is more danger in running than in fighting, and if you don't stop and fight, you will all be killed!' "[48] John Skain, one of three brothers serving with Hughes, was killed. A local tradition recalls that Colonel Thomas Brandon, leading by example, killed three British dragoons with his sword.[49]

A similar flight occurred in Hayes's Little River Battalion, where more men went down under dragoon sabers. Jeremiah Files "was wounded . . . on the left Arm and on the right hand each wound was made with a sword." Files's father was killed at the same time, probably in close proximity to his son. As officers tried to restore order, some went down. James Carlisle's "company officer Capt. [James] Caldwell was mortally wounded."[50]

As pursuit continued, Hughes and other officers like him brought about some order, but the militia "were not rallied until Gen. Morgan did it in person." Hughes's company "was induced to make a stand on the brow of a slope, some distance from the battle-line, behind a clump of young pines that partially concealed and protected them from Tarleton's cavalry. Others now joined them for self-protection. Their guns were quickly loaded and they were themselves again. Morgan galloped up and spoke words of encouragement to them."[51]

Light dragoons and militiamen reached the militia horses at the same time. "Our company when just about to catch up our horses . . . [the British] fell upon us with great fury." "They overtook us and began to make a few hacks at some, however, without doing much injury." "The Whigs reserved their fire till the enemy were so near, that it was terribly effective, emptying many a British saddle, when the survivors recoiled."[52]

The militia were relieved by their own rifles and a sudden overwhelming attack by Washington's dragoons, who outnumbered the 17th at least three to one. Washington had seen the crisis and acted immediately, leading his dragoons over Morgan Hill to hit the British head on. The American cavalry "enabled the militia to regain the tranquility necessary for returning to a state of order." James Collins, his hide now safe, noted that militiamen "being relieved from the pursuit of the enemy began to rally and prepare to redeem our credit, when Morgan rode up in front, and waving his sword, cried out, 'Form, form, my brave fellows! give them one more fire and the day is ours. Old Morgan was never beaten.' We then advanced briskly, and gained the right flank."[53]

As the militia rallied and began moving around Morgan Hill, a crisis occurred on the main line and nearly cost Morgan his victory, until events conspired to change American fortunes on the day. As the main line shifted, the militia put themselves in order, reformed, and headed back into battle. The militia who moved to engage the British on the American right flank in the last stages of the American counterattack were chiefly from the Spartanburg Regiment and Hammond's South Carolina State Troops. They had not been as discomforted and maintained some order. Men from the Little River and Fair Forest Regiments who returned to action did so in two groups on the American left. Some caught their horses, mounted, and participated in the counterattack and pursuit. Others on foot acted in the traditional role of riflemen, firing at long range. There were many targets for them because the main line had achieved something of a miracle.

7 : The Main Line

The fire on both sides . . . produced much slaughter.
—*Banastre Tarleton,* History of the Campaigns of 1780–1781

Maryland lieutenant colonel John Eager Howard led the Virginians and Continentals, forming the most powerful opposition to Tarleton's infantry. Out of sight until the British crested the ridge in front of the militia, even then they were not clearly visible due to thicker woods behind the militia line. During the militia firefight, Morgan and Howard kept them in good order, quietly waiting for the British.[1] The Continentals stood in the "beaten zone," a term referring to ground where projectiles missing their initial target fall with effect. Bullets that missed militiamen and did not hit trees were still lethal. The weight and momentum of the .75 caliber Brown Bess musket ball made it dangerous 150 yards behind the militia. At least one officer went down from such a hit, crippled for life with a wound in his right hip.[2]

When the British initially appeared, Morgan rode down toward the skirmishers, but returned to the militia line. He remained behind Pickens's men until they opened fire, then moved to the Continentals. He steadied the main line as the British advanced. Delaware private Henry Wells recalled, "the powerful & trumpet like voice of our Commander drove fear from every bosom, and gave new energies to every arm."[3]

Since the militia withdrawal might create a disaster, Morgan and Howard made it clear the militia were supposed to retreat. The advance warning helped; when the militia pulled back, "the Continentals[,] . . . undismayed by the retreat of the militia, maintained their ground."[4] Morgan prepared for the withdrawal by aligning the Virginia companies *en échelon* to the center. As the militia moved rearward, Morgan moved to the foot of Morgan Hill across the swale. Here the militia could see him as they passed through the line toward the left rear.

During the two or three minutes it took the militia to pass through, the British reformed their own lines. The redcoated infantry had been badly hurt by the militia rifle fire, but their officers still maintained control. "The

Enemy Seeing us Standing in such good Order Halted for Some time to dress their line Which Outflanked our[s] Considerably The[y] then advanced On boldly."[5] The British had to reform when they saw the Continentals. They were too disordered by the militia gunfire and subsequent bayonet charge to take on the well-disciplined American regulars. The unengaged Continentals must have been quite disconcerting to Tarleton's infantry. Just having seen victory in the backs of the militia, they now saw trouble in the solid ranks wearing blue coats faced with red, outlined by white belts supporting cartridge box and bayonet scabbard. Skirmishers and militia had done their duty well. Tarleton's force was hurt, and there is evidence to suggest that the fighting spirit of some men had been broken. With losses from bullets and lack of enthusiasm, the British were now facing their sternest test.

The British dressed all three battalions across the front. The British Legion infantry had their left flank on the road and their right flank adjoining the light infantry. Casualties suffered against the militia meant these two battalions were now covering a smaller front than they had against the militia. Shortening the linear distance opposite the Virginians was necessary, moreover, because the canebrake and boggy ground at the head of Suck Creek constricted the battlefield. Instead of open order, the two battalions now formed a more solid line opposite Triplett's Virginians. The 7th Regiment Fusiliers dressed right on the road to maintain contact with the British Legion. As their casualties mounted, the line shortened and its front did not extend beyond the Continental's right flank, if it even reached that far. The 71st Regiment, moving forward behind Ogilvie's dragoons, was not yet positioned beyond the Continental right flank as the main-line fighting began.

British officers corrected problems before advancing farther. Their men closed up and dressed ranks under fire as the main-line riflemen opened up as soon as the militia were clear. At a range well under 100 yards, Hammond's skirmishers and Gilmore's Rockbridge riflemen had easy targets; "a warm fire ensued, and the advance of the enemy was not with such a quick step."[6] Once reformed, the British infantry line advanced, ready to engage.

While the British reformed their ranks, the last militiamen passed through the main line. "As soon as the militia were cleared away from before the second line, the musquetry then had orders to fire."[7] Continental muskets now joined the rifles of Gilmore and Hammond. Their fire covered the movement of the four Virginia companies onto line. Once the militia cleared the front of Lawson's Virginia State Troops and Tate's Augusta riflemen, they stepped forward. A half minute later, Buchanan's and

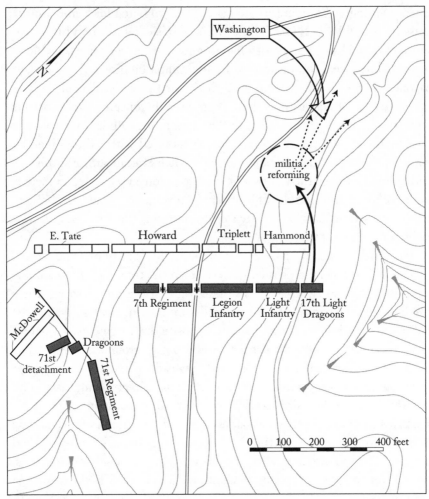

Note: British Legion and light infantry frontage reduced by 25%, 7th Regiment frontage reduced by 20% in allowance for casualties at militia line.

MAP 14. *Main-Line Positions after Militia Withdrawal*

Combs's riflemen advanced, closing all gaps in Howard's line. A solid wall of infantry now blocked any further British advance.[8]

Morgan reported to Greene that "when the enemy advanced on our lines they received a well directed and incessant fire," or, as Virginia private Richard Swearingen said, "the Regulars came up and began to Pour it into them nicely."[9] Continental officers reported the British advanced "under a Very heavy fire until the[y] got Within a few yards of us" and Howard's "regiment commenced firing." The firing "was kept up with coolness and constancy."[10] Howard's solid line was arranged into three battalions for firing purposes. Wallace's Virginia Continentals, Anderson's Maryland Continentals, and Gilmore's Virginia militia fired first for their respective battalions. In the center, Kirkwood fired after Anderson, then Mangers, then Dobson. When each Virginia company came on line, they fired. Then the cycle started again. Thomas Young, watching from Morgan Hill, was impressed: "when the regulars fired, it seemed like one sheet of flame from right to left."[11]

Once the volleys began, they quickly developed into a very hot fire. The deeper crash of musket volleys was punctuated by the higher crack of individual rifles and massed rifle volleys. The Americans "received [the British] with unshaken firmness." "The fire on both sides was well supported, and produced much slaughter."[12] The fight grew more intense as both sides closed the range and kept up the pace of firing. Both British and Continentals "maintained their ground with great bravery; and the conflict between them and the British troops was obstinate and bloody." "All the officers and men behaved with uncommon and undaunted bravery."[13]

Mounted officers stood out and were observed by soldiers. Maryland private Andrew Rock knew Morgan by sight and "saw him frequently at the battle of the Cowpens." Virginia's Private Jeremiah Preston saw Tarleton across the lines, an indication of how close the fighting was and confirming that gunsmoke was blown away. "The contest became obstinate; and each party, animated by the example of its leader, nobly contended for victory. Our line maintained itself so firmly."[14]

The fighting grew in intensity. Virginia rifleman Jeremiah Preston checked his cartridge pouch later and found he "fired 17 rounds."[15] Seventeen shots provides insight into the battle's duration. A rifle could be fired no faster than about one shot every fifteen seconds in the hands of an expert. This estimate provides a short-term parameter of about five minutes for the main-line fighting. A longer time is indicated by Johnson, who claimed it lasted "near thirty minutes."[16] It is likely that the infantry fight lasted less than ten minutes from the first shots to the American withdrawal.

In combat, distances seem foreshortened. When a person is in desperate straits, time seems to slow down; action seems to occur in slow motion. Other thoughts intrude as the musketeer, under the eyes of watchful sergeants, mechanically follows the manual of exercise that will guarantee his survival. During loading and firing, soldiers noticed little increments of their task. The dry taste of black powder and waxed paper cartridges was one step. Then, a rattle of ramrods in the barrels as new charges of buck and ball were forced home against the breech plug with a distinctive *ping*. Platoon and division volleys crashed with bright yellow flashes from pan and barrel, highlighting the firing sequence. The blast of noise and light was so dramatic a soldier could not tell if his own musket fired. During priming, only a wisp of smoke coming out of the barrel's touch hole would show that the gun went off. The acrid smell of burnt powder, greasy black smears on hand and face from ramrods grown slick with sweat and powder residue, and cut thumbs from mishandling the musket's cock added to individual perceptions of the fight. There was a disconcerting *whiz* of balls going overhead, *thwacking* against trees, *thudding* into the ground, or the awful *thunk* of lead striking flesh and bone. A growing undertone of groans was punctuated by shrill screams of the wounded. Cutting across these distractions came the commands as officers called out, "Prime and load!; Shoulder; Make Ready; Take Aim!; Fire!" and then repeated the cycle.

During the fighting, senior officers noted the impact of their fire and their own casualties. American casualties provide a key to locating British units and assessing their strength. If an American unit suffered few or no casualties, it is unlikely that a British unit was opposite them. Officer casualties suggest a moderate level of fighting in the road where Combs's Fauquier Company was located and Preston fired his seventeen shots. "I was in the Road all the time of the actions I covered Captain Combs he was killed." The shocking indication of mortality was not lost on Private George Rogers, who stood next to Captain Combs; "the Captain . . . was killed and fell by his Side." Lieutenant Dearing, another officer in Combs's company, received a mortal wound as he "was wounded through his hand . . . and bled to death."[17] Enlisted casualties in Combs's company were not heavy, but they did occur and Private William McCoy "received two wounds."[18]

Given constriction of space and American casualties, both the light infantry and the British Legion infantry were much reduced by the time they engaged the Virginians.[19] Triplett's companies suffered about equally, so they had equal opposition, indicating the British right may have been reduced to less than 200 men. Since Triplett had about 160 men and Hammond 115 when the battle began, the Americans brought more guns to this firefight than the British did. The reduced light and legion infantry faced a numerically superior, rifle-armed force at close range. The Virginians were not vulnerable in this fight because they had rifles. They were protected by the cycle of firing which left one company always loaded, and by the bayonets of adjacent Continentals.

On the right, casualties suggest Wallace and Lawson were under fire only just before their withdrawal. The two right Maryland companies under Anderson and Mangers, and Buchanan's Augusta riflemen, had no

TABLE 3. *Wounds in American Main-Line Companies*

Gilmore	Tate	Combs	2M	1D	3/5M	1/7M	Buchanan	Lawson	Wallace
3	4	4	3	16	3	2	1	6	5

(N=47)

British unit opposite them and could fire virtually unopposed into the 7th Fusiliers. A complete absence of gunshot wounds in the two right Maryland companies suggests they had an easy time, at least until the counterattack. Dobson's left Maryland company, located between Combs and Kirkwood, appears to have been in virtual dead space facing a gap between the 7th Fusiliers and the British Legion infantry. Dobson's low casualties suggest the 7th Fusiliers closed up on their colors opposite Kirkwood as their casualties mounted rather than dressing on the road. If so, they left Dobson's Marylanders free to fire at targets of opportunity.

The fusiliers advanced slightly later, so they were farther away when the South Carolina militia fired. While they may have escaped the worst volley fire from Thomas and Roebuck, they were shot up by McDowell's flankers who retreated only as far as British pressure forced them. The British Legion and the light infantry, closer to the guns of Brandon and Farr, suffered more. If the reduced 7th Fusiliers dressed on their cannon and colors instead of the road, they were formed directly opposite the Delaware Company. The compression is a reflection of how badly they had been hurt by the skirmishers, the flanking fire from McDowell, and the militia line.

Kirkwood's men suffered because the brunt of the fusilier fire fell on them. If casualties are any indication, Kirkwood's Delawares saw the most intense fighting of all American units at Cowpens. No other American company suffered anything like the 25 percent casualties at Cowpens that the Delawares endured. One-third of the Delawares were wounded by bayonet during the counterattack. Ensign Bivins was badly wounded in the hip, probably by a stray musket ball or grapeshot during the militia fighting. Besides Bivins and those wounded in the final stages of the battle, ten Delawares, one-sixth of the company's strength, were killed or wounded in the main-line firefight.

Most Delaware casualties were gunshot wounds, and an examination of their wounds is instructive. Of the sixteen Delaware men injured at Cowpens, one was killed outright, four others died before 1 February, and six were so badly wounded they saw no further service. As an added insult, many suffered multiple wounds. Multiple wounding was the result of repeated volley fire as well as the use of buck-and-ball cartridges.[20]

Five Delawares were wounded in the arm; three "through the arm," suggesting musket balls. Sergeant McGuire was listed as having been wounded "in the hand." Private John Mitchel was wounded "in the arm and leg"; John Todd, wounded "through" the arm, was also wounded "through" the neck. John Harriss and Thomas Walker both suffered multiple wounds in their lower extremities.[21]

So many wounds were in the lower extremities and belly that it is likely fusilier officers were particularly effective in getting their muskets "presented" lower than other British units, keeping their fire down where it was more likely to strike home.[22] Most Delaware wounds occurred during the firefight, so the high casualty rate reflects a strong British presence opposite them. The 7th Regiment's cannon fired while engaging Kirkwood, but wounds inflicted by artillery fire are difficult to identify. It is possible that Private Richard Treasure, who "lost" his leg, was struck by grapeshot. Other wounds suggestive of musketry might be from artillery as well.

Despite the losses, the disciplined regulars fought obstinately. "The contest between the British infantry in the front line and the continentals seemed equally balanced, neither retreating."[23] The British infantry was approaching exhaustion by this time. After their approach march, the earlier fighting against the militia, and now, intense fighting against the Continentals, they were reaching a point at which they could not go forward but were unwilling to retreat. The Continentals and Virginians were just as stubborn.

Tarleton realized that musketry would not break the formidable Americans, but he had cavalry ready on both flanks. The 71st Regiment and cavalry reserve were already moving forward on his left behind a screen of Ogilvie's troopers. He "thought the advance of the 71st into line, and a movement of the cavalry in reserve to threaten the enemy's right flank, would put a victorious period to the action. No time was lost in performing this manoeuvre. The 71st were desired to pass the 7th before they gave their fire. . . . The cavalry were ordered to incline to the left, and to form a line, which would embrace the whole of the enemy's right flank."[24] Tarleton's orders caused two separate actions. On the British right, the 17th Light Dragoons broke through Hammond's skirmishers and attacked the reforming militia in action already described.

On the British left, the initial impact fell on McDowell's flanking skirmishers in a now-forgotten encounter that was critical to American success.

Main-line veterans only reported that the British "thought to surround our right flank."[25] The men moving against the American right were British Legion dragoons under Ogilvie and MacArthur's 71st Regiment. The remaining dragoons were a reserve, ready to exploit any breakthrough. They were "ordered to charge the right flank of the Americans." Already posted on the left flank, the dragoons only had to "form a line."[26]

The main American battle line curved forward on the extreme flanks because the skirmishers were outside the British flanks and moving back only when pressed. Initially, the Highlanders did not see the full extent of the American line behind the ridge. They simply followed the dragoons over the crest, then attacked toward McDowell. It may be that one or two companies were detached on line while the remainder of the 71st came forward in column. Their movement opened a gap between the 7th and 71st Regiments. Only a part of the 71st moved against the skirmishers, but Chesney reported that this "detachment of the 71st Regt under Major McArthur broke the Riflemen without difficulty."[27]

The distance covered by the Highlanders provides another timeframe, confirming that the main-line fighting did not last very long. If the 71st covered 300 yards from their reserve position, the distance is about 450 paces. At the quick step they would take 4.5 minutes, but they ran, so the time was shorter. Even so, McDowell's flanking skirmishers caused a crucial delay.[28]

With the Highlanders running forward, the dragoons advanced at a canter, at least until the North Carolinians directed their fire against them. McDowell's skirmishers offered some resistance before Ogilvie "cut his way through their line."[29] Sword wounds reported by North Carolinians occurred here because McDowell was not attacked on the skirmish line, nor is there any evidence his men were involved in the militia rout behind the main line.[30]

Wounds reported by Surry, Wilkes, and Burke County men were similar. All blade-related injuries suffered by North Carolinians fell on these two companies. Burke County's Joseph James was "charged on by a British Dragoon and struck on the head with his sword and left on the ground for dead . . . his ribs were broken loose from his back as he supposes by the horse of the Dragoon."[31] A Surry County man "received a blow on the head with a sword from one of the enemy which felled him to the ground." Others received combinations of wounds indicating both cavalry and infantry fought their way through the North Carolinians.

Wilkes County private William Meade "received severe wounds . . . a rib broken by the point of a bayonet, had his scull badly fractured by a sword

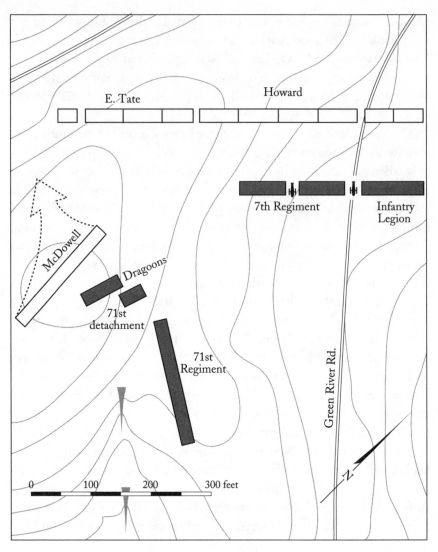

MAP 15. *McDowell's Right-Flank Action*

and had a leg badly wounded by the stroke of a cutlass of a British Lieutenant."[32] Meade was originally on the front line as a skirmisher. He withdrew,
continuing the fight as the militia line retreated. He was hacked over the
head by a saber, which fractured his skull. This wound put him on the
ground, where a Highlander made certain he was out of the fight by bayo-
netting him, breaking a rib. Meade may have been writhing in agony on the
ground when cut by the cutlass, a weapon more likely to be a Highland
broadsword carried by a Scottish officer. Meade is precise in making a distinction between the head wound by a saber and the lieutenant's "cutlass."

The fight was a bitter struggle with no opportunity to surrender. Before they went into battle, the 71st were told to give no quarter, and North Carolina riflemen with saber wounds confirm how vicious a fight it was by also reporting bayonet wounds.[33] In the short, brutal fight on the right flank, the North Carolinians were driven off but not beaten; they simply moved farther to the right rear, into the boggy ground of Maple Swamp, where they continued to fire at long range in relative safety. They covered the right flank, and bought just enough time for an American victory.

The American cavalry were protecting the left-flank militia and driving off the 17th Light Dragoons. McDowell gave Washington enough time to return to Morgan Hill, reform, and cover the right flank. Even then, he was just in time because Ogilvie's troopers were riding, virtually unopposed, toward the American rear. The vicious little flank fight was less than five minutes in duration, the time taken for the main body of the 71st to run about 300 yards and take position opposite Wallace. As the Highlanders swung their line to enfilade Wallace, Ogilvie's dragoons charged toward the American rear.

While the North Carolina flankers bought time, the main line fought the British infantry to a standstill. Although neither commander mentioned the right-flank fight, noise and smoke called attention to the threat. Howard "soon observed, as I had but about 350 men and the british about 800, that their line extended much further than mine particularly on my right, where they were pressing forward to gain my flank." "Their line Was So much longer than ours," "they gained our flanks, which obliged us to change our position."[34]

The dual threat to the American right was part of a double envelopment; Tarleton sent the 17th Light Dragoons against the American left, where they scattered the militia reforming behind the main line. To make matters worse, "the advance of M'Arthur reanimated the British line, which again moved forward; and, outstretching our front, endangered Howard's right."[35]

Howard was "apprehensive that the reserve could not be brought up in time to defend his exposed flank, or if it were, that it would leave his other flank too much ex-posed."[36] Upon "seeing my right flank was exposed to the enemy, I attempted to change the front of Wallace's company." The order required the Virginians "to wheel backward on their left, and face the turning enemy."[37] Something went wrong in the execution of the order. "Whether my orders were not well understood or whether it proceeded from any other cause, in attempting this movement some disorder ensued in this company which rather fell back than faced as I wished them."

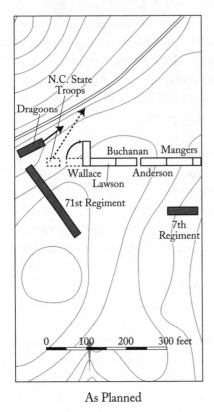 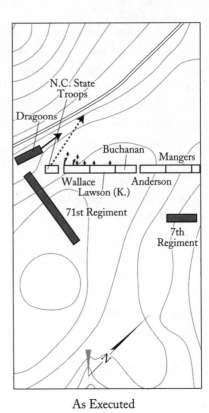

As Planned   As Executed

MAP 16. *The Misunderstood Order*

I can account for the retreat. . . . This company on my right were
Virginians, commanded by Capt. Wallace who some time previous had
formed a connexion with a vile woman of the camp, and the infatuation
was so great that on guard or any other duty he had this woman with him
and seemed miserable when she was absent. He seemed to have lost all
sense of the character of an officer. He was in this state of mind at the
time of the action.[38]

The proper sequence of commands to refuse the right flank is, "To
the right about—Face"; then, "To the right wheel—March"; then "Halt";
and finally, "To the right about—Face." After completing the ninety-
degree wheel and the facing movement, the company would be facing the
Highlanders.[39]

Some thought "the retreats [*sic*] was ordered by mistake by one of Morgan's officers."[40] Initially, the person responsible for the "misunderstood
order" seemed to be Captain Andrew Wallace. He commanded the company on the right, was a Virginian, and died later in battle. Howard de-

scribed the mistake as an affair of honor.[41] When Howard ordered Wallace to refuse the right flank, Wallace, an experienced combat veteran, began the maneuver by facing his men to the rear. Wallace then gave the order to wheel right. Instead of a right wheel, they marched to the rear.

Captain Conway Oldham commanded the second platoon under Wallace. Oldham was probably assigned to Wallace's company at Charlotte in December 1780. At that time, the light infantry companies were built up to strength, and one soldier who served under Oldham reported joining Wallace's company then.[42] In the noise of battle, Oldham and his platoon, having faced to the rear, may not have heard the entire order and heard only "March!" The men may have been guilty of wishful thinking, and so the platoon marched forward instead of wheeling. At that point, Wallace had no choice but to countermand his own order and march rearward because Oldham's platoon was stepping into the first platoon, making a bad situation even worse.[43]

Coincidentally, a volley from the 71st was fired at virtually the same instant Wallace ordered his men to wheel. In Wallace's company, John Brownlee was "wounded in two places, receiving a ball in his cheek, and One in his thigh," and William Warren "was shot in the thigh."[44] Leg wounds show the Scots kept their musket barrels down and took good aim as well.[45] The enfilade volley from the 71st was shattering and created precisely what eighteenth-century tacticians strove for, disorganization and confusion in the opponent's ranks.

To compound the crisis, Lawson's Virginia State Troops on Wallace's left had a command crisis at the same time. The company commander, "Capt John Lawson was shot at the battle of the Cowpens both the balls in and under the Right arm from which wound he died immediately. My Lieutenant Thomas Taylor held command of my Company." One of Lawson's men, Thomas Crowell, was also "wounded by a shot in his leg."[46] In the confusion of replacing commanders, Lieutenant Taylor saw Wallace's Continentals move off. As the Virginia Continentals withdrew, the right flank of the Virginia State Troops was exposed, and Taylor ordered his company to withdraw, following Wallace to the rear.

The 71st fired only a single volley, which came as the Americans were refusing their flank. The volley lashed the Virginians at precisely the right time to create maximum confusion. A single volley is suggested by American casualties, as well as an immediate charge by Highlanders moving to exploit the confusion their fire created. An all-out rush upon their enemy with swords or bayonets was a Highlander tradition.[47]

As the Virginians maneuvered, "some confusion ensued, and first a part, and then the whole of the company commenced a retreat. Officers along the line seeing this, and supposing that orders had been given for a retreat, faced their men about, and moved off." The accidental withdrawal "was very fortunate as we thereby were extricated from the enemy."[48] Seeing the flank companies moving in formation, apparently under orders, other officers followed the Virginians rearward. "The rest of the line expecting that a retreat was ordered, faced about and retreated but in perfect order."[49] The ripple effect reached the Delawares, where "Captain Kirkwood with his company wheeled to the right," and Virginia private John Thomas noted, "they fired before they retreated."[50] Continentals fired by platoon, company, or division. Firing, and then withdrawing, bought time and indicates the companies withdrew *en échelon*, not as an entire battle line.[51]

As the Continentals disengaged and marched off, the movement surprised Morgan and he immediately confronted Howard. Howard recalled that Morgan, who "had mostly been with the militia, quickly rode up to me," "and in a loud tone of voice" "expressed apprehensions of the event; but I soon removed his fears by pointing to the line, and observing that men were not beaten who retreated in that order."[52] Morgan, seeing the line under control, issued Howard a fragmentary order and, "pointing to the rising ground in the rear of the hollow way, informed him that was the ground which he wished him to occupy, and to face about."[53] The "maneuvre being performed with precision, our flank became relieved, and the new position was assumed with promptitude."[54] While the exact pace of withdrawal is unknown, the men moved "rather in an accelerating step, but still in perfect order."[55]

The Americans fell "back Some Distance" "in good order," for "about 80 yards."[56] The actual distance depends on how far a unit moved from the main line. Morgan had been in the rear but rode forward after the retreat began and met Howard about halfway across the swale. Thomas, in Combs's Virginia company, said they retreated about 240 feet. Morgan reported they withdrew about 100 feet, indicating some Continentals were halfway across the swale when he and Howard spoke.

As the Americans came off the line, the British saw the retrograde movement and related it to the force of British arms, because, as Tarleton noted, "upon the advance of the 71st, all the infantry again moved on." Charles Stedman later reported that the "continentals, no longer able to stand the shock, were forced to give way. This was the critical moment of the action, which might have been improved so as to secure to the British troops a complete victory."[57] The British soldiers, seeing the backs of their opponents, started forward to keep the pressure on. Their physical and

TABLE 4. *Seventy-first Regiment Firing Distance on American Right Flank*

Initial Distance	Time	71st Covers	Distance to Wallace	Wallace Covers
50 yds.	70 secs.	116 yds.	31.33 yds.	97.33 yds.
45 yds.	70 secs.	116 yds.	26.33 yds.	97.33 yds.
40 yds.	70 secs.	116 yds.	21.33 yds.	97.33 yds.
35 yds.	70 secs.	116 yds.	16.33 yds.	97.33 yds.
30 yds.	70 secs.	116 yds.	15.33 yds.	97.33 yds.
25 yds.	70 secs.	116 yds.	10.33 yds.	97.33 yds.
20 yds.	70 secs.	116 yds.	5.33 yds.	97.33 yds.

Note: Assumes a 20-second delay in 71st movement.

psychological systems were recharged with energy for the conflict's final resolution. "The British rushed forwards."[58] The charge was probably spontaneous, perhaps by individuals, then units, as Americans withdrew from their front. The first were the Highlanders on the American right, but then the 7th Regiment opposite the Delawares, "thinking that We Were broke set up a great Shout Charged us With their bayonets but in no Order."[59] Officers may have ordered pursuit, but privates, sensing victory, went after the Americans with a vengeance. They "shouted victory, and advanced rapidly and in disorder, within thirty yards of Howard's rear."[60] This charge disordered the British infantry, which maintained good discipline up to this point. The British fell into disarray, not only because of the headlong charge, but because the tree cover was somewhat thicker.

A withdrawal, especially an unplanned one, in the face of an enemy was a most difficult operation, regarded as the height of an officer's ability to command troops. A retreat "done in sight of an active enemy, who pursues with a superior force . . . is, with reason, looked upon as the glory of the profession. It is a manoeuvre the most delicate, and the properest to display the prudence, genius, courage, and address, of an officer who commands . . . a good retreat is esteemed, by experienced officers, the master-piece of a general."[61]

As Morgan marked the halting point for Howard, he saw the withdrawal took the American line out of a tight spot. He went back to Howard's men and "rode along the rear of the line reminding the officers to halt and face as soon as they reached their ground." He also found the British infantry "unable to come up with his corps" because they were "enfeebled by their fatiguing march in the morning . . . and by the subsequent exertions in the action."[62]

TABLE 5. *Distances Covered at Common and Quick Step*

	Common Step		Quick Step		Double-Quick	
	Feet	Yards	Feet	Yards	Feet	Yards
1 sec.	3.30	1.10	5	1.66	5.45	1.81
2 sec.	6.60	2.20	10	3.12	10.90	3.62
3 sec.	9.90	3.30	15	5.00	16.35	5.43
4 sec.	13.20	4.40	20	6.66	21.80	7.24
5 sec.	16.50	5.50	25	8.33	27.25	9.05
10 sec.	33.00	11.00	50	16.66	54.50	18.10
15 sec.	49.50	16.50	75	25.00	91.75	27.15
20 sec.	66.00	22.00	100	33.33	119.00	36.20
30 sec.	99.00	33.00	150	50.00	173.25	54.30
45 sec.	148.50	49.50	225	75.00	265.00	71.45
60 sec.	198.00	66.00	300	100.00	346.50	108.60
75 sec.	247.50	82.50	375	125.00	438.25	135.75
90 sec.	297.00	99.00	450	150.00	519.75	162.90
120 sec.	396.00	132.00	600	200.00	693.00	217.20

The withdrawal was a race to see if the Americans could reach safety before the British caught them. In less than two minutes, at the rate of eighty paces a minute, Wallace's Virginians reached Morgan Hill where they formed a rallying point for the main line. If they went faster, "accelerating" as they marched, it would have taken even less time. The withdrawal had been accomplished. Now the inertia of a rearward movement had to be stopped and the ranks dressed, to what Howard later described as "perfectly formed."[63] Then, they could turn and renew the battle.

While the distances depend on where the Highlanders fired and started their charge, an idea of the timeframe and firing distances can be worked out. The timeframe of American retreat and British pursuit was not long. It can be calculated to some extent by computing time, pace, and distance prescribed from manuals. Table 5 provides comparative time and distance information using these figures. American and British infantry had been trained to march and charge at certain speeds. The normal marching pace was 24 inches, but this actually meant "the space between the two feet of a man in walking, usually reckoned at 2 1/2 feet."[64] Charging men, moving at the "quick step," were calculated at the same distance. When the final order to charge was given at very close range, the men were to "quicken their step" even more. The number of paces per minute changed from 80 to 120 at the quick step and was even faster at the final charge. At the common step's 80 paces per minute, over 66 yards were covered in one minute. With the quick step, soldiers moved 100 yards in one minute.[65] The Americans were under control and must be seen as initially withdrawing at the common step, and then slightly faster. The initial slower pace was, in part, because the men were reloading their muskets.

The American withdrawal was a crisis of time versus space. Howard was moving his men to a new position, where they must stabilize, turn, and fire before the Scots ran up their backs. Since the 71st came from the right and pursued Wallace and Lawson, they were not an immediate threat to Continentals farther left who started later. The 7th Regiment seems to have charged only after the Delawares moved off.

The sequence of firing, facing to the rear, and marching off involved a certain amount of time. The Highlander pursuit was almost instantaneous. If five seconds are allotted as the time for firing, facing about, and commencing the rearward march, each unit departed the main-line position five seconds after its right neighbor.[66] If the Americans withdrew by division, Triplett started retreating only twenty seconds after Wallace. Anything longer than five seconds per company allowed the 71st to catch Wallace before Triplett left his position.

The Virginia Continentals retreated a hundred yards in a minute and a half at the common step. Wallace probably kept his men at this pace so other American units could catch up with him and keep the line intact. In those same ninety seconds, the 71st covered 151 yards at the quick step of 120 paces per minute. If the Scots started five seconds after Wallace, they covered 141 yards in eighty-five seconds. Since the 71st did not overrun the Americans, the distance initially separating them from Wallace when the 71st fired was approximately 40 yards.[67]

Triplett's left-flank Virginians, last to move, retreated only 80 yards to their firing point.[68] They covered that distance in less than seventy-two seconds because they sped up during the withdrawal. The time and distance allowed the Virginia riflemen to fire a volley within ten to twelve seconds of Wallace without endangering Washington's dragoons. Other Continental units reached their turning points between 80 and 100 yards from their original position. The signal to halt and fire may have been Wallace's Continentals reaching 100 yards. When Wallace halted, the other units halted, faced about, and fired in sequence.

The Americans went off the battle line with empty muskets and reloaded as they moved, giving the appearance of "trail arms," reported by

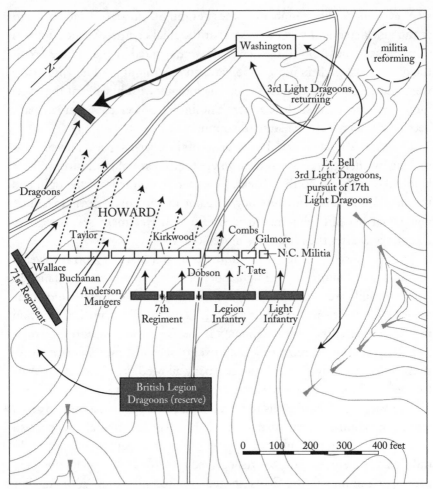

Note: British Legion and light infantry frontage reduced by 25%, 7th Regiment frontage reduced by 20% in allowance for casualties at militia line.

MAP 17. *Main-Line Withdrawal*

Johnson. The men were trained to keep their muskets off the ground while reloading, and the timeframe was more than adequate to reload while moving.[69] As they marched, American officers steadied the line.

The precise retrograde movement was spelled out in manuals and drilled into the men. "When a battalion is obliged to retire, it must march as long as possible, but if pressed by the enemy, and obliged to make use of its fire, the commanding officer will order, *Battalion! Halt! To the Right About,— Face!* and fire by battalion, division, or platoon, as before directed."[70] Howard virtually quoted Von Steuben. "As soon as the word was given to halt and face about the line was perfectly formed in a moment. The enemy pressed upon us in rather disorder, expecting the fate of the day was decided. They were by this time within 30 yards of us . . . my men with uncommon coolness gave them an unexpected and deadly fire." The Continentals "commenced a very destructive fire, which they little expected, and a few rounds" devastated the Scots.[71]

Howard's comment about a few rounds suggests firing was company fire, not a single volley. Since the manual calls for the men to fire "as before directed," the Americans continued their earlier firing pattern, which Stewart confirms by noting "destructive volleys."[72] Multiple smaller volleys are implied by Johnson, who stated "the order flew to right and left . . . promptly obeyed; the enemy were within thirty yards . . . scarcely a man of the Americans raised his gun to his shoulder; when their fire was delivered, they were in an attitude for using the bayonet."[73]

When Howard marked the turning point, he was met by "a messenger from Colonel Washington, who . . . had a fair view of the confusion existing in the British ranks. 'They are coming on like a mob. Give them a fire and I will charge them,' was the message delivered."[74] The British "coming on like a mob" were the 71st. Washington, having just completed a sweep through Ogilvie's British dragoons, had seen disorder in the 71st.

With that little coordination, the Americans halted, faced about, and fired. The 71st was shocked when "Howard faced about, and gave it a close and murderous fire." At a range of "ten or fifteen yards," "the fire was destructive," and "nearly one half their number fell." The damage was magnified by surprise. Some British soldiers simply "threw down their arms and fell upon their faces." The "unexpected fire . . . stopped the British, and threw them into confusion. Exertions to make them advance were useless [and] an unaccountable panic extended itself along the whole line." "The ground was instantly covered with the bodies of the killed and wounded, and a total rout ensued."[75]

Howard saw the firing "occasioned great disorder in their ranks . . . [and] ordered a charge with the bayonet, which order was obeyed with great alacrity." The Americans "taking advantage of the present situation, advanced upon the British troops, and augmented their astonishment."[76] "Howard ordered the drums to beat the charge—the inspiring roll was promptly obeyed." The Americans "charged them home They not expecting any Such thing put them in Such Confusion."[77]

The Continentals delivered their bayonet charge on the 71st at the same time Washington's dragoons attacked the Highlanders's left flank and rear.[78] As the volleys fired, Washington's cavalry reformed on Howard's

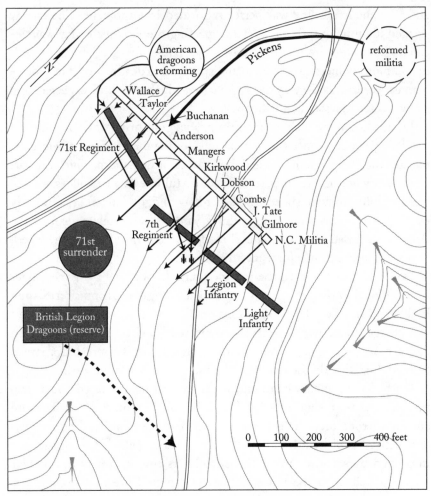

Note: British Legion and light infantry frontage reduced by 25%, 7th Regiment frontage reduced by 20% in allowance for casualties at militia line.

MAP 18. *The American Counterattack*

right and rear; an interval between firing and charge was necessary to keep the dragoons out of the line of fire. Once the infantry fired, the cavalry charged without danger from American bullets.

After the Americans fired, the Scots "who remained were so scattered . . . they could not be united." "They were checked."[79] Delaware's Lieutenant Anderson recalled the Americans "were in amongst them With the Bayonets Which Caused them to give ground and at last to take to the flight But We followed them up so Close that they never Could get in Order again until We Killed and took the Whole of the Infantry Prisoners."[80] The counterattack was relentless, both "officers and men behaved with uncommon and undaunted bravery, but more especially the brave Captain Kirkwood and his company, who that day did wonders, rushing on the enemy without either dread or fear."[81]

The Highlanders "did not fall back immediately, probably expecting that the first line and cavalry would push forward to their support." The 71st fought back with "irregular firing" and American casualties occurred. Jacob Taylor, a private with Wallace, "was shot through the thigh with several buck shot and was stabed in the leg with a bayonet."[82] Marylander John Bantham "received three severe wounds in my right side by a bayonet."[83]

Pickens and his militia chose this moment to reenter the battle. They came forward and a few completed a circuit behind Morgan Hill, but since no Spartanburg veterans mention the 17th Light Dragoon charge as a personal experience, they reformed farther to the right rear and were not disrupted. Now under control, Pickens moved them forward over Morgan Hill, where they "pushed forward to the right flank of the Highlanders."[84] Only after the militia came back on the field did the 71st break. The militia kept the pressure on, firing rifles as the Scots tried to regroup while the collapse spread to other units. After being blasted by musketry, assaulted by bayonet, and sabered from behind, the 71st was in dire straits. The Scots "saw no prospect of support, while their own numbers were diminishing, and the enemy increasing. They began to retire, and at length to run, the first instance of a Highland regiment running *from* the enemy," and their retreat "communicated a panic to others which soon became general."[85]

The surprising American volley was bad enough, but the bayonets made it worse. Then the American dragoons struck the Scots in their left flank and rear. A feeling of isolation, being attacked on all sides, struck the Highlanders because they "were farthest advanced, [and] receiving this unexpected charge, fell back in confusion, and communicated a panic." The British "fled with the utmost precipitation" in "general flight," and a "total rout ensued."[86]

The sudden collapse of the 71st is not unexpected. They had endured a night march and gone without sleep on 15 January. On 16 January, they were awake during the day, moving but more often standing around, while advance troops cleared the route. After four hours' sleep on the night of 16–17 January, they marched twelve miles over wet, churned-up roads. They stood in the beaten zone during the militia-line fight, then ran almost a quarter mile, fired a volley, and made a headlong hundred-yard downhill charge. The Highland charge was a very simple tactic but difficult to control. Against an enemy who "was properly trained and armed to stand up to the Highlanders, the latter had no alternative," and the Scots broke when confronted by disciplined volleys fired by bayonet-armed Americans who then charged.[87]

The militia coming over Morgan Hill as the Highlanders collapsed indicates how rapidly battle sequences occurred. Most returning militiamen were under Thomas and Roebuck, but McDowell's men swarmed up out of Maple Swamp to cut off any further retreat. The militia's decision to get back into the fighting was made easier once they saw Howard's fire stagger the Scottish Highlanders. "The militia who had fled, seeing the fortune of the day changed, returned and joined in the pursuit." They moved forward, following the path of Washington's dragoons and Howard's infantry, who swept through the Highlanders and went down the battlefield.[88]

As the militia rejoined the battle, the Continentals followed Howard toward the cannon. "Their artillery *was not thrown in the rear*, but was advanced a little at the head of the line."[89] The artillery position indicates some British infantry either failed to pursue or retreated more rapidly than the Highlanders.[90] The gunners were left alone—a fatal situation for artillerymen. Howard noted the British cannon a short distance away and "called to Captain Ewing, . . . to take it. Captain Anderson . . . hearing the order . . . kept pace until near the first piece."[91] "When within a few yards, he saw the man at one of them about to put the match to it, levelled at them. At this critical moment he ran up, and, with the assistance of his spontoon, made a spring, and lit immediately upon the gun, and spontooned the man with the match."[92]

Anderson and Ewing, from companies on opposite ends of Howard's battalion, were in close proximity because of the clustering effect caused by the bayonet charge and because Anderson moved his company by the left oblique after hearing Howard's shout. "There were two pieces of cannon as stated, but they were not stationed together, one was on the [British] right and the other on the left, opposed to col. Howard's command, only one of them was taken by capt. Anderson, the other was taken by some other officer."[93] At the other gun, Howard "saw some of my men going to bayonet the man who had the match," "who appeared to make it a point of honour not to surrender his match. The men, provoked by his obstinacy, would have bayonetted him on the spot, had I not interfered, and desired them to spare the life of so brave a man. He then surrendered his match."[94] The gunners fought to the end, "till the whole of the artillery-men attached to them were either killed or wounded."[95]

Tarleton, seeing his artillery in danger, tried "to rally the infantry to

Andrew Pickens; engraving by James Barton Longacre, after a painting by Thomas Sully (National Portrait Gallery, Smithsonian Institution)

protect the guns . . . the effort to collect the infantry was ineffectual: Neither promises nor threats could gain their attention."[96] After Tarleton's infantry failed to rally, he tried to get his reserve dragoons to save the guns. A few dragoons came galloping toward the melee around the cannon but were intercepted by Continentals and Virginians moving beyond the guns. Maryland private Andrew Rock "received a severe cut with a saber from one of the Brittish Cavalry upon his left arm." Delaware private Henry Wells "was struck across the left shoulder by one of Tarleton's Troopers,

With his Sword with Such violence, that the colar of my coat, my vest and my Shirt, were each cut through, and the flesh & skin Sleightly scratched and bruised so much so that there was a considerable not or welt on my Sholder."[97] Some Virginia State Troops were sabered in this encounter, too. James Braden "received a saber wound in the right hand." Isaac Way "was severly wounded on the Side, back, arms, head and in the face by the cutt of the sword of a British draggoon."[98] Virginia injuries show Edmund Tate's men covered Howard's right as he advanced into the swarming fugitives.

After Tate's men went past the Highlanders, Pickens and McDowell's militiamen filled the gaps and surrounded the 71st. Hammond led his men around to the Scots' left and rear and opened fire on them, cutting off their escape into Maple Swamp. Despite the rout and rifle fire, the Highlanders appear to have rallied after running a short distance back up the slope. They "stood . . . after they retreated, and had formed into some compact order." This did not last long. After taking the guns, Howard's Continentals stormed into this last resistance. Howard personally went "towards the right, in among the 71st, who were broken into squads, and as I called to them to surrender, they laid down their arms, and the officers delivered up their swords. Captain Duncanson, of the 71st grenadiers, gave me his sword, and stood by me. Upon getting on my horse, I found him pulling at my saddle, and he nearly unhorsed me. I . . . asked him what he was about. The explanation was that they had orders to give no quarter, and they did not expect any. . . . I admitted his excuse, and put him into the care of a sergeant." Warned by Duncanson, and "exclaiming 'Give them quarters,'" Howard tried to prevent a massacre.[99]

The situation was volatile. Georgian James Jackson, Pickens's brigade major, ran "the utmost risque of my life in attempting to seize the colours of the 71st Regiment . . . being saved by an exertion of Colonel Howards."[100] Pickens claimed "the 71st which was there surrendered to me and I believe every officer of that Regiment delivered his sword into my hands. . . . Major McCarthur surrendered to me some distance from the battle ground and delivered his sword to me. . . . I sent back to Gen'l Morgan, by Major Jackson, Major McCarthur with the sword."[101]

The British right also collapsed. The Carolinians, including Brandon and Hayes, "among which were the Virginia militia, pushed them so close that they gave them no time to form." The militia "advanced at the same time and repulsed their right flank, upon which they retreated off, leaving us entire masters of the field." "We then advanced briskly, and gained the right flank of the enemy, and they being hard pressed in front, by Howard, and falling very fast, could not stand it long. They began to throw down their arms, and surrender themselves prisoners of war." "Two British light infantry companies laid down their arms to the American militia."[102]

Some North Carolina militiamen, after retreating to their horses, mounted and returned to the fray. Being mounted, they had an ideal opportunity to apprehend isolated fugitives. Hugh McNary remembered that "when the Enemy first gave way the Americans pursued them deponent was in front, and got far enough ahead of his company, to stop a British officer, the officer Surrendered. Deponent dismounted and took from the officer his Holsters and pistols, after getting them he discovered that his company had stoped pursuit, and was returned back; he mounted his horse, and returned leaving the British officer, but took the Holsters and pistols which he afterwards sold."[103]

As the Americans gained the upper hand, Thomas Young saw that the "British broke, and throwing down their guns and cartouch boxes, made for the wagon road, and did the prettiest sort of running!" "Tarleton's quarters" had already rung out from the Americans as they rampaged over the field, from the swale south past militia ridge, gathering up individual soldiers and driving on. Their own success left the Americans scattered and disorganized. Seeing the confusion, Tarleton tried to seize an advantage.[104] In the meantime, Washington's cavalry continued the effort to totally destroy the British force.

8 : *Cavalry* Actions

We made a most furious charge.
—*Thomas Young, "Memoir of Major Thomas Young," 1843*

Cavalry activity is part of the larger battle chronology but has been separated for clarity, in part because separate battle increments moved in such rapid sequence. Cowpens mounted action was widely scattered and took place as part of several battle stages.[1] Preliminary clashes were incidental to the main flow of the combat along the Green River Road axis, but dragoon clashes around the main line were crucial to the American victory. The cavalry movements explain American success and British failure at Cowpens. American cavalry met British dragoons head on in the American left rear, on the American right, and during the counterattack. These episodes led to a clash around the cannon and culminated in the celebrated personal combat between Lieutenant Colonel William Washington and three British officers near the battle's end. Finally, the American pursuit of Tarleton was primarily a cavalry operation.

Mounted operations are a major key to understanding Morgan's victory even though they were the least orchestrated by his tactical planning. The delicate timing of American cavalry movements underscores the key role played by Washington's Third Continental Light Dragoons, mounted state troops, and militia volunteers. Cavalry action's sequential order is only partially related to the infantry fighting.

When the American mounted groups mustered on the morning of 17 January, Washington had more than 150 men. These numbers were only half the British cavalry's strength, but judicious selection of when and where to use his dragoons allowed Washington to achieve success every time he engaged. Tarleton's advantage in cavalry strength was negated because he violated economy of force while Washington utilized all his men at the right time and place to achieve mass.[2]

American dragoons formed up on Morgan Hill. From this central location they were free to move and still be in position to block a militia retreat. The probable arrangement of cavalry units was as troops formed up in columns. The front rank of each troop formed a line facing south across the swale. This formation allowed rapid deployment to either flank or the front.

Morgan instructed Washington to respond to a crisis or opportunity. His role as reserve permitted only a general plan, and Morgan gave Washington a great deal of freedom "to be able to charge them should an occasion offer."[3] Washington wanted his dragoons fighting at close quarters with the sabers he personally preferred. To implement his plans, he issued "positive orders to his men not to fire a pistol."[4]

Tarleton posted "a captain, with fifty dragoons" on each flank. The detachments protected his flanks, threatened Morgan's, and left Tarleton a mounted reserve of four troops. Captain David Ogilvie commanded the left-flank British Legion dragoons; Lieutenant Henry Nettles led the 17th Light Dragoons on the right.[5] As infantry fighting began, British dragoons moved along with the infantry while the reserve waited on the Green River Road behind the battle line. American dragoons sat on their horses on Morgan Hill, but British artillery "opened so fiercely upon the centre, that Col. Washington moved his cavalry from the centre towards the right wing."[6] Slightly west of their original position, American dragoons now protected Morgan Hill, positioned behind the American right center.[7]

As the main-line firefight intensified with no result, Tarleton ordered a double envelopment of the American main line. "The cavalry on the right were directed to charge the enemy's left."[8] They burst through Hammond's flanking skirmishers and attacked reforming militia. At the same time, British Legion dragoons moved forward, supported by the 71st, and drove off McDowell's flankers. The 71st assaulted the American right flank while Ogilvie moved against the American rear.[9]

When the 17th hit the militia, Washington's dragoons were concealed behind Morgan Hill. Upon learning "cavalry were cutting down our riflemen on the left," "Washington's cavalry made an attack upon them, . . . defeated them with considerable loss," and "obliged them to retire in confusion."[10] Washington's movement countering the 17th Light Dragoons was in keeping with his role responding to a crisis. His "charge was made on the enemy's cavalry . . . , leaving . . . eighteen of their brave 17th dragoons dead on the spot."[11] The 17th Light Dragoons, outnumbered at least four to one, suffered losses in their advance and had just been staggered by close-range rifle fire. Finally, they "had pretty much scattered."[12] Surprised, opposed by greater numbers, and lacking unit cohesion, they were overwhelmed. The survivors rode for safety, pursued by some white-coated 3rd Light Dragoons. Washington's action stabilized the dangerous situation on the American left. After the cavalry covered the militia, "we retired to the rear," and reformed.[13] This first clash occurred while Ogilvie fought his way through McDowell on the American right. As the dragoons reformed, Continental infantry retreated. Washington was seen by Lieutenant Colonel Howard, who noted his position "on the summit; for I had a full view of him as we retreated from our first position."[14] Howard, withdrawing his infantry, also saw "the enemy's cavalry retreating the way they had advanced, by our left flank, and Washington in pursuit of them."[15] "Lieutenant Bell, having previously taken off with him, in pursuit of the enemy on our left, nearly a fourth part of your regiment."[16] Howard saw Bell's white-coated Americans chasing the British, recognized them as Washington's dragoons, and thought Washington was with them.

Ogilvie's troop, finished with McDowell's skirmishers, passed the American right flank. When Tarleton saw Wallace's Virginians move off the main line, "an order was dispatched to the cavalry to charge."[17] The British reserve moved forward to militia ridge but did not charge. Their lack of enthusiasm left Ogilvie unsupported as the Highlanders pursued the Continentals. McDowell's two- or three-minute delaying action on the American right flank was critical. Without McDowell's stand, Ogilvie's troopers would have reached the American rear while Washington was engaged with the 17th Light Dragoons. Washington, given time, reacted to this crisis and moved "to cover with his dragoons the rear of the broken provincials."[18] Thomas Young described the action, "the command to charge was given. . . . We made a most furious charge, and cutting through the British cavalry, wheeled and charged them in the rear. In this charge, I exchanged my tackey for the finest horse I ever rode."[19]

Once again, Washington's entire force achieved numerical superiority over a single British troop. Captain Ogilvie's troop, "which did not exceed 40 men . . . exposed to a heavy fire, and charged at the same time by the whole of Washington's dragoons, was compelled to retreat in confusion."[20] Washington's men slashed their way through Ogilvie, wheeled, and rode back through the disorganized troopers while the British reserve watched from the crest of militia ridge less than 200 yards away. The ride out and back through Ogilvie took Washington less than two minutes and covered about 200 yards. The charge kept the British Legion's reserve out of the fight, because when they saw Washington ride over Ogilvie they did not attack. Alexander Chesney thought the British Legion "was filled up from the prisoners taken at the battle of Camden . . . on seeing their own Regt opposed to them in the rear [they] would not proceed against it."[21]

Now the withdrawing American infantry was almost ready to stop. As they halted, faced about, and fired, Washington's dragoons passed beyond the American line. As his cavalry cleared the infantry's line of fire, Washington sent a messenger to Howard reporting, "They are coming on like a mob. Give them one fire and I'll charge them."[22] Washington's dragoons wheeled on Morgan Hill as Howard's infantry began firing into the 71st. "The critical moment lost on the one side was eagerly seized on the other. . . . Washington charged with his cavalry." Thomas Young described his third charge of the morning, "the bugle sounded. We, about half formed and making a sort of circuit at full speed, came up in rear of the British line, shouting and charging like madmen. At this moment Col Howard gave the word 'charge bayonets!' "[23]

This third American cavalry charge was timed very closely to the Continental bayonet charge. The short instant while the dragoons "half formed" was crucial as Howard's volleys struck down the British and the cavalry wheeled out of the line of fire. "At the Same time that We Charged [bayonets], Col Washington Charged the horse Which Soon gave Way." "This charge was made at the same moment that I charged the infantry."[24]

Washington's dragoons hacked their way through the 71st and rode on. Washington next encountered "Legeonary Infantry, intermixed with the Battalion of the Brave 71st . . . who, under the Operation of a Universal panic . . . instantly surrendered."[25] Washington's troopers passed through the infantry and headed for Tarleton's reserve cavalry. Their path passed the artillery, "whom you immediately made prisoners, but the Drivers of the Horses who were Galloping off with 2–3 pounders, you could not make Surrender until after Repeated Commands from you, you were obliged to order to be Shot."[26] The artillerymen may have tried to limber up the guns to get them away, but Washington prevented this, leaving the guns for Howard's infantry. Simons overstated the cavalry role as the artillerists fought to the death against Howard's infantry.[27]

After passing the guns, the Americans rode screaming after the British Legion reserve troops. Their calls were so loud that Sergeant Everheart, still a prisoner, "could hear them distinctly cry out as their watchword, 'Buford's play.' "[28] The intimidated British dragoons still refused to advance. "These dragoons never fought well . . . neither at Blackstocks, in this affair, or any other . . . fair conflict."[29] "Tarleton sent directions to his cavalry to form about four hundred yards to the right of the enemy, in order to check them, whilst he endeavoured to rally the infantry to protect the guns. The cavalry did not comply with the order."[30] When his infantry did not rally, Tarleton tried to get his dragoons into the fighting around the guns, but "it was in vain that Tarleton endeavoured to bring his legion

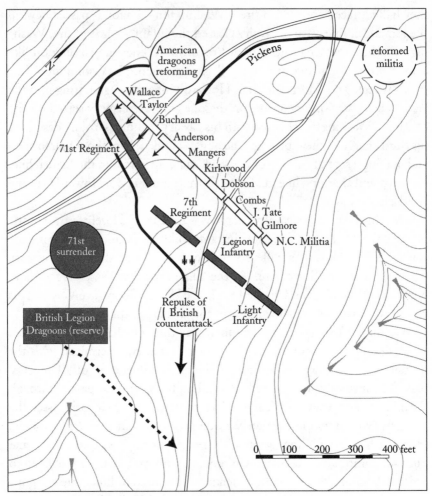

Note: British Legion and light infantry frontage reduced by 25%, 7th Regiment frontage reduced by 20% in allowance for casualties at militia line.

MAP 19. *Cavalry Movements in the Counterattack*

cavalry to charge and check the progress of the enemy: They still stood aloof, and at length fled in a body through the woods, leaving their commander behind."[31]

Tarleton and his officers went to extreme lengths to rally their men. George Hanger responded to charges that Tarleton failed by noting, "exertions were used, and most vigorous ones, to enforce obedience to the orders . . . some officers went so far as to cut down several of their men, in order to stop the flight." "In this last stage of defeat Lieutenant-colonel

Tarleton made another struggle to bring his cavalry to the charge. The weight of such an attack might yet retrieve the day . . . but all attempts to restore order, recollection, or courage, proved fruitless. Above two hundred dragoons forsook their leader, and left the field of battle." The British Legion dragoons rode off to fight another day.[32]

To rally his dragoons, Tarleton went down the road, perhaps 200 yards ahead of the Americans swarming around the artillery. He was well to the rear when he commenced a last attempt to win the battle. "Fourteen officers and forty horsemen were, however, not unmindful of their own reputation, or the situation of their commanding officer. Colonel Washington's cavalry were charged, and driven back into the continental infantry by this handful of brave men."[33]

Some British dragoons advanced and tried to save the cannon, but Washington's troopers came between Tarleton and the American infantry. "The affair in this quarter now became very animated."[34] Too few of Tarleton's men got into action. "Tarleton says that 14 officers & 40 men charged Washington's horse and drove them back into the continental infantry. . . . This is not correct. This affair checked Washington's pursuit, but he did not fall back."[35] Whether Washington fell back or not, British dragoons reached the American infantry. Continentals reported being wounded by British dragoons, and the only encounter between them came when Tarleton charged into the melee around the guns. This encounter was the worse part of the battle for the American cavalry. South Carolina dragoon James Simons claimed "It was at this period of the Action that we sustained the greatest loss of Men."[36] James Busby, "wounded in the Neck by a Sword from a British horseman while he was in a charge under Col Washington," was probably hurt at this time.[37]

At least one British Legion dragoon was a former Delaware Continental. Michael Dougherty "should have escaped unhurt, had not a dragoon of Washington's added a scratch or two to the account already scored on my unfortunate carcass." He was in Captain Nathaniel Vernon's troop and reported as a prisoner in the 23 February 1781 muster roll. Since Dougherty was wounded by one of Washington's men, he must have been involved in this last-ditch attack because Vernon's British Legion troop did not encounter Americans anywhere else.[38]

The British response was too little and too late, and the Americans could not be overcome. "Tarleton prudently commanded a retreat. Being of course in the rear of his men, and looking behind, he perceived that Washington was very near him and full thirty yards ahead of his troops."[39] "It was

Washington's custom, to be in advance of his troops in the day of battle." "In the pursuit he had got a head of his men, perhaps 30 yards. Three of the british officers observing this wheeled about and made a charge at him."[40]

Word of the ensuing "duel" spread quickly after Cowpens.[41] The earliest account dates from February 1781, when Samuel Shaw wrote fellow officers in the North that, "Col. Washington . . . opposed himself three several times personally to Tarleton, who declined any engagement of that sort. He wounded Washington's horse with a pistol, but received a cut on the arm from one of our dragoon officers."[42] Howard made a more circumspect statement: the third officer, "who was believed to be Tarleton, made a thrust at him, which he parried."[43] "In this engagement colonel Washington . . . displaying his personal valour in a combat with colonel Tarleton, in which he cut off two of Tarleton's fingers & would have cut off his head, had it not been for his stock-buckle, which . . . saved the life of the British officer."[44]

A differing British version identifies participants. "A party of the cavalry retreated with such expedition, that they lost their way, and encountered a party of the enemy's cavalry of nearly the same strength. Each party marched up at full trot, threatening mutual destruction. They drew up at the distance of ten paces, and dared each other to advance. Both were timid, and not a man moved." "Cornet Paterson, of the 17th Light Dragoons . . . coming up at that instant, and indignant at seeing such backwardness in British troops, penetrated the ranks, dashed at Colonel Washington, who commanded, and, in the act of making a stroke at him, was cut down by the Colonel's orderly serjeant."[45]

Once Patterson was disabled, Washington, with a broken sword, was still in danger because "the officer on the left . . . was preparing to make a stroke at him when a boy, a waiter, who had not strength to wield his sword, drew his pistol and shot and wounded this officer, which disabled him."[46] Washington escaped his first two opponents thanks to his staff. The third officer "retreated 10 or 12 steps and wheeled about and fired a pistol which wounded Washington's horse." "The noble animal that bore Washington was destined to receive the ball that had . . . been aimed at his rider."[47] Militia dragoon William Shope rescued Washington "by giving the colonel his horse" after Washington's horse was killed on the battlefield.[48] Howard's comment that the British officer was "believed to be Tarleton" sums up the "duel."

Tarleton's dragoons were some distance from the artillery when the fight around the guns began. The open field gave them room to maneuver, but clear sight lines allowed militia rifles to be brought into play. "Pickens' marksmen had now opened upon them, and they literally broke away with a *'sauve qui peu.'* "[49] The men firing on the British dragoons were militia who fled to their horses, remounted, and resumed the fight. With the mobility to operate against cavalry and the weaponry to engage at long range, "we then advanced briskly, and gained the right flank of the enemy, and they being hard pressed in front, . . . could not stand it long. They began to throw down their arms, and surrender themselves prisoners of war."[50]

James Collins, the Fair Forest private, was one militiaman who re-mounted and returned to the fight. "I fired my little rifle five times."[51] If Collins fired two shots on the militia line with Brandon, and one against the 17th Dragoons, he fired only twice more at British soldiers reforming after Howard's bayonet charge. Collins was not alone in firing at the British during this phase; a fairly heavy long-range fire was directed against Tar-leton's legion. It was too much for the British, and "two hundred and fifty horse which had not been engaged, fled through the woods with the utmost precipitation, bearing down such officers as opposed their flight."[52]

About this time, Kinlock's headquarters troop was overrun. As Lieuten-ant Simons later told William Washington, "they could no longer Keep Everhart a Prisoner [and] Shot him with a Pistol, in the head, over one of his eyes . . . being then intermixed with the enemy, Everhart pointed out to me the man who shot him, . . . who by my order, was instantly Shot, and his horse as well as I can recollect, was given to Everhart, whom I ordered in the rear to the Surgeons."[53]

Alexander Chesney did not mince words. Tarleton's "force disperced in all directions the guns and many prisoners fell into the hands of the Ameri-cans." Washington, now remounted on Shope's horse, set off in pursuit. "The retiring enemy were pressed," as the Americans swarmed after the British.[54] Some men did not wait for the order to chase after the British. Howard mentioned other pursuers: "We had a German a volunteer . . . He with some five or six militia men well mounted had pushed down the road and got a head of Tarletons horse and had taken the baggage which he was obliged to leave."[55]

The incident involving Tarleton's baggage train has been presented in many ways, often implying Tarleton scattered Tories plundering his bag-gage. William Johnson first reported that "a party of about fifty loyalists . . . These men . . . finding the baggage abandoned, very laudably entered upon the work of saving what they could . . . by appropriating it to their own use. . . . [T]he wrath of the mortified dragoons was let loose upon all who were not fortunate enough to make good their retreat."[56] When the frus-trated British dragoons came on their baggage train, they attacked. After all, it was virtually impossible to tell Tory from Whig, since both were wearing civilian clothing.

The baggage guard was "a party of men under Ensign Fraser, of the 71st." Fraser and the wagons "had not reached the Cowpens at the time of the action: Early intelligence of the defeat being conveyed . . . by some friendly Americans, he immediately destroyed whatever part of the baggage could not be carried off, and mounting his men on the waggon and spare horses, retreated to the main army unmolested." In the little time it took to cut the wagon horses loose, and flee, it was difficult to destroy much of anything so that the victorious Americans could not use these spoils of war. Morgan described the British baggage as "immense," and thirty-five wagons that Fraser did not destroy were captured. Many Americans "had not for months seen candles, coffee, tea, sugar, pepper or vinegar" until they captured Tarleton's baggage.[57]

When Tarleton reached his baggage, Americans with the German volunteer Glaubeck were there. Glaubeck's party included Major Benjamin Jolly and Thomas Young, who had "resolved upon an excursion to capture some of the baggage. We went about twelve miles, and captured two British soldiers, two negroes, and two horses laden with portmanteaus. One of the portmanteaus belonged to a paymaster in the British service, and contained gold. Jolly insisted upon my returning with the prize to camp."[58] The precise accounting of two soldiers, two servants, and two horses indicates Jolly's party encountered British batmen. These officer servants were moving in advance of the slow-moving baggage wagons. When Glaubeck, Jolly, and Young reached the wagons, Fraser was gone, since no Americans engaged the baggage guard. Abandoned wagons were spread out along the road, following the line of march. The Americans plundered some wagons, sent Young rearward, and then "dashed onward, and soon captured an armorer's wagon."[59]

Tarleton reported that he encountered the "Americans, who had seized upon the baggage of the British troops on the road from the late encampment, [where they] were dispersed."[60] It is possible some baggage was destroyed by Tarleton after he "retook the baggage of the corps, cut the detachment who had it in possession to pieces, destroyed the greater part . . . [and] retired with the rest to Hamilton's Ford."[61] Tarleton's party was not further molested after the baggage incident.

No American reported being set upon by Tarleton after the battle except Thomas Young, returning to Cowpens with his prisoners. When he saw British dragoons, he wheeled, put spurs to my horse, and made down the road . . . three or four dashed through the woods and intercepted me. . . . My pistol was empty, so I drew my sword and made battle. I never fought so hard in my life. . . . In a few minutes one finger on my left hand was split open; then I received a cut on my sword arm by a parry which disabled it. In the next instant a cut from a sabre across my forehead . . . the skin slipped down over my eyes, and the blood blinded me so that I could see nothing. Then came a thrust in the right shoulder blade, then a cut upon the left shoulder, and a last cut . . . on the back of my head—and I fell upon my horse's neck.[62]

Young's capture places American Whigs at the baggage train. What happened to Young clearly reflects "the wrath of the mortified dragoons," but "they took me down, bound up my wounds, and placed me again on my horse a prisoner of war . . . Col. Tarlton sent for me . . . I begged him to parole me, but he said, 'if he did, I should go right off and turn to fighting again.'"[63]

As Tarleton retreated, he learned "that the main army had not advanced beyond Turkey creek: He therefore directed his course to the south east, in order to reach Hamilton's ford, near the mouth of Bullock creek, whence he might communicate with Earl Cornwallis."[64] While Tarleton rode south, more American pursuit was organized. Pickens "sent Col. Washington with his cavalry in pursuit of Tarleton, I ordered Jackson, who was brave and active, to return as quickly as possible with as many of the mounted militia as he could get."[65] "After the battle was over the company . . . mounted and went in pursuit of Tarleton under the command of Collonel Washington—They pursued on towards Cornwallis camp and then return to the Cowpens." "We pursued them on to where Corn Wallies Army was laying."[66]

Militia pursuing Tarleton included men from four different battalions who mounted, perhaps after withdrawing from the militia line. They joined the Continental dragoons and "pursued with Col. Washington 22 miles and made prisoners of several in Tarleton's rear but could not bring him to an action. We did not get back to the battle ground till the next morning."[67]

As soon as some order was restored, Kirkwood's infantrymen were sent after the British, an independent role they performed often in 1781. Despite 25 percent casualties in the battle, the Delawares went about twelve miles to serve as a reserve for the mounted troops. Kirkwood's men marched about three hours and halted around noon. Kirkwood's party, "among which were the Virginia militia," halted to rest while waiting to see if Washington needed help farther down the road. They also secured the captured wagons and additional prisoners. After waiting, the Delawares "returned back to the field of Battle . . . late in the afternoon." It was about to rain, although none of the Delawares, worn out by fighting and marching twenty-four miles since the battle, mentioned it. Along with Sergeant Major William Seymour, they "lay amongst the Dead & Wounded Very Well pleased With Our days Work." They had been "instrumental in taking a great number of prisoners."[68]

A day or two after the formal pursuit ended on 18 January, a party of militia snapped up some of Tarleton's baggage train that had escaped. The Newberry militiamen had "left their homes to unite with Morgan before the battle of the Cowpens. . . . [The] battle was fought and won; and the news reached them on the way. . . . They fell upon a part of Tarleton's baggage train at Love's Ford, . . . and captured it; horses, negroes, wagons and all other property, they managed to get safely into the block house on Pacolet."[69] The victims in this case must have been the heavy baggage and people Tarleton did not want during the pursuit of Morgan. They were working their way up the Broad River's east bank, moving toward Cornwallis's camp slightly farther north when they were taken.

When Kirkwood and Washington returned to Cowpens, Morgan was already gone. Before the Flying Army left, Morgan did not neglect intelligence gathering and local conditions. Men were "detached by order of Genl. Morgan to look into Cornwallis' Camp on the Broad River, to report his movements and communicate with Genl. Pickens or himself daily until further orders. This service was performed regularly until the british took up Camp at Ramsour's Mill."[70] Some units were directed to suppress the Tories.

The British used several routes to escape. Some took the Green River Road to the Pacolet crossings they used on 16 January. Others, including Tarleton, retraced the approach march as far as Adam Goudelock's farm near Burr's Mill on Thicketty Creek. With Tories such as Chesney no longer present, Tarleton impressed a guide. "Tarleton and his cavalry fled before Washington for sixteen miles, to Goudelock's, where they pressed Mr. Goudelock to pilot them across the Pacolette at Scull Shoals, which was the nighest route to Hamilton's ford, on Broad River."[71] Tarleton seized the civilian because his escape route was not well known and would not appear on maps even in the early nineteenth century.

Mrs. Goudelock's fear "for the safety of her husband, saved . . . Tarleton and the remnant of his legion from captivity."[72] Tarleton left a clear trail as he headed for Cornwallis, at least as far as Goudelock's. Military travel over the last three days apparently so obscured the road Tarleton took after Thicketty Creek, that Mrs. Goudelock was able to mislead Washington and sent him down the familiar road toward Grindal Shoals. Washington got back to the Cowpens later, driving "before him near one hundred straggling prisoners collected on his route."[73] Others, including Triplett's Virginians, continued through the night, scouring the region for British fugitives until "the next day when we returned from the pursuit. We then followed after Morgan who had gone on with the prisoners."[74]

Tarleton, following Goudelock's directions, made his way via Skull Shoal, retreating "with the remains of this small but brave and faithful band of adherents, to Hamilton's Ford (Pinckneyville), upon Broad River," "near the mouth of Bullock creek."[75] Thomas Young reported what happened when Tarleton "got to Hamilton Ford about dark. Just before we came to the river, a British dragoon came up at full speed, and told Col. Tarlton that Washington was close behind in pursuit. It was now very dark, and the river was said to be swimming. The British were not willing to take water. Col. Tarlton flew into a terrible passion, and drawing his sword, swore he would cut down the first man who hesitated. They knew him too well to hesitate longer."[76]

The alarmed dragoon was mistaken since Washington was already back at Cowpens. Militia units *were* covering the roads, sweeping up stragglers. Captain Samuel Otterson and his company pursued "until night at which period all of his men had falled off by their horses giving out except ten men when we overtook the enemy Kill one Took twenty twenty [*sic*] two white Prisoners & twenty seven negroes sixty head of horses 14 sords & 14 braces of pistols amongst the white prisoners was an officer with the rank of Captain." Otterson had an advantage since his home was located near Hamilton's Ford and he knew the countryside.[77]

Otterson fell upon British dragoons who salvaged some of Tarleton's more portable baggage. They included a fourteen-man mounted detachment and a sergeant's guard of eight infantrymen based upon the captured weaponry. They evaded Washington's pursuit and were working their way back to Cornwallis. A dragoon who escaped Otterson reported Washington's approach to Tarleton. In the darkness and confusion, Young made his escape from Tarleton's party.

A young Virginian by the name of Deshaser . . . and myself, managed to get into the woods. In truth a British soldier had agreed to let us escape, and to desert if we would assist him in securing the plunder he had taken. We slipped away one at a time up the river, Deshaser first, then myself. I waited what *I* thought a very long time . . . and I gave a low whistle—Deshaser answered me, and we met. It was now very dark and raining . . . we pressed on and soon arrived at old Captain Grant's where I was glad to stop.[78]

Tarleton crossed the Broad, but remained at the ford overnight, collecting men who escaped and reached the river. By 18 January, "above two hundred cavalry who had fled to the main army, and several other fugitives, joined Lieutenant-colonel Tarleton . . . at Hamilton's ford."[79] "Few of the legion cavalry were missing: One division of them arrived the same evening in the neighbourhood of the British encampment, with the news of their defeat, and another under Tarleton, who in his way had been joined by some stragglers, appeared the next morning."[80] Not all the British continued moving toward Cornwallis. Some tried to hide and wait out the cold, rain, and pursuit. "We approached a barn. It had a light in it, and I heard a cough. We halted and reconnoitred, and finding it occupied by some British soldiers, we pressed on."[81]

Except for isolated incidents over the next few days, the pursuit ended by midnight. A new phase in the southern campaign was beginning as Cornwallis sought to recover the Cowpens prisoners, and Morgan moved to evade him. The pursuit ended in the "Race to the Dan" as Morgan, and then Greene, kept away from Cornwallis and his army during a series of forced marches across North Carolina and into Virginia.

9 : The Aftermath

You have done well, for you are successful.
—*Daniel Morgan to John Eager Howard,*
about 8:45 A.M., 17 January 1781

As fighting ended, four new activities began: plundering, treatment of the wounded, pursuit, and prisoner collection. Kirkwood's infantry, mounted militia, and Washington's dragoons pursued the British, while militia and Continentals secured prisoners and collected weapons, the trophies of victory. Medical personnel began trying to cope with the numerous wounded of both sides.[1]

Militiamen looting the rows of British knapsacks and accoutrements found welcome booty. "Our poor fellows, who were almost naked before, have now several changes of clothes . . . as the British officers . . . carried every thing with them."[2] The dead and wounded also attracted men seeking plunder. General Andrew Pickens's servant, Dick Pickens, "came across a young British officer elegantly dressed, with fine fair top boots on, and badly wounded . . . Dick brought the boots to Pickens."[3] Major James Jackson encountered an American "sergeant . . . dealing the wine out to all in his way. A wounded militia man at some distance requested me for a drop to revive him, which the sergeant refused on my application. I then ordered the men with me to drive him off and take possession of the cask."[4]

Traditional military trophies were captured, including the colors of the 7th regiment, two field pieces, 800 muskets, and a portable forge.[5] The cannon and forge went north with the first militiamen to leave the battlefield.[6] Captured ammunition was distributed to replace militia expenditures during the battle. "After receiving some small share of the plunder, and taking care to get as much powder as we could, we were disbanded."[7]

Another trophy was an officer's badge of office, his sword. Surrendering his sword meant an officer was no longer in command; to be given an enemy's sword symbolized honor gained because capturing an officer meant great risk. "Howard, holding seven swords of British officers who had personally surrendered to him, was complimented by General Morgan: 'You have done well, for you are successful; had you failed, I would have shot you.' Col. Howard replied: 'Had I failed, there would have been no need of shooting me.'"[8] South Carolina's Major James Dugan took a British officer's sword, too. The course of the war had changed, but there was much to be resolved before it finally ended. The next night, Robert and James Dugan, along with two neighbors, were killed. Tories "put them to death by the most savage and deliberate use of their swords . . . literally hewed in pieces."[9]

Cowpens was a short battle and American casualties were relatively light; still, more than a hundred American wounded exceeded the capabilities of the few surgeons on the scene, one of whom, John Whelchel, was critically wounded himself. British casualties placed a further strain on the doctors, surgeons, and surgeon's mates, even though British medical personnel were present, and Tarleton quickly sent "Doctor Stewart and the Surgeon's Mate of the Seventh Regt."[10]

Medical personnel dealing with the carnage varied greatly in their training and knowledge of medical practices. Some with little training probably did seem to be "Quacks and Empiricks . . . whose education and knowledge of the animal oeconomy should render them incapable of low artifice, or ignorance of nature's admirable effort for her own relieve."[11] One manual indicated a sense of modern-day triage in that certain wounds, such as those to the heart and major arteries, were seen as "inevitable death."[12] Those who could be treated were; the other wounded were made as comfortable as possible.

Manuals and medical ideals bore slight resemblance to the treatment soldiers received after battle. Yet, it was state of the art, even if some practitioners were not particularly adept. The large number of wounded, coupled with the small number of medical personnel, compounded the difficulties. This situation was well known to military doctors who faced the same crises on every battlefield where many wounds, "themselves not mortal, may be rendered so by neglect or erroneous treatment; this frequently happens to soldiers and seamen in the day of battle, when the multiplicity of cases prevents the Surgeons from paying a proper attention to all."[13]

Initial treatment was administered on the field. Those who could travel went with the army. William Meade completed the march "to Gilbert Town in North Carolina . . . and remained under the care of the Surgeon . . . until the month of September."[14] A few days after the battle, wounded men unable to leave the field were either dead or stabilized enough to be moved for long-term treatment. Many were "taken to the house of Doctr Robert Nelson . . . within five miles of the battle ground." Lawrence Everheart was treated by Dr. Richard Pindell, who "dressed my wounds."[15] William Warren of Wallace's Virginia Continentals was "taken to the house of Kit Hicks by Mrs Hicks and daughter where he was nursed."[16] Others were "taken to Mr Sanderer's," a local resident, and treated.[17] Pindell recalled, "I was left on the field to take care of the Wounded, without any Aid or force Except a Lt Hanson . . . & our two waiters. . . . I obtained from the British Surgeons a Rect for 87 prisoners, even after a Guard of at least 24 Soldiers and about an Equal number of Waggoners had arrived with waggons to carry them to Charleston."[18]

Those who survived their wounds and the first days of medical treatment had a fair chance of surviving. Some wounded, motivated by patriotism or unwilling to leave their comrades, tried to carry on.[19] Others were mutilated for life. Benjamin Trusloe "received a shot over the left eye which caused him to lose the sight." Joseph Croes "lost two of his fingers." Some wounds healed but left a victim like James Busby with scars which had an "electric effect . . . when . . . [he] exhibit[ed] the mark of the wound which had nearly severed his head from his body."[20]

Others were judged unable to continue in military service. Virginian John Brownlee was "wounded in two places, receiving a ball in his cheek, and One in his thigh. Shortly after that, his wounds being uncured and rendering him unfit for Service, he was discharged, in or near Salisbury, NC." Delaware ensign William Bivins, wounded in his first battle "by a ball in the right hip, . . . continued in the hospital near the Cowpens under the care of the Surgeons . . . till his term of service expired."[21]

Some hardy men survived their wounds *and* the medical care, only to die after a lifetime of suffering from Cowpens injuries that never healed. Jacob Taylor reported "the wound in his leg by the bayonet has ever since that time been running lose and at times very putrified." William McCoy "received two wounds and one ball is at this time in my thigh." Nathaniel Dickison was "wounded in his left groin by a musket ball . . . being so badly wounded that to this day he is a cripple." John Simmons, "wounded by a musket ball passing between the tendon & bone of the left leg, . . . [was] totally disabled from Service . . . [and] finally died of Said wound in Talbot County[, Georgia,] in the year 1837."[22]

Cowpens casualties do not fit generalized eighteenth-century wound patterns because the battle lacked large numbers of cavalry and artillery. European cavalry wounds were usually on the right side, typically the wrist and forearm, and this was true of 71 percent of the wounded horsemen. John Gunnell, Third Continental Light Dragoons, was wounded "by a Saber in the Sword Arm & hand & also in the head."[23]

European infantry were more frequently wounded on the left side, but 70 percent of the American infantry wounded at Cowpens were struck on the right.[24] At Cowpens, infantry did not close with bayonets except during the counterattack, and many bayonet wounds were on the right side. A number of saber wounds were reported by militia infantrymen, ridden down and hacked by British cavalry.

A comparison of infantry and cavalry wounds indicates that mounted men were more likely to be injured by blows to the head or upper torso than the lower limbs. This reflects the nature of mounted combat and a general reluctance of cavalrymen to attack unbroken infantry who were bearing bayonets. The solid wall of men armed with bayonets on muskets kept cavalry back, and neither the dragoon nor his horse wanted to be stabbed with the bayonet. Few infantrymen were likely to be hit in the head by a dragoon's saber, and then only if they were broken and retreating without order.

At Cowpens, 25 percent of the infantry wounds were to the head and only two proved mortal. Of the 33.7 percent lower-limb wounds, three were mortal. Of the 43.7 percent with torso and upper-limb wounds, two were fatal. Eighteen fatal, otherwise unidentified, wounds can be distributed according to known wound percentages. An adjusted distribution allows an inferential total of seven head, ten torso, and nine lower-limb fatalities.

Many officers were injured. The largest number of officer casualties occurred among the South Carolina militia, where men "led from the front," by example. This seems all the more true because most South Carolina officer casualties occurred when the militia were routed by the 17th Light Dragoons. Officers stood fast, providing rallying points while fighting off British dragoons.

There was also a low, but steady incidence of smallpox among the soldiers. Smallpox was a virulent, debilitating, and disfiguring disease. A person with smallpox passed on the infection from the first rash until the last scabs drop off, a period of about forty days. Smallpox did not spread rapidly and depended on contact.[25] By taking the first signs of smallpox and subtracting a twelve-day incubation period, it is possible to identify men infected while with Morgan. Four men had smallpox immediately before Cowpens. At least five men apparently contracted the disease with the Flying Army, and two others are related cases.

James Neill, Robert Long, and John Verner all came down with smallpox within two weeks of the battle. James Neill returned home to Rowan County, North Carolina, the night of 1 February 1781, "very sick with the small pox." Robert Long remained with Morgan until the Catawba crossing on 31 January, when he "took the Small Pox." John Verner "marched back to Abbeville and was taken down with the Small Pox." Verner and Long were in Hayes's Little River Regiment.[26]

Joseph Brown, a private in Lindsey's Company of the Little River Regiment, was one of Hayes's men "taken with the small pox and confined about three weeks. . . . As soon as he was able to march again . . . he went and joined Morgan" before the battle. After three weeks' confinement, he was still contagious.[27] Given the way smallpox spreads, it is likely that Hayes's men were infected by Joseph Brown or one of his immediate associates. The cases of James Neill and James Dawson are harder to isolate. Dawson could have associated with Long and Verner, since Hayes and the 3rd Light Dragoons made the Hammond's Store raid together. Joseph McJunkin contracted smallpox after the fight at Fletcher's Mill on 2 March 1781. James McCall died of smallpox in May 1781.[28] James Dawson, a light dragoon, missed the battle at Guilford Courthouse on 15 March "by having the small pox." Since scabs are still present up to forty-one days after the first onset of the disease, he almost certainly contracted it while with Morgan's forces.[29]

Hayes's Little River Battalion is an ideal focal point for smallpox. They were refugees and provided a vehicle for spreading it. Removed from their relatively isolated farms in the Ninety Six District, they came together with whatever they had, including smallpox. Whoever the carrier, a steady incidence of smallpox was associated with the South Carolina militia. Unlike Continentals who were immunized, even early in the war, militia were usually unprotected.

While Morgan marched north with the prisoners, local militia looked after the dead and wounded. "Soon after the battle was over Genl. Morgan moved off with the prisoners leaving this applicant with his company to bury the dead of both parties." For the men at the battlefield, "the sight was truly melancholy. The dead on the side of the British, exceeded the number killed at the battle of King's Mountain, being if I recollect aright, three hundred, or upwards."[30]

Immediately after the battle, the militia had other tasks. Assigned to protect the wounded and local Whigs, they repressed Tories and searched out British stragglers. Some went north and "were then ordered away to disperse some tories who were assembling near Inoree [sic] River." Militiamen remembered particularly unsettled conditions after Morgan left South Carolina. "Morgan & his army having retreated from our State it was now almost Fire & Faggot Between Whig & Tory, who were contending for the ascendancy it continued so till the 15th or 20th May. I was almost constantly out."[31]

Many British soldiers were captured. Prisoners were taken as individuals

TABLE 6. *British Casualties*

Rank	Morgan	Seymour	N.C. State Records	Stevens
Prisoners not wounded				
Major	1	1		
Captain	13	5		
Lieutenant	14	13		
Ensign	9	4		
Adjutant		1		
Cornet		1		
Officer total	37	25	29	
NCOs and privates	550	502	502	
Prisoners wounded				
Officers		3	29	
NCOs and privates	200	180	150	200–300
Total prisoners				
Officers	29	37	28	
NCOs and privates	500	730	652	502
Killed				
Officers	10	10	10	10–12
NCOs and privates	100+	190	200	100
Total British losses				
Officers	39	37	38	39
Privates	800	920	852	800+
Total	839	957	890	839+

Sources: Daniel Morgan to Nathanael Greene, 19 Jan. 1781, Showman, *Greene Papers,* 7:152–55; Seymour, *Journal of the Southern Expedition,* 14; *North Carolina State Records,* 15:419; Edward Stevens to Thomas Jefferson, 24 Jan. 1781, Boyd, *Jefferson Papers,* 4:440–41.

and in large groups. Manuel McConnell, a militia dragoon, "had the honor & pleasure of delivering five British prisoners to the prisoners guard." Adam Rainboult, a North Carolinian on Triplett's left, claimed "the party to whom he belonged took Sixty three prisoners."[32] Organizing prisoners and starting them off in manageable groups was a priority. Prisoners were assembled and divided into "small Squares or Companies" of perhaps "a hundred."[33] Counts were made, both for control purposes and for publicizing the victory.

British prisoner figures are complicated because overlapping categories—officers, privates, Tories, wounded, and prisoner—were used by veterans in reckoning British losses.[34] Morgan claimed "the enemy's loss was 10 commissioned officers and over 100 rank and file killed and 200 wounded, 29 commissioned officers and about 500 privates prisoners." A more precise account claimed "in the action were killed of the enemy one hundred and ninety men, wounded one hundred and eighty, and taken prisoners one Major, thirteen Captains, fourteen Lieutenants, and nine Ensigns, and five hundred and fifty private men."[35]

If the killed, wounded, and prisoners are added together, the 800 captured muskets approximates Morgan's total British casualties.[36] On 23 January, Morgan reported 600 prisoners, reflecting additional men brought in after the army left Cowpens.[37] At least 87 wounded British soldiers were left at Cowpens because they could not be moved.[38] The total number of wounded was undoubtedly higher because some soldiers, especially dragoons, escaped and were not counted by the Americans.

Morgan took immediate steps to keep the prisoners. As soon as it was practical, British prisoners were marched north, ahead of the main force.[39] Prisoners would slow Morgan's march and deplete supplies. More important, Cornwallis was positioned to cut off Morgan's retreat and would move to recapture them. The British recognized they lost a sizable force at Kings Mountain, and should have tried to get them back. American prisoners observed that Lord Cornwallis, while "he listened to Tarleton's narrative, was leaning on his sword; he pressed it so hard in his fury, that it broke, and he swore he would recover the prisoners at all hazards."[40] As it turned out, Cornwallis did move, but not fast enough, in part because Morgan moved so rapidly.

The night of 17 January, Americans and prisoners camped at Island Ford. The Broad River bivouac was tactically sound and necessary. Morgan's men needed rest and the river would interrupt a sudden British move. The halt gave the wounded a chance to recover before moving again. Some wounded could hardly go much farther. One man, "carried in a Horse Bier three days . . . was taken to Gen Charles McDowells at the Quaker Meadows on the Catawba River and there with one Michael Cane an American and Sixteen wounded British soldiers were placed under a surgeon by the name of Rudolph."[41] Waiting overnight allowed pursuit units to rejoin the Flying Army, as North Carolina private Josiah Martin reported, "We returned from the pursuit. We then followed after Morgan who had gone on with the prisoners. After overtaking them Morgan & regulars left us, & we with Col Washington conducted the prisoners to Burk town."[42]

The next day, Pickens headed toward Gilbert Town. After Gilbert Town, Pickens and Washington marched their men and the prisoners to the Catawba's Island Ford and Shallow Ford on the Yadkin.[43] The prisoners were guarded by Triplett's Battalion. Morgan sent the Virginians home but used them as guards even though their enlistments had expired.[44] North Carolina militia from Surry, Wilkes, and Rowan Counties, having to march north anyway, guarded prisoners, too. As one private reported, the militia "marched as a guard over the Brittish Prisoners untill he reached Wilks County North Carolina." Rowan County militiamen only guarded the "prisoners till they reached the Cataba where he with others was left under command of Col Davidson."[45] Already near home, Rowan men were reassigned to block the Catawba River fords by Morgan and Davidson.

Once they reached Virginia, the prisoners were turned over to local militia who marched them on to the Winchester prison camps. The British would spend the war here or farther north in Maryland.[46] Some Prince of Wales American Regiment light infantry men ultimately mustered as prisoners at Lancaster, Pennsylvania, on 24 June 1782.[47]

Some British soldiers quickly escaped and rejoined Cornwallis. They went on north to battles at Guilford Courthouse and Yorktown. Other prisoners eventually returned to British colors. Maneuvering before Yorktown, the First Battalion, 71st Regiment, encountered "a deserter and a little drummer boy [who] came from the enemy . . . this boy belonged to the 71st regiment: he had been taken prisoner at the Cow-pens, enlisted with the enemy, and now, making his escape, was received by the piquet which his father commanded."[48]

Morgan placed the Flying Army between his prisoners and British pursuit after moving north of the Broad River. The Flying Army struck east and crossed the Catawba at Beattie's Ford, then moved up the east bank to Sherrill's Ford, where other units joined them.[49] As the Flying Army moved north, it began to dissolve. Western North Carolina militiamen "guarded prisoners into Burk County, [where] applicant was then honorably but verbally discharged."[50] At the Catawba River, South Carolina State Troops and many militiamen were relieved and sent back to South Carolina.[51]

The march was not an easy one for soldiers or prisoners. Sergeant Major Seymour reported "the troops suffered greatly in their return to Salisbury N. Carolina with the prisoners from the high waters cold rains and want of provisions at Broad River, Catawba there was several lives lost from high waters." "[W]e had very difficult marching, being very mountainous, the inhabitants, who were chiefly Virginians, living very poor, except one settlement on the other side the Catabo, being excellent good land inhabited by the Dutch."[52]

Nathanael Greene rode immediately to join Morgan and plan how to best deal with the British. Greene and Morgan did not move until forced to; they prepared to dispute a Catawba River crossing while the prisoners marched north. Greene probably conceived the "Race to the Dan" at Sherrills Ford when he learned Cornwallis destroyed his baggage at Ramseur's Mill. The Flying Army remained with Morgan and Greene, between the prisoners and Cornwallis. By traveling on parallel routes, each group would be able to obtain provisions through foraging and supplies brought in by militia. Both routes would then be of little use to the British because the Americans took all readily available food. They also removed or disabled boats at river crossings.

Cornwallis finally moved after Morgan's men. Left behind to cover the fords and delay the British, North Carolina general William Lee Davidson and a few men were killed as the British poured across Cowan's Ford.[53] Once the British crossed the Catawba, the Americans had to get past another river, the Yadkin beyond Salisbury.

After the British crossed Cowan's Ford, five miles downstream, Greene and Morgan moved rapidly away from Sherrill's Ford. Greene ordered Rowan County militia to assemble, but they failed to turn out.[54] Greene ordered supplies halted at Guilford Courthouse, except some being sent on with Captain John Smith and needed by the withdrawing Americans who crossed the Yadkin at Trading Ford.[55] High water that slowed the British on the Catawba made it necessary to use boats on the Yadkin, where "the Americans sunk the flat boat by boring holes through her bottom after the prisoners were set over and waiting her down with rock."[56]

After crossing, the Americans briefly waited at Trading Ford, then marched to Guilford Courthouse.[57] The main army arrived on 8 February. Here, Morgan was granted permission to leave the army "untill he recovers his health.[58] The main army conducted a forced march into Virginia, and crossed the Dan River to safety on 13 February 1781.[59] The Flying Army, now under Otho H. Williams and known as light infantry, crossed on 14 February, just ahead of Cornwallis.[60] The American army movements now became part of the Guilford Courthouse campaign."[61]

As soon as Cornwallis reached Salisbury, he wrote Greene requesting a prisoner exchange, hinting that coming warm weather would be hard on American prisoners in Charleston. He suggested it might be necessary to

Nathanael Greene; oil painting by Charles Willson Peale
(Independence National Historical Park Collection)

move them to the West Indies.[62] Cornwallis offered the several hundred American prisoners in Charleston in exchange for the men lost at Cowpens. He failed in his effort to retake the prisoners, either by force or by exchange.

In mid-March, the two armies fought at Guilford Courthouse, an action that crippled the British army but left the American army intact.[63] Cornwallis then marched his men to Wilmington, North Carolina. After resting and partially refitting his troops, the British marched north into Virginia.

The summer 1781 campaign was inconclusive. When Washington's Northern Army and the French army under Rochambeau arrived in Virginia, Cornwallis fortified Yorktown and waited for help. The British navy was driven off by the French fleet under the Compte de Grasse. Alternatives exhausted, Cornwallis surrendered on 19 October 1781.

Following Guilford Courthouse, Greene returned to South Carolina. His army fought, and lost, three pitched battles, but subordinate commands won many smaller engagements. At summer's end, Americans controlled the South except for a coastal enclave between Charleston and Savannah. The British lost the South, and ultimately the Revolutionary War, largely because the Continentals, state troops, and militia from Delaware, Maryland, Virginia, the Carolinas, and Georgia never gave up. The episode that started the British downslide can be identified as Cowpens, in large part because the British reaction ultimately led to Yorktown.

The Cowpens American veterans represent a thin section of southern society at the time of the battle. The small group of elite leaders and the large body of yeomen took a variety of paths after the war. Some became governors, representatives, and the like; others filled lower positions, such as justice of the peace and sheriff. Many moved west, taking up land earned by their military service.

Frederick Jackson Turner conceived a notion of the frontier as a safety valve providing opportunities for Americans to expand spatially.[64] This hypothesis has been hotly debated ever since, but it has a general ring of truth.[65] More than 900 names identified as Cowpens participants provide a group to statistically test Turner's hypothesis by identifying where Cowpens veterans resided in the 1830s.[66] American participants mirror society at large because they came from the same society. While they share many things with the larger civilian populace, they are a distinct group because they were all at Cowpens on 17 January 1781. That event serves as a starting point for examining their earlier and later activity.

The 638 men in Moss who filed pension applications can be subdivided by rank, military unit at Cowpens, birthplace, residence in 1781, and residence at pension filing.[67] They can be examined about social and spatial mobility in terms of their past and their military unit with information provided in pension declarations.

Eighty-six officers' histories are known. Officers born in the state where they enlisted were less likely to move from that state after the war when compared with those who changed residence before Cowpens.[68] Of those officers not born in the state from which they served, slightly more than half moved to another state after the war. Of thirty-nine South Carolina officers, seventeen moved out of the state. Those who stayed had family and economic reasons for remaining. In many cases, they held political office before the war. Men who moved were usually little known before the war and in lower ranks such as lieutenant. In any case, officers, the elected and appointed leadership at Cowpens, seem much more likely to have held political office after the war.[69]

Of 552 enlisted men traced through the pensions, only 107 were born in the state where they enlisted. Both those born outside and in their enlistment state were likely to move on. Of the 552 men, 394 (71.3 percent) moved out of state after Cowpens. Those who enlisted in their birth state and moved after the war outnumbered those who stayed by about four to one. Over twice as many South Carolina enlisted men moved out of state than stayed. One reason for this mobility is the opportunities available after the war.[70]

Most men drafted for military service were surplus population. These young men had few ties, and very little investment in, their home community. Most had no trade other than farmer or laborer. During the war they became used to moving. With no trade or property of their own, they had little or no economic reason to remain home when the government offered free land after the war. They left. Men with a trade were more likely to remain in their home community.[71]

Most Carolina enlisted men moved on to Georgia, Alabama, Tennessee, and Kentucky. Virginians and Marylanders primarily chose Tennessee or Kentucky, but many went to Ohio and Indiana, as did the Delaware men. The Cowpens pension information shows Turner was right; men did move. The pension documents provide a very strong argument for the Turner hypothesis because "Officers were more likely to stay in the state they served to return to their land or start a political career. When officers did move to new states or territories, they still pursued political careers. The enlisted men moved for new opportunities to gain land."[72]

Many British soldiers survived the hard southern campaigning and were granted land in Canada. At least 125 British Legion enlisted men took up land in Nova Scotia in 1784. Many of these men were Cowpens participants.[73] Veterans whose names come down to the present usually had something bad happen to them. Christian Tager of Sandford's Light Dragoon Company was badly wounded at Cowpens. He settled in Nova Scotia, "restless and embittered by the war, living somewhere near Amherst on his half-pay and drinking himself to dementia in the village inn."[74] Another Sandford's Company dragoon came to a bad end, perhaps confirming what Delaware private, and sometime member of the troop, Michael Dougherty said about them being the worst set of fellows he ever encountered. Michael Hayes murdered his wife on Christmas Eve, 1785. Convicted by the first "full dress trial" held in Queens County, Nova Scotia, he was hung in Liverpool, 10 July 1786.[75]

John Christy of Captain Miller's infantry company drowned "wading the creek at Little Port Jolly," Nova Scotia. Dr. Edward Smith, surgeon, settled in Nova Scotia after the war. Sergeant George Hammett, after being paroled following Yorktown, went to Nova Scotia and settled in Port Mouton.[76] Some, perhaps predictably, officers, prospered. Lieutenant Walter Willett and Cornet Samuel Willett of Captain Sandford's Light Dragoon Company were "granted lands at Wilmot Nova Scotia in 1784 . . . Formed a militia unit called Barclay's Legion in 1793."

Some British soldiers ended up in the country they fought for and lost. Sometimes they even turn up in American pensions. "Amongst these prisoners there was one John Hailey an Englishman who now lives a near neighbor to this Declarant in White County Tennessee, but to whom he was not then personally known . . . said Hailey's son has married the stepdaughter of this Declarant." Hailey is John Hailey of Captain Daniel Lyman's Company, Prince of Wales American Regiment, which served at Cowpens as light infantry.[77] Samuel Moore's recollection sums up something of the American experience. Both Moore and Hailey fought for a country, moved west, raised a family, then saw their children marry into an "enemy" lineage. Those two in-laws must have had some interesting recollections of their service to pass on to their grandchildren.

Epilogue

When this project began, the research was directed at learning how many men actually fought with Morgan. After the Little Big Horn Battlefield archaeology research was published, it seemed Cowpens could be treated the same way. A research proposal for Cowpens battlefield archaeology raised questions about positioning and how one could identify units involved with their material culture.

As research continued, other questions were raised. These circulated around casualty figures, the role of North Carolina troops after they served as skirmishers, and the South Carolina militia withdrawal. The mistaken order was another intriguing part of the battle that became clearer. Why did the British infantry, especially an elite unit such as the 71st Regiment, collapse? The most confusing battle segments involved the role of the American cavalry. Finally, what happened to Tarleton's baggage train, and how long did the battle actually last? All these questions forced a reevaluation of documentary sources and material culture and led to this book.

Tarleton said Morgan had about 2,000 men, but Morgan claimed only a few over 800 as his total force. It is highly unlikely that more than two-thirds of 900 participants survived forty more years and then swore to participating at Cowpens, as pension documents indicate. Given men who died between 17 January 1781 and the first pension act in 1818, a sizable number of veterans did not survive to file pension applications. Where unit size is known, the pension application rate is less than one to three or four. That is, one pension application equaled at least three or four Cowpens soldiers—and this is a low figure. Some 600 men filed pensions, so the total of Americans at Cowpens should thus be between 1,800 and 2,400 men. This figure agrees more closely with Tarleton's estimate of 2,000 than Morgan's 800.

The next question is why such a discrepancy occurred. The militia performance against British troops before 1781 exasperated American military leaders. Washington thought so little of militia he wanted to fight in the European fashion, and so did other experienced officers.[1] After Kings Mountain, southern political leaders felt militia could defend their states without relying on a standing army of Continentals who were expensive to feed, clothe, arm, and pay. If Morgan wanted Cowpens to stand as a Continental victory against British troops, following an agenda related to a regular army, he had to show that regulars won the battle. In his original report, Morgan claimed 800 men won against "chosen" British troops. He amplified this impression by naming only Continental and long-service Virginia militia officers who had served with him since the fall of 1780, and he omitted some Virginia Continentals and state troops, such as Wallace, Oldham, and Lawson. Pickens was mentioned only in passing. McDowell was slighted entirely, yet he had been a mainstay of the Flying Army since September 1780.

Morgan's "regulars," Continentals and long-service Virginia militia, numbered about 600 men: 300 Continental infantry, 82 Continental dragoons, 160 Virginia militia under Triplett, and about 50 Virginia State Troops. This total does not include Carolina and Georgia militia, nor does it include state troops. On paper, at least, Morgan counted his "regulars," and perhaps threw in another 200 men to allow for the militia. Sergeant Major William Seymour of the Delaware Company validates this interpretation by stating explicitly that "we [had] not eight hundred of standing troops and militia."[2] If Seymour meant 800 regulars ("standing troops") augmented by militia, then Morgan, Seymour, and Tarleton agree. Eliminating the militia made the victory seem more important because American regulars won the battle.

Casualty lists support this interpretation. Morgan reported 12 killed and 60 wounded. By name, at least 24 Americans were killed and 104 were wounded. By assigning casualties to units, it is obvious that Morgan counted only his "regular" casualties, the Continentals and Triplett's Virginians. Furthermore, none of the many wounded men who were not hurt badly enough as to miss time in ranks were reported.[3] Just as Morgan ignored the militia in counting his troop strength, he ignored their casualties. An entry in the North Carolina State Records supports the idea that Morgan counted only "regular" casualties.

3 officers wounded and 55 non Comd. & Privates.
10 Privates killed.
American, 60 cavalry, 20 Infantry, Militia[4]

This list shows two groups of casualties. The first consists of regulars and reports 58 wounded and 10 killed. This is remarkably close to Morgan's claim of 60 wounded and 12 killed. The second group appears to list 80 additional militia casualties. The total casualty figures for this cryptic entry are 148 men. This is over the 128 named casualties, but very close to a doubling of Morgan's figures.

If Morgan considered that his 800 "standing" troops suffered 72 killed and wounded, documented casualties nearly double that total, suggesting the Americans had at least 1,600 men who suffered 127 to 148 casualties. Morgan had at least 600 men on the main line, and Tarleton claimed 1,000 men were on the militia line. There were, at the barest minimum, 125 American cavalrymen. Morgan did not lie. Even if he had accurate counts of the militia, which is unlikely, he chose his words carefully to advocate a specific cause, an American standing army. This is ironic because Cowpens is known today as a victory of militia working with regular troops.

As research continued, it became clear that Morgan's tactical genius had not been given enough credit. Participant narratives indicate Morgan had a well-thought-out tactical plan, flexible enough to take advantage of events as they developed. While Morgan's tactical arrangements at Cowpens are praised as sound,[5] they are never clarified, in part because he changed from a written plan for battle *if attacked* to an orally given *deployment for a battle he wanted to fight.* The change occurred after Pickens and others brought in more men sometime after Morgan prudently issued a written plan for action *in case* Tarleton caught up with the Americans.[6]

The traditional three-line, European-style, defense in depth formation does not explain the fighting Morgan had in mind. His genius lay in reversing the strength of his linear formations and creating progressively stronger defensive lines. Working within traditional European military thinking, Morgan constructed a mental, as well as a physical, trap for Tarleton.[7] As the British drove successive American lines from the battlefield, they anticipated victory only to encounter another, stronger line after exerting themselves. The depth of the American lines soaked up the shock of British thrusts.

Where Tarleton ultimately used all his men in a long battle line with a mounted reserve, Morgan deployed his men in three lines and a reserve according to their weapons. In order to aid his men as much as possible, Morgan utilized the known tendency of British infantry to fire high by placing his men downhill. Low American casualties seem to be a reflection of overshooting, which also silhouetted the British against a light skyline.

The skirmish line retired under pressure, firing as opportunity offered. They took new positions behind the militia line and on its flanks. The militia withdrawal was not intended to go very far to the rear; their rally point was behind the main line. Morgan prepared for the militia withdrawal by positioning his Virginia units *en échelon* to channel the militia toward their second position. Accounts suggesting the militia retreated around the left flank ignore British accounts, Morgan's prefight main-line positioning, and common sense. Morgan stationed himself at the end of a channel where he directed militia toward their next position. Morgan and his staff then rallied the militia behind a wall of regular troops, so they could be used where needed as the fighting developed.

The Continentals stood firm and shot it out with the British infantry. When pressed, they withdrew, and fought again. They protected the militia, stopped, and then shattered the British infantry. The American dragoons moved rapidly in a very short time span to cover both flanks. At each encounter, Washington had many more men than the British unit he drove off.

Private soldiers probably did not understand the subtleties of Morgan's tactics. They knew what they, and their company, were expected to do, and did it. Their diverse backgrounds and incorporation into cohesive fighting units is another vital part of the Cowpens story.

Tarleton had little choice but to attack at the first opportunity. He knew "of a corps of mountaineers being upon the march from Green river." Since British numbers would get no larger, Tarleton could not allow American strength to increase. To encourage his troops and intimidate the Whigs, Tarleton ordered the 71st Regiment to take no prisoners.[8] Tarleton deployed infantry behind the protection of dragoons and placed cavalry on both flanks. His primary reserve was initially the 71st Regiment because there was no room to deploy them beyond the 7th Regiment's left flank. At the militia line, the field was wider and he started the 71st forward. His reserve then became four troops of British Legion dragoons.

Tarleton planned on overwhelming Morgan's militia with a quick infantry charge, denying them any opportunity to use their rifles. When the British charge broke through, the fleeing militia would be attacked by his dragoons. If faced with heavy resistance, Tarleton was disposed to send units around both flanks to surround them while his infantry used their bayonets to their front. He was unable to do this at Cowpens.

Creating the battle maps demonstrated other facets about the Cowpens deployments. Computerized scaling of units indicates that the battlefield *was* constricted and that both Morgan and Tarleton misrepresented things. Morgan's flanks were covered, on his right by the west ravine and then by the headwaters of a small creek. On the left, the skirmish line's left flank was in the air, but militia and main lines were covered by canebrakes and wet ground unsuitable for cavalry operations. Placing units on the battlefield shows that the only times Tarleton's men were "loosely formed" may have been when they initially deployed east of the Green River Road to drive in the skirmishers. The field narrows at the militia-line position. At the main line, British infantrymen were compressed, but their casualties before this point meant they did not cover much ground. American casualty distributions suggest the British were probably in a tight formation at the main line.

Initially, Tarleton did not deploy his cavalry against the American battle lines because he could not use them. American flanks were covered by ground unsuitable for mounted operations. An additional factor was the skirmishers on both flanks who used ground cover well. Only when open ground presented itself on the main-line flanks did Tarleton order dragoons forward. They were devastating when they dashed through Hammond, hit the militia, and went through McDowell's flankers. Ultimately, the British dragoons were not successful because they were outnumbered when Washington confronted them.

Morgan countered British tactics to rout his riflemen by supporting militia with Continentals, the "regular force" Hanger mentioned. Morgan fed his men who waited with freshly loaded weapons and clear instructions about their roles. He opted to attack the British leadership. "Morgan's marksmen . . . presented the means of introducing disorder into the ranks of the enemy."[9] Morgan's men used a devastating first fire twice at Cowpens, on the militia line and on the Continental line. Morgan used this "precious resource" very shrewdly. The British infantry, on the other hand, faced a first fire from two different lines, one armed almost exclusively with rifles, without having a chance to get their own volley in first.

North Carolina militia not only fought as skirmishers. They continued fighting throughout the battle, and on the right flank bought a crucial minute or two that saved the Americans. South Carolina militia did not cross the field, obstructing Continental fields of fire because Morgan carefully planned their withdrawal to avoid any disruption of his main line. The South Carolina militia withdrew quickly, in good order, through the main line. They were reforming and reloading, behind Triplett's Virginians, when surprised by the 17th Light Dragoons and a panic occurred.

The mistaken order causing a withdrawal from the main line was the result of a series of mishaps. The fault appears to lie with Captain Conway Oldham, who did not comprehend what Wallace wanted to do. The error was compounded when Wallace gave his order at the same instant the 71st Regiment fired a volley into the Virginians. Once Wallace saw confusion, he had no choice but to stabilize his men by continuing their march to the rear, dressing their ranks on the move and then halting.

The error might be due to misunderstanding the drum beatings, but veteran troops would not confuse the beat for "right wheel" with "forward march" even if the preparatory command were missed.[10] If the preparatory command "To the right wheel" given by Wallace and his drummer came at precisely the same time the 71st Regiment volley struck the Virginians, it is likely Oldham and his platoon heard only the command of execution and stepped off to the rear. The error was compounded by the Virginia State Troops to their left. Their company commander, John Lawson, was killed by the same volley. His replacement saw Wallace moving off and ordered his men to withdraw as well.

American cavalry struck several times in rapid succession. The keys to understanding what they did lie in the recollections of Thomas Young and James Simons, and a knowledge of how narrow the battlefield actually is. Once their accounts were reduced to specific episodes, Washington's actions could be linked with infantry activity. After a charge of less than 100 yards, Washington hit the 17th Light Dragoons on the American left flank immediately after the South Carolina militia fired a volley into them. The British dragoons were outnumbered four to one at the point of contact and routed. Approximately one-fourth of the 3rd Light Dragoons pursued the British while Washington withdrew.

Washington quickly reformed and attacked Ogilvie's British Legion troop that penetrated the American right flank. Again, it was a question of mass. Washington had well over a hundred men while Ogilvie had fewer than fifty. Washington rode through Ogilvie, then turned and rode back through the stunned British. The distance covered in this second charge was less than 200 yards out and back and took less than two minutes.

While Howard's infantry turned about to fire their surprise volleys, Washington reformed. When Howard charged bayonets, American dragoons rode into the 71st, sabers flashing, and knocking men down with their horses. Washington then rode about eighty yards through small groups of British infantry toward the cannon. Here they may have shot the artillery horses. As Continental infantry swarmed over the cannon, Tarleton brought some dragoons forward. The two mounted parties clashed, then the British drew off. As they withdrew, three British officers engaged Washington. It is unlikely that Tarleton participated since MacKenzie, who harbored an intense dislike for Tarleton, did not mention it.

The collapse of the British infantry seemed incredible to Tarleton and later historians, especially the Scots. He described the failure as "unaccountable" and astonishing, due to "some unforeseen event."[11] Three British infantry disintegration episodes affected the outcome of Cowpens. The first occurred when the South Carolina militia volley fire hit the British.

The second occasion involved the 71st Regiment when it was blasted by surprise fire after the Continentals had withdrawn. Then, some British soldiers involved in the main-line firefight failed to pursue the Americans when they withdrew. These failures can be described as two different psychological problems resulting from similar causes.

In the five days before Cowpens, the British were subjected to stress that could be alleviated only by rest and proper diet. Tarleton had four days' rations before commencing his operations.[12] He moved rapidly after Morgan, averaging about fourteen miles a day, but operating for long hours. The average distance traveled each day is misleading because so much of it was stop-and-go movement as streams were crossed and potential ambush sites cleared. There was no time to rest or forage when a unit was likely to be moving immediately. In the forty-eight hours before the battle, the British ran out of food and had less than four hours' sleep. Loss of sleep has a pronounced impact on effectiveness, especially in combat operations. When sleep deprivation occurs in conjunction with hunger, the impact of both is magnified.[13]

The British were suffering nutritionally, too. Their regulation daily ration consisted of bread (1.5 pounds), meat (either 1 pound beef or .5 pound pork), peas (.25 pint), one ounce of rice, and one ounce of butter.[14] This approximates 2,500 calories per day. Tarleton's men marched rapidly and did not have time to supplement basic rations which ran out. Unless foraging was more successful than initially appears, Tarleton's men got no meat because cattle were not driven with his force. In the absence of meat, the men should have gotten three pounds of flour or bread, but their four-day flour resource collected before 12 January and before the rapid pursuit of Morgan began was exhausted by 16 January. A typical army march during the southern campaign rarely involved carrying more than two days' food unless the units were on a forced march,[15] so Tarleton's 16 January comment that the American camp "afforded plenty of provisions" is an important indication of food shortages.[16]

The damp, cold weather made additional demands on energy reserves beyond those needed for marching. If temperatures ranged from fifteen to forty degrees with high humidity and a wind chill, the men required additional calories for maintenance of body temperature. During their march to contact, the infantry waded at least two streams and used roads badly churned up by the Americans on 16 January. Instead of simply marching at the rate of three miles an hour, the British crossed rugged terrain on a bad path. Additional British infantry caloric needs due to the cold, wet, windy weather and the increased exertion can be estimated as approximately another 500 to 1,000 calories, which they had no way of obtaining.

British Legion infantry and light infantry initially led Tarleton's force during the approach march. During this movement, they were exposed to bitterly cold weather, clearing obstructions in the road, and crossing streams, and subjected to at least three separate, but brief encounters with American scouts. While the sudden engagements did not physically involve most infantrymen until they deployed, the firing and uncertainty added additional stress. The cumulative impact on their nervous systems was similar to that noted during World War II when, "if a skirmish line was halted two or three times during an attack by sudden enemy fire, it became impossible to get any further action from the men, even though none had been hurt."[17]

In combat situations, stress, or fear, is applied when lives are at stake. The threat may be real or imagined, but the reaction is still an onset of metabolic processes that consume energy.[18] Early consumption of already depleted energy reserves to deal with psychological and physical stress (fear, cold, marching) led to failure later in the battle.

Once the battle began, British infantry deployed and marched forward under rifle fire that they did not return. Their final advance to engage involved moving approximately 300 yards during which they were under irregular skirmish fire. At a range of less than fifty yards, the officers were subjected to deliberate, aimed rifle fire by sharpshooters, some of whom definitely hit their marks.[19] After advancing another ten to fifteen yards, they were struck by a volley fired by Brandon's Battalion, and then by four more South Carolina volleys.[20]

Here, according to MacKenzie, between a third and a half of the infantrymen went down and many were physically wounded.[21] It is significant that British authors mention fatigue here as a factor of the approach march.[22] Since the references deal with the night march to Cowpens, fatigue was already a factor the minute the British arrived on the battlefield. The cumulative impact on the British infantry of four days' marching, poor rations, bitter cold, and the American militia volleys is described in modern terms as combat, or battle, shock. Despite physical and psychological stress, many British soldiers kept on and moved forward to engage the American main line of resistance.

The 71st Highlanders experienced a similar shock but had different reactions. They underwent the same approach march at the rear of the column. Since the British kept halting to clear stream crossings, checking for ambushes, and waiting for scouting reports, the rear was subjected to periods of waiting and chilling, then periods of heavy exertion as they hurried to catch up. If anything, by the time the Scots got on the field, they were more debilitated than other British units.

On the battlefield, the Scots deployed, mixed with the 7th Fusiliers, and were sorted out. Then they stood in reserve behind the 7th Regiment, where any bullet missing the fusiliers likely fell into their ranks. Then, after trotting uphill over 300 yards and firing a volley, they saw the Americans retreat and reacted with exhilaration. After charging over more than one hundred yards, they ran into surprise volley fire that staggered them. After all their exertions in cold, damp weather, the sudden turnaround, accompanied with noise, injury, and flashes of light stunned them. This is an even better example of classic combat shock than what happened in front of the South Carolina militia.

Combat, or battle, shock is an acute form of combat fatigue.[23] For the 71st, it was precipitated by massed, and sudden, fire power of the Continental volleys. Onset was so debilitating as to render some of the Scots incapable of flight, much less fighting. Aspects of combat shock can be seen in those Highlanders who fell stunned to the ground, leaving very few individuals to resist the Continental bayonet charge. Shock was followed by flight, as the 71st simply broke and ran, an episode Tarleton described as an "unaccountable panic," which was quickly communicated to other British soldiers.[24]

When the Highlanders stopped running and tried to reform, militia fired into them from two, perhaps three, sides, and bayonet-wielding Continentals advanced on them from another. Howard described the 71st as "broken into squads," although others said they had "formed into some compact order."[25] The phrasing describes "crowding" or "bunching" behavior as men drew closer for security.[26] As Richard Fox pointed out in reference to the Little Big Horn in 1876, "mass flight following disintegration . . . is most dangerous. Once men take to flight, they do not stop until overcome by some obstacle or exhaustion."[27] At Cowpens, a combination of uphill running and exhaustion, and their two light infantry companies in "compact order," brought them to a halt.[28]

Disorganized, under heavy fire, and facing another onslaught of Continental bayonets proved too much, even for Highland officers, to bear.[29] The 71st was unable to continue fighting and surrendered. What is remarkable about the 71st Regiment is that they experienced all the earlier trials without breaking, even though "fatigued troops—hungry, thirsty, tired—will very readily break under even moderate stress,"[30] as the legion and light infantry soldiers demonstrated in front of the militia.

The lack of support for the 71st demonstrates another, lesser impact of stress in combat. The light infantry, legion infantry, and 7th Fusiliers did not pursue the withdrawing Americans with the same vigor as the Scots.[31] Their failure was due to combat fatigue. MacKenzie noted fatigue "enfeebled the pursuit, much more than loss of blood."[32]

Combat fatigue is the gradual onset of mental breakdown in battle. It usually takes four stages during prolonged combat operations.[33] At Cowpens, the preliminary stages were accelerated by poor diet, lack of sleep, and physical exertion over the four days before 17 January. Analysis of World War II combat fatigue casualties provides an understanding of what befell the British Legion infantry and the light infantry. "Rapid exhaustion due to additional noise, as well as heat or cold, has to be mentioned . . . stress accelerates all those bodily functions important for survival, and thus speeds up the metabolic process . . . this accelerates exhaustion."[34] Many British infantrymen, aside from the 71st, were victims of combat fatigue and simply unable to move forward, even though they advanced to the main line and engaged it in a stubborn firefight. When the Americans moved off, some were too spent to pursue.

The Scots' greater resistance to combat fatigue may have been due to their being an elite unit.[35] The physical activity of the 71st involved two different sorts of bodily-reserve depletion. One was similar to a marathon in terms of the approach march. The other was the run into position followed by the charge after the Continentals. Both types of exertion reduced resistance to the onset of fatigue.

The cumulative outcome of all factors—diet, cold, humidity, psychological stress, and physical exertion—was pronounced, as virtually all British infantry ceased functioning as combat soldiers. Some did not move, others panicked and ran; the few hardy soldiers whose bodies and souls still endured put up a fight but they were too few and too scattered. Tarleton's infantry were broken, routed, and captured.

Tarleton's baggage train was not plundered by Tories. Americans, including Thomas Young, were the culprits. Young explained what happened at the baggage train as well as why the British panicked when crossing the Broad River. Young's account coincides closely with the Tarleton and Otterson accounts to explain the American militia pursuit.

Finally, there is the question of how long the battle lasted. Participant recollections varied from less than an hour to all day. The time depends on when a soldier thought it started and when he finished his duties. Duration would be lengthened by anyone who considered that the battle included dragoon skirmishing, reconnaissance by fire, and pursuit. Actual fighting, from the time the British advanced infantry to the rivulet, until Tarleton's dragoons fled the field, lasted well under forty minutes.

If the battle began as the British discharged their cannon and started up the slope, it was about thirty-five minutes or less before the British fled. Time can be measured in space covered at a fixed marching rate. It can be reckoned by the number of volleys one side fired. When different measures of time are applied to battle duration, a chronological framework from British infantry deployment to mass flight is well under forty minutes.

I hope that this study will generate interest in the southern campaign, where the Revolutionary War was ultimately won, so the Cowpens veterans will not be forgotten. There are more accounts still to be located. An archaeological investigation of the battlefield will support or deny conclusions reached here but will also certainly raise new questions. Such is the nature of scientific inquiry.

Notes

PREFACE

1. Moss, *Patriots at the Cowpens.*
2. Scott and Fox, *Archaeological Insights*; Scott, Fox, Connor, and Harmon, *Archaeological Perspectives*; Fox, *Archaeology, History, and Custer's Last Battle.*
3. Moss, *Patriots at the Cowpens.*
4. Henry Lee, *Memoirs of the War*; Stedman, *American War*; Tarleton, *Campaigns of 1780–81.*
5. Bearss, *Battle of Cowpens*; Fleming, *Cowpens*; Roberts, *Battle of Cowpens.*
6. As an example of cumulative error, several modern authors report that when Tarleton initially sent his dragoons forward to contact a reconnaissance by fire, fifteen were shot from their horses. See, for example, Fleming, *Cowpens*, 63; Higginbotham, *Daniel Morgan*, 136–37; Rankin, "Cowpens," esp. 356; Roberts, *Battle of Cowpens*, 86; and Treacy, *Prelude to Yorktown*, 100. None of these authors cite a source following that statement.

   The earliest statement made about reconnaissance casualties seems to be James Graham's *Life of General Daniel Morgan*, 299, with David Schenk's *North Carolina*, 213, only slightly later. No citation is given in Schenk, but his source was probably Graham, who also gave no source but probably used Thomas Balch's *Papers*, 45–46. Balch cited James Simons's 3 November 1803 letter to William Washington. Simons actually described action behind the left flank of the main line involving men of the 17th Light Dragoons "leaving in the course of ten minutes eighteen of their brave 17th dragoons dead on the spot." This is the earliest quote referring to British dragoon casualties with the approximate number others have so repeatedly cited.

7. Lambert, *South Carolina Loyalists*; Morrill, *Southern Campaigns*; Pancake, *This Destructive War.*
8. S. L. A. Marshall, *Men Against Fire*, and his *Soldier's Load*. Marshall's observations and conclusions have been challenged; see, for example, Smoler, "The Secret of the Soldiers." Post-battle interviews are still done by the U.S. Army to determine combat lessons to avoid future mistakes.
9. Keegan, *Face of Battle.*
10. A good discussion of "point of view" and its impact on battle history can be found in Keegan, *Face of Battle*, 128–33.
11. Anderson, "Journal"; John Eager Howard to John Marshall, 1804, Bayard Papers (Marshall prepared specific questions about Cowpens which Howard answered in his letter); MacKenzie, *Strictures on Lt. Col. Tarleton's History*; Daniel Morgan to Nathanael Greene, 19 Jan. 1781, Showman, *Greene Papers*, 7:152–55; Seymour, *Jour-*

nal of the Southern Expedition; James Simons to William Washington, 3 Nov. 1803; Balch, *Papers*, 45–47; Tarleton, *Campaigns of 1780–81*.

12. Hanger, *Address to the Army*; Henry Lee, *Memoirs of the War*; Samuel Shaw, "Revolutionary War Letters to Captain Winthrop Sargent"; Stedman, *American War*.

13. "Account of Christopher Brandon" in Draper, *King's Mountain*, 285–86; John R. Shaw, *Narrative*; Gordon, *Independence of the United States of America*; John Marshall, *Life of George Washington*; William Johnson, *Sketches of Nathanael Greene*; Moultrie, *Memoirs of the American Revolution*; Ramsay, *History of the American Revolution*; Ramsay, *History of the Revolution in South Carolina*; Saye, *Memoirs of Major Joseph McJunkin*; Young, "Memoir," 84–88. McJunkin later became something of a "professional veteran" and gave talks about the battle.

14. A good description of problems inherent in using pension documents may be found in Dann, *Revolution Remembered*, xix–xxi.

15. Recent work shows "shadows" of military action can be detected by bullets and accoutrements recovered archaeologically. The two most recent are Lees, "When the Shooting Stopped," and Scott and Hunt, "Civil War Battle of Monroe's Crossroads."

INTRODUCTION

1. The long roll is one of the rudiments, or basic drum beatings, of eighteenth-century music. In the military, the long roll was a call to bring men immediately into ranks, preparatory to fighting. Moon, *Instructor for the Drum*, 22.

2. The issues involved and the British interpretation of American sentiments are covered by Pancake, *This Destructive War*, 25–30.

3. Campbell, *Expedition against the Rebels of Georgia*; Lawrence, *Storm over Savannah*.

4. Moultrie, *Memoirs of the American Revolution*, 1, 60–115; Pancake, *This Destructive War*, 60–71; Tarleton, *Campaigns of 1780–81*, 9–32; Uhlendorf, *Siege of Charleston*.

5. Pancake, *This Destructive War*, 67–72, contains a good summation of British efforts and their problems. Lambert's *South Carolina Loyalists*, 93–125, provides greater detail and examines Loyalist motivation.

6. Lambert, *South Carolina Loyalists*, 120–21; Pancake, *This Destructive War*, 81–82. One example is Tarleton burning Thomas Sumter's plantation on 28 May 1780. Tarleton later wrote "without any thing material happening on the route." Tarleton, *Campaigns of 1780–81*, 27. Another is the burning of Andrew Pickens's farm in December 1780; Pancake, *This Destructive War*, 85.

7. Lambert, *South Carolina Loyalists*, 84–85; Pancake, *This Destructive War*, 128.

8. Wickwire and Wickwire, *Cornwallis*; Lamb, *Original and Authentic Journal*, 362; Pancake, *This Destructive War*, 57–59; Tarleton, *Campaigns of 1780–81*, 85.

9. Henry Lee, *Memoirs of the War*, 208–10; Pancake, *This Destructive War*, 120–21; Stedman, *American War*, 217–18; Tarleton, *Campaigns of 1780–81*, 165–69.

10. Lambert, *South Carolina Loyalists*, 59–60, 143–44; Henry Lee, *Memoirs of the War*, 209. Rankin, *North Carolina Continentals*, 266, briefly indicates southern ideas about militia.

11. Henry Lee, *Memoirs of the War*, 215–16; Pancake, *This Destructive War*, 123–27; Tarleton, *Campaigns of 1780–81*, 168–70, 182–83.

12. Nathanael Greene to Thomas Jefferson, 6 Dec. 1780, Greene to Abner Nash, 6 Dec. 1780, Greene to George Washington, 7 Dec. 1780, Greene to Henry Knox, 7 Dec. 1780, Showman, *Greene Papers*, 6:530–31, 533, 542–45, 547; Henry Lee, *Memoirs of the War*, 233–34; Seymour, *Journal of the Southern Expedition*.

13. Greene to John Butler, 13 Dec. 1780, Greene to Joseph Marbury, 4 Dec. 1780, Showman, *Greene Papers*, 6:516, 566, 521–22.

14. Baron Von Steuben to Greene, 24 Nov. 1780, John Gunby to Greene, 13 Dec. 1780, Showman, *Greene Papers*, 6:503, 567.

15. Henry Lee, *Memoirs of the War*, 244–45; Greene to Jefferson, 6 Dec. 1780, Greene to Abner Nash, 6 Dec. 1780, Greene to Nicholas Long, 6 Dec. 1780, Greene to North Carolina Board of War, 7 Dec. 1780, Greene to George Washington, 7 Dec. 1780, Showman, *Greene Papers*, 6:530–31, 532, 533–34, 541, 542–45.

16. Conrad, "Nathanael Greene and the Southern Campaigns," 70; Henry Lee, *Memoirs of the War*, 244–45, 247; Rankin, *North Carolina Continentals*, 261; Showman, *Greene Papers*, 6:xvi–xix.

17. Seymour, *Journal of the Southern Expedition*, 10; William Smallwood to Nathanael Greene, 6 Dec. 1780, Showman, *Greene Papers*, 6:538–39. Many Virginians mentioned this episode in their pension applications: Samuel Brown, pension, 1 June 1835, M804, Roll 377; James Emmons, pension, 2 Oct. 1832, M804, Roll 927; Lawrence Everheart, pension, 7 Apr. 1834, M804, Roll 944.

18. Greene to Daniel Morgan, 16 Dec. 1780, Showman, *Greene Papers*, 6:589–90.

19. Greene to Samuel Huntington, 7 Dec. 1780, Greene to George Washington, 7 Dec. 1780, Showman, *Greene Papers*, 7:7–11.

20. Conrad, "Nathanael Greene and the Southern Campaigns," 71; Tarleton, *Campaigns of 1780–81*, 208. Had Greene known British reinforcements were nearing Charleston, he might not have chosen to divide his forces.

21. Economy of force and mass are modern principles of war used to guide analysts in evaluating combat. Economy of force means having enough resources to complete the mission. Mass means having superior force at the critical place and time. For additional discussion, see Matlof, *American Military History*, 6–7.

22. Conrad, "Nathanael Greene and the Southern Campaigns," 76; Nathanael Greene to Alexander Hamilton, 10 Jan. 1781, Showman, *Greene Papers*, 7:87–91.

23. Greene to Hamilton, 10 Jan. 1781, Showman, *Greene Papers*, 7:87–91; William Johnson, *Sketches of Nathanael Greene*, 1:362; Rankin, *North Carolina Continentals*, 265; O. H. Williams to Elie Williams, 14 Jan. 1781, Merritt, *Calendar*, 35.

24. Greene to Lafayette, 29 Dec. 1780, Showman, *Greene Papers*, 7:18–19; William Johnson, *Sketches of Nathanael Greene*, 1:362; Seymour, *Journal of the Southern Expedition*, 11–12.

25. James Collins, pension, 8 Apr. 1834, M804, Roll 613; Aaron Guyton, pension, 1 Oct. 1833, M804, Roll 1149; Robert Long, pension, supplementary statement, 7 Oct. 1835, M804, Roll 1581; Henry Lee, *Memoirs of the War*, 248–51; Tarleton, *Campaigns of 1780–81*, 183–84. Wider views of backcountry unrest can be found in Crow and Tise, *Southern Experience*, and Hoffman et al., *Uncivil War*.

26. Lambert, *South Carolina Loyalists*, 104–36; Pancake, *This Destructive War*, 73–90.

27. Henry Lee to Nathanael Greene, 25 Jan. 1781, Showman, *Greene Papers*, 7:197–98. Other attacks were planned but put off after Greene's withdrawal to Virginia in February. See Francis Marion to Greene, 27 Jan. 1781, ibid., 7:207.

28. Henry Lee, *Memoirs of the War*, 223–25; Daniel Morgan to Greene, 31 Dec. 1780, 4 Jan. 1781, Showman, *Greene Papers*, 7:30–31, 50–51.

29. MacKenzie, *Strictures on Lt. Col. Tarleton's History*, 95–96.

30. Conrad, "Nathanael Greene and the Southern Campaigns," 69; Tarleton, *Campaigns of 1780–81*, 169.

31. Tarleton, *Campaigns of 1780–81*, 182–83.

32. Lord Cornwallis to Banastre Tarleton, 2 Jan. 1781, Tarleton, *Campaigns of 1780–81*, 244–45.

33. Tarleton, *Campaigns of 1780–81*, 211–12, 245–46.

34. Lord Cornwallis to Banastre Tarleton, 5 Jan. 1781, Cornwallis to Henry Clinton, 18 Jan. 1781, ibid., 246–47, 249–50.

35. Samuel Shaw, "Revolutionary War Letters to Captain Winthrop Sargent"; Tarleton, *Campaigns of 1780–81*, 249.

36. James Simons to William Washington, 3 Nov. 1803, Balch, *Papers*, 45–47: Joseph Johnson, *Traditions and Reminiscences*, 303; Tarleton, *Campaigns of 1780–81*, 214.

37. Daniel Morgan to Nathanael Greene, 15 Jan. 1781, Showman, *Greene Papers*, 7:127–28; Seymour, *Journal of the Southern Expedition*, 11.

38. Greene to Morgan, 16 Dec. 1780, 6:589–90; E. Alfred Jones, *Journal of Alexander Chesney*, 126–30.

39. Morgan to William Snickers, 19 Jan. 1781, Horatio Gates Papers.

CHAPTER ONE

1. Cornwallis noted that Tarleton's "disposition was unexceptionable"; Charles, the Earl Cornwallis, to Banastre Tarleton, 31 Jan. 1781, Tarleton, *Campaigns of 1780–81*, 252; George Smith, *Universal Military Dictionary*, 241. A Scotsman noted Morgan's arrangement was "on this occasion . . . judicious"; Stewart, *Sketches of Highlanders*, 2:73.

2. Peterson, *Continental Soldier*, 29, 37, 60; Neumann, *History of Weapons*, 5–10, 13–15, 32–38.

3. The best explanation of infantry drill for the American Revolution is Ernest W. Peterkin's *Exercise of Arms*.

4. References to British muskets include George C. Neumann's *History of Weapons* and Anthony C. Darling's *Red Coat and Brown Bess*. The South Carolina militia being partially armed with muskets is a detail derived from a letter from John Eager Howard to John Marshall, 1804, Bayard Papers. The use of French muskets by Continental forces is based on artifacts from Guilford Courthouse, N.C. (John R. Beaman, personal communication with author, 3 June 1991); from Camden, S.C. (Meryl McGee and Joe Henderson, personal communications with author, 24 Apr. 1990); and from Ninety Six, S.C. (Holschlag and Rodeffer, *Ninety Six*, 52; and Holschlag, Rodeffer, and Cann, *Ninety Six: The Jail*, 205–7). Documents reporting French weapons given to British Loyalist militia after Camden include George Turnball to Charles, the Earl Cornwallis, 1 Oct. 1780, Reese,

Cornwallis Papers, 26. A return showing large quantities of .69 caliber ammunition in an American supply depot was by Joshua Potts, "An Account of Stores Deposited at Harrisburg 40 Miles E. N. E. of Hillsborough Left There June 1st, 1781," in Walter Clark, *State Records of North Carolina*, 485.

5. The precise quotation is, "A soldier's musket, if not exceedingly ill bored and very crooked, as many are, will strike the figure of a man at 80 yards; it may even at a hundred; but a soldier *must be very unfortunate indeed* who shall be wounded by a *common musket* at 150 yards, PROVIDED HIS ANTAGONIST AIMS AT HIM; and, as to firing at a man at 200 yards with a common musket, you may just as well fire at the moon and have the same hopes of hitting your object." Hanger, *Sportsmen*, 205.

6. Ibid., 126–28. Hanger *is* discussing rifles, but the observation about practice is just as true for muskets. Works citing Hanger on muskets without reference to practice include Peterson, *Continental Soldier*, 27; Morrill, *Southern Campaigns*, 16; Fleming, *Now We Are Enemies*, 230–31; and Galvin, *Minute Men*, 63–65.

7. The author accomplished this on at least two occasions. Both times, conditions were dry and windless, the musket bore was clean, and new flints were used. To increase speed, balls were .63 caliber but the musket was .75 caliber. The extreme windage did not cause any loss of accuracy, but balls could be run to the breech without a ramrod, speeding the loading process dramatically. Starting with a loaded musket, six shots were fired in one minute. A silhouette of a British soldier was placed at a distance of 75 yards and five hits were recorded on one silhouette. More hits would have been obtained using buck and ball. Inspiration for this firing came from Robert Rogers's Rangers, who also used buckshot. Cuneo, *Robert Rogers of the Rangers*, 53.

8. George Washington, "General Orders, Perkiomy, 6 October 1777," Peterson, *Arms and Armor*, 61, 81. Multiple loads were used at Kings Mountain; Draper, *King's Mountain*, 293. Americans reported buckshot wounds in southern battles: Hezakiah Carr, pension, 8 Apr. 1818, M804, Roll 473; Joseph Cox, pension, 14 Aug. 1821, M804, Roll 671; and John Newton, pension, 9 Apr. 1818, M804, Roll 1815. Holschlag and Rodeffer, *Ninety-Six*, 65, reported a buck-and-ball cartridge found during excavation of the American approach trench at Ninety Six.

9. Neumann, *History of Weapons*, 134.

10. Hanger, *Sportsmen*, 125, 143; Peterson, *Continental Soldier*, 40, 62.

11. Hanger, *Sportsmen*, 144.

12. Joseph Marbury to Nathanael Greene, 22 Jan. 1781, Showman, *Greene Papers*, 7:170.

13. Hanger, *Sportsmen*, 208–10.

14. Robert E. Lee, *American Revolution in the South*, 266–67.

15. Draper, *King's Mountain*, 279.

16. Ibid., 279.

17. Robert E. Lee, *American Revolution in the South*, 275.

18. Schenk, *North Carolina*, 109.

19. Robert E. Lee, *American Revolution in the South*, 356.

20. Peterson, *Continental Soldier*, 64; Otho Holland Williams Orderly Book, 35, 43; Young, "Memoir," 527.

21. Neumann, *Swords and Blades*, 26–27, 37–38, 41–42, 45–50.

22. Christian Peters, pension, 17 Sept. 1832, M804, Roll 1917.

23. Neumann, *Swords and Blades*, 228, 232–38, 253–75.

24. Edward Harvin was wounded by a British officer's spontoon at Hobkirk's Hill, pension, 14 Oct. 1833, M804, Roll 1214. John Eager Howard reported Captain Richard Anderson using a spontoon at Cowpens in a letter to Henry Lee Jr. in *Campaign of 1781*, 97–98. For descriptions of spontoons, see Neumann, *Swords and Blades*, 191. "Platoon officers [are to be armed] with swords and espontoons," according to the Von Steuben manual. See Riling, *Regulations*, 5, for additional armament. A drill manual for the spontoon is included in Peterkin, *Exercise of Arms*, 218–21.

25. Darling, *Red Coat and Brown Bess*, 10; Peterkin, *Exercise of Arms*, 10–11; Riling, *Regulations*, 6–7.

26. Riling, *Regulations*, 8.

27. Duffy, *Military Experience*, 211–12.

28. Riling, *Regulations*, 65. A timespan for volley firing can be calculated accurately because eighteenth-century soldiers were trained to fire in specified sequential order. In Revolutionary War Bicentennial tactical demonstrations, battalion-sized units maneuvered and fired in accordance with the Von Steuben manual. Based on a tape recording of demonstrations in Paris and Versailles in September 1983, a battalion fired eight platoons in sequence in 70 seconds, with one platoon volley every 9 seconds. Four divisional firings took 30.3 seconds with a volley every 7.5 seconds. When the battalion fired full volleys, the interval was 41 seconds from first to second firing. These observations seem correct even for slower-loading riflemen. During competitions for speed and accuracy, riflemen in the Brigade of the American Revolution get off a shot every 15 seconds. Reloading time in the military, however, is based on the slowest loaders, not the fastest.

29. Smith and Elting, "British Light Infantry," 88. At Cowpens, Tarleton reported that his men used two ranks in the "loose manner of forming which had always been practiced by the King's troops in America." Tarleton, *Campaigns of 1780–81*, 221. In earlier engagements, the British compensated for loose formations by using multiple lines, but this was not done at Cowpens.

30. Campbell, *Expedition against the Rebels of Georgia*, 16–17; Governor Abner Nash to Delegates in Congress, 23 August 1780, in Walter Clark, *North Carolina State Records*, 60.

31. Duffy, *Military Experience*, 200.

32. Hanger, *Sportsmen*, 199–200.

33. Hanger, *Address to the Army*, 82.

34. Neumann, *History of Weapons*, 37, 118, 120–23.

35. Ibid., 150, 156–65, 180–85.

36. Joshua Graham, "Narrative of the Revolutionary War," 255–56.

37. Robert E. Lee, *American Revolution in the South*, 91n.

38. One saber used in the South is marked "3 RD LD NO 35 3-t," probably indicating Third Regiment Light Dragoons, Number 35, Third Troop. It was carried by Captain Peter Jaquett of the Delaware Line, and other infantry officers were similarly equipped. Neumann, *Swords and Blades*, 177; "Minutes of the North Carolina Board of War, 30 Oct. 1780," *North Carolina State Records* 14, 438.

39. Collins, *Autobiography*, 34–35.

40. William Washington, "Comment on the Sword," and Major Richard Call to Governor Thomas Jefferson, 29 Mar. 1781, both in Palmer et al., *Virginia State Papers*, 1:605. American dragoons, reflecting Washington's preference, had specific orders not to fire pistols, but to rely on sabers at Cowpens. See John Eager Howard to John Marshall, 1804, Bayard Papers.

41. James Collins, a militiaman who fought with the infantry at Cowpens, described the manufacture of these caps. The militia would go to "a turner or wheelwright, and get headblocks turned, of various sizes, according to the heads that had to wear them . . . ; we would then get some strong upper, or light sole leather, cut it out in shape, close it on the block, then grease it well with tallow, and set it before a warm fire, still on the block, and keep turning it round before the fire, still rubbing on the tallow, until it became almost as hard as a sheet of iron; we then got two small straps or plates of steel, made by our own smiths, of a good spring temper, and crossing in the centre above, one reaching from ear to ear, the other, in the contrary direction; the lining was made of strong cloth, padded with wool, and fixed so as to prevent the cap from pressing too hard on the ears; there was a small brim attached to the front, resembling the caps now worn, a piece of bearskin lined with strong cloth, padded with wool, passed over from the front to the back of the head; then a large bunch of hair taken from the tail of a horse, generally white, was attached to the back part and hung down the back; then, a bunch of white feathers, or deer's tail, was attached to the sides, which completed the cap. The cap was heavy, custom soon made it so that it could be worn without inconvenience" (*Autobiography*, 35).

42. William Johnson, *Sketches of Nathanael Greene*, 1:378–79.

43. Caruana, *Grasshoppers and Butterflies*, 4, 16–20; Muller, *Treatise of Artillery*, 115. McConnell, *British Smooth-Bore Artillery*, 48–49, raises questions about Caruana's interpretive drawings.

44. Gooding, *British Artillery*, 40–42, 46; McConnell, *British Smooth-Bore Artillery*, 281–90, 315–23; Muller, *Treatise of Artillery*, 161. McConnell abstracts much detail about projectiles and powder, drawing, in part, from Muller's technical descriptions in eighteenth-century prose.

45. Caruana, *Grasshoppers and Butterflies*, 31–32.

46. Ibid., 6, 31–32; Muller, *Treatise of Artillery*, 152, 161–62; Keegan, *Face of Battle*, 160. Muller's work derived from experience and experiments conducted by the Royal Artillery and had a major impact on gunnery. At Cowpens, the effect of shot initially aimed at the militia line caused William Washington to shift his cavalry farther to the right. This was probably bouncing shot, although the distance was well within the range of the three-pounder.

47. Muller, *Treatise of Artillery*, 163; Caruana, *Light 6-Pdr. Battalion Gun*, 8.

48. Caruana, *Grasshoppers and Butterflies*, 25–30; Muller, *Treatise of Artillery*, 161; George Smith, *Universal Military Dictionary*, 213. Although several participants mention artillery at Cowpens, only a secondary account gives the rate of fire. This oral tradition is somewhat suspect, but it does have a ring of truth because it reports that they fired in pairs eight times. Haggis, "Firesides Revisiting."

49. Tarleton, *Campaigns of 1780–81*, 15–16, 20, 30, 114, 159; Samuel C. Williams, "General Richard Winn's Notes," 9.

CHAPTER TWO

1. The entire quotation begun by the chapter epigraph is: "I give this the name of a flying Army; and while its numbers are so small, and the enemy so much superior, it must be literally so; for they can make no opposition of consequence." Nathanael Greene to Marquis de Lafayette, 29 Dec. 1780, Showman, *Greene Papers*, 18–19.

2. Henry Lee, *Memoirs of the War*, 1:393–94; Thomas Lovelady, pension, 8 Jan. 1833, M804, Roll 1591; Manuel McConnell, pension, 18 Sept. 1832, M804, Roll 1670.

3. Higginbotham, *Daniel Morgan*, 7; Henry Lee, *Memoirs of the War*, 386, 393–94; William Neel, pension, 29 Oct. 1832, M804, Roll 1804. See also supplementary statement to 1836 pension.

4. "Recollection by a British Officer," 6:204–11. See also Robert E. Lee, *American Revolution in the South*, 580, where Morgan says it was 500 and 499 lashes.

5. Henry Lee, *Memoirs of the War*, 386–87.

6. Berg, *Encyclopedia*, 77, 130, 132; Higginbotham, *Daniel Morgan*, 365; Lancaster, *American Revolution*, 292; Henry Lee, *Memoirs of the War*, 388–91. Lee, who knew Morgan well, stated that he took leave for health reasons.

7. Henry Lee, *Memoirs of the War*, 392; Daniel Morgan to Nathanael Greene, 6 and 7 Feb. 1781, Greene to Morgan, 10 Feb. 1781, Showman, *Greene Papers*, 7:256, 271, 354–55.

8. James Graham, *Life of General Daniel Morgan*, 448; Henry Lee, *Memoirs of the War*, 392–93.

9. George Smith, *Universal Military Dictionary*, 112–13.

10. William Neel, pension, 29 Oct. 1832, M804, Roll 1804; see also supplementary statement, 19 Mar. 1836; Henry Lee, *Memoirs of the War*, 393; Otho Williams to Daniel Morgan, 31 Oct. 1780, James Graham, *Life of General Daniel Morgan*, 245.

11. Nathanael Greene to Morgan, 16 Dec. 1780, Morgan to Greene, 15 Jan. 1781, Showman, *Greene Papers*, 6:589–90, 7:127–28; Riling, *Regulations*, 136. Captain C. K. Chitty was Morgan's commissary of purchases. Captain Benjamin Brookes was Morgan's brigade major.

12. John Eager Howard to John Marshall, 1804, Bayard Papers; Morgan to Greene, 19 Jan. 1781, Showman, *Greene Papers*, 7:152–55; Richard Pindell to Otho Holland Williams, 16 Dec. 1816, Pindell, "Militant Surgeon of the Revolution," 316.

13. Berg, *Encyclopedia*, 136; Moss, *Roster of South Carolina Patriots*, 10, 18, 84, 103, 240, 1012; Dennis Tramell, pension, 10 Dec. 1833, M804, Roll 2408. Otho Holland Williams Orderly Book, 17 Sept. 1780, shows Brigadier Generals William Smallwood and Mordecai Gist with personal guard details. A number of men from Frederick County, Virginia, Morgan's home area, may have served him in this fashion. Two other likely candidates are John Moore, personally recruited by Morgan in North Carolina, and a Massachusetts man who served with Morgan at Saratoga. See Moss, *Patriots at the Cowpens*, 58, and John Moore, pension, 15 Aug. 1832, M804, Roll 1756.

14. Seymour, *Journal of the Southern Expedition*, 8, 9, 11; Otho Holland Williams, "Notebook Extract," 23 Jan. 1781, Merritt, *Calendar*, 36, Otho H. Williams, "Narrative of the Campaign of 1780," 390.

15. Nathanael Greene to ?, 14 Nov. 1782, Showman, *Greene Papers*, forthcoming;

Henry Lee, *Memoirs of the War*, 409; Cary Howard, "John Eager Howard"; Read, "John Eager Howard," 277–79; Ward, *Delaware Continentals*, 416–17.

16. Samuel Shaw, "Revolutionary War Letters of Captain Winthrop Sargent," 321; Steuart, *History of the Maryland Line*, 61, 134. These interpretations are based on the two men's known presence at Cowpens, along with their seniority and lack of command. It is possible that either Brookes or Somerville, or both, actually served on Morgan's staff and not on Howard's.

17. Robert E. Lee, *American Revolution in the South*, 185.

18. Anderson, "Journal," 208; William Bivins, pension, 22 Sept. 1834, M804, Roll 249; "Pay Roll of Cap't Robert Kirkwood's Comp'y of Foot in the Delaware Reg't . . . Mar. 1st 1780," Delaware, *Delaware Archives*, 1:117–18, 242; Otho Holland Williams Orderly Book, 1780–81. In Delaware, *Delaware Archives*, 1:117–18, there is a transcription error in which "Infantry" should be "Light Infantry." This interpretation is based on names in the "Return of the Men Killed and Wounded in Capt. Kirkwood's Company at the Cowpens, 17th Jan'ry 1781" (1:254).

19. Robert Downs, pension, 13 July 1818, M804, Roll 847, Draper, *King's Mountain*, 366; John Hackney, pension, 7 Sept. 1819, M804, Roll 1150; Schenk, *North Carolina*, 97; Ward, *Delaware Continentals*, 8, 551. Possibly related to "Blue Hen's Chickens," but it is difficult to know if either nickname was actually used during the war.

20. Delaware, *Delaware Archives*, 1:115–18, 254–56; Moss, *Patriots at the Cowpens*; Riling, *Regulations*, 6–7; Otho Holland Williams Orderly Book, 13, 23, 25, and 29 Sept. 1780.

21. Delaware, *Delaware Archives*, 1:115, 117–18, 254–56; Otho Holland Williams Orderly Book, 16 and 20 Sept. 1780.

22. Steuart, *History of the Maryland Line*, 49–50, 76; Otho Holland Williams Orderly Book.

23. Benjamin Martin, pension, 25 Mar. 1833, M804, Roll 1637; Steuart, *History of the Maryland Line*, 20, 73–74, 79, 130–34; Otho Holland Williams Orderly Book, 16 Dec. 1780.

24. Hall et al., *Muster Rolls*, 388–93; Moss, *Patriots at the Cowpens*, 41, 86; Steuart, *History of the Maryland Line*, 110, 116, 145; Otho Holland Williams Orderly Book, 16 Dec. 1780.

25. Berg, *Encyclopedia*, 131; Abraham Hamman, pension, 13 Nov. 1832, M804, Roll 1174; Heitman, *Historical Register of Officers*, 418–19, 566; John Eager Howard to John Marshall, 1804, Bayard Papers; Sanchez-Saavedra, *Guide to Virginia Militia Organizations*, 180–81; Seymour, *Journal of the Southern Expedition*, 8; Tarleton, *Campaigns of 1780–81*, 29, 83; Joseph B. Turner, *Journal of Captain Robert Kirkwood*, 11; Otho H. Williams, "Narrative of the Campaign of 1780," 506. The best-known composite Virginia unit was commanded by Lieutenant Colonel Abraham Buford when it was attacked by Tarleton's British Legion at Waxhaws, S.C., on 29 May 1780.

26. Berg, *Encyclopedia*, 119–20, 128; Posey, *General Thomas Posey*, 78; Richard Gentry, pension, 12 Sept. 1834, M804, Roll 1061; George Keller, pension, 28 Jan. 1833, M804, Roll 1462; William Knight, pension, 30 Dec. 1833, M804, Roll 1503. Links

between Posey and the pensioners are difficult to establish, but agreement between movements, arrival times, and company officers supports the conclusions made.

27. Henry Connelly, pension, 15 Aug. 1833, M804, Roll 628; Rankin, *North Carolina Continentals*, 248, 255–62. After the battle of Camden, S.C., fourteen N.C. Continentals were placed in the advance force that became the Flying Army. A few recruits came in and their commander, Captain Yarborough, was in Salisbury in January 1781, but they were not sent to join Morgan because they had no shoes.

28. Long, "Statement of Robert Long"; Andrew Pickens et al. to Nathanael Greene, 8 Dec. 1780, Showman, *Greene Papers*, 6:557–58; Samuel Hammond, pension, 31 Oct. 1832, M804, Roll 1176.

29. Logan, *History of the Upper Country*, 2:104.

30. Otho H. Williams, "Narrative of the Campaign of 1780," 483.

31. Jacob Taylor, pension, 18 May 1840, M804, Roll 2347. The quote appears in his 1819 interrogatory statement. For an overview, see Shy, *A People Numerous and Armed*.

32. William L. Shea presents a good overview of southern militia antecedents in his *Virginia Militia in the Seventeenth Century*. For an overview of militia at the start of the war, see Shy, *A People Numerous and Armed*. Call-ups for militia service late in the war tried to distribute duty by classifying men into various groups, each of which was required to provide a certain number of men.

33. Josiah Martin, pension, 3 Oct. 1832, M804, Roll 1640; O'Neall and Chapman, *Annals of Newberry*, 38.

34. Draper, *King's Mountain*, 224; E. Alfred Jones, *Journal of Alexander Chesney*, 22; Josiah Martin, pension, 3 Oct. 1832, M804, Roll 1640; O'Neall and Chapman, *Annals of Newberry*, 37.

35. Salley, *Hill's Memoirs of the Revolution*, 6. Salley's two "colonels" were actually a lieutenant colonel and a colonel. The distinction settled any question of seniority or superior rank.

36. James Martin, pension, 8 Mar. 1832, M804, Roll 1639; William Young, pension, 16 Aug. 1833, M804, Roll 2666. Barber's "Company" was placed under Captain Thomas White at Cowpens.

37. See Papenfuse and Stiverson, "General Smallwood's Recruits," 117–32; Arthur J. Alexander, "How Maryland Tried"; and Diehl, "Rockbridge Men at War," 261–65, 360.

38. James Stewart, pension, 6 Oct. 1832, M804, Roll 2290; Jesse Morris, pension, 27 May 1834, M804, Roll 1771. Stewart's service "was rendered in behalf of John Work who was then a Drafted man for the term of three months."

39. A last class of soldier is difficult to classify. They were neither Continentals nor state troops but could be militia. These men served as "Volunteers." This "volunteer" is different from those Morgan called "Volunteers from Georgia and South Carolina" and might mean they came as individual soldiers. Daniel Morgan to Nathanael Greene, 19 Jan. 1781, Showman, *Greene Papers*, 7:153; Moss, *Patriots at the Cowpens*, 106.

40. Aaron Guyton, pension, 1 Oct. 1833, M804, Roll 1149.

41. John Collins, pension, 29 Sept. 1832, M804, Roll 613; Diehl, "Rockbridge Men at War"; John Irby, pension, 22 Jan. 1833, M804, Roll 1394; Samuel Sexton, pension, 17 Sept. 1833, M804, Roll 2154.

42. William Capps, pension, 27 Mar. 1845, M804, Roll 466; Adam Rainboult, pension, 3 Oct. 1832, M804, Roll 1994.

43. Draper, *King's Mountain*, 227, 244; Benjamin Martin, pension, 25 Mar. 1833, M804, Roll 1637; Dennis Tramell, pension, 10 Dec. 1833, M804, Roll 2408.

44. Martin, pension, 1833; Russell and Gott, *Fauquier County in the Revolution*, 69; Sanchez-Saavedra, *Guide to Virginia Militia Organizations*, 145; Seymour, *Journal of the Southern Expedition*, 9.

45. Jeremiah Preston, pension, 20 Dec. 1843, M804, Roll 1972; John Thomas, pension, 9 Aug. 1832, M804, Roll 2370. Lieutenants in this company were Keith Alexander and William Dearing.

46. Jacob Lemmon, pension, 8 July 1833, M804, Roll 1547. If Lemmon's recollection is correct, this company may have been partially armed with muskets. The Continental Army usually required riflemen to bring their own weapons into service when they were called to duty.

47. Diehl, "Rockbridge Men at War," 262.

48. John McPheeters, pension, 6 Apr. 1833, M804, Roll 1700.

49. Jacob Taylor, pension, 18 May 1849, M804, Roll 2347.

50. Robert E. Lee, *American Revolution in the South*, 227; Moss, *Patriots at the Cowpens*.

51. Ewell's Company of Campbell's Militia "joined General D. Morgan on the field just at the time he had secured his victory at the Cowpens." John Powell, pension, 25 July 1820, M804, Roll 1962. Powell, a member of the First Virginia State Regiment, was sick in the Hillsborough, N.C., hospital. He was sent to Morgan with Campbell's Militia.

52. William L. Davidson to Nathanael Greene, 16 Jan. 1781, and Greene to Daniel Morgan, 8 Jan. 1781, Showman, *Greene Papers*, 7:73, 134.

53. One company was under a captain variously called Robinson, Robertson, or Richardson. This unit can be identified from an arrival time just before the battle began and by the names of other officers. The other company was commanded by a man named Hanley, Handley, Hunley, or Hanson. Men in this second company reported joining Morgan the afternoon of 16 January, before the Flying Army moved to Cowpens. David M. Ellington, pension, 17 Mar. 1834, M804, Roll 911; Drury Ham, pension, 8 Oct. 1833, M804, Roll 1168; William Lilly, pension, 19 Oct. 1833, M804, Roll 1563.

54. See, for example, Schenk, *North Carolina*, 200, 210–11.

55. Bailey, *Commanders at Kings Mountain*, 343–51, 367–68; Hugh McNary, pension, 5 Sept. 1832, M804, Roll 1698; Phifer, *Burke*, 309.

56. Bailey, *Commanders at Kings Mountain*, 358; Phifer, *Burke*, 308–9.

57. Phifer, *Burke*, 308.

58. Richard Crabtree, pension, 2 Aug. 1834, M804, Roll 674; Joseph McPeters, pension, 15 Oct. 1832, M804, Roll 1699; John Wallace, pension, 14 Aug. 1833, M804, Roll 2479. See also Wallace's supplementary statement, 1833. Platoons in this company were under Captain James Alexander and Captain Alexander Erwin.

59. William Capps, pension, 27 Mar. 1845, M804, Roll 466; Adam Rainboult, pension, 3 Oct. 1832, M804, Roll 1994.

60. Jeremiah Files, pension, 4 Feb. 1833, M804, Roll 973; William Lorance, pension, 3 Dec. 1832, M804, Roll 1584. One platoon was probably commanded by Captain William Alexander.

61. Nathaniel Dickison, pension, 23 June 1835, M804, Roll 814; Draper, *King's Mountain*, 173, 175, 184, 332; Thomas Morris, pension, 2 Dec. 1833, M804, Roll 1772; Abraham Potter, pension, 26 Nov. 1833, M804, Roll 1958; Henry Smith, pension, 21 Oct. 1833, M804, Roll 2214. Consolidating these men, platoons were under Captain William Lewis and Captain Joseph Cloud. Captain Henry Smith was under Cloud. Surry County's Captain Bell was wounded at Cowpens; he was likely a "squad" leader, as was Oliver Charles.

62. Draper, *King's Mountain*, 265; Powell, *North Carolina Gazetteer*, 430.

63. Bailey, *Commanders at Kings Mountain*, 195; Josiah Martin, pension, 1 Oct. 1832, M804, Roll 1641; Alexander McLaen, pension, 18 Mar. 1833, M804, Roll 1693; Christopher Waggoner, pension, 27 Oct. 1834, M804, Roll 2468. Platoons were probably under Thomas White and Samuel Martin.

64. Daniel Morgan to Nathanael Greene, 23 Jan. 1781, Showman, *Greene Papers*, 7:178.

65. Henry Lee, *Memoirs of the War*, 594–95; Pickens, *Skyagunsta, the Border Wizard Owl*; Ferguson, "General Andrew Pickens."

66. Ferguson, "General Andrew Pickens," 109–11; Lambert, *South Carolina Loyalists*, 161–62; Long, "Statement of Robert Long," 5; McCrady, *South Carolina in the Revolution, 1780–1783*, 18–23.

67. Moss, *Patriots at the Cowpens*, 122–23; Joseph Johnson, *Traditions and Reminiscences*, 353–60; George White, *Historical Collections of Georgia*, 219–21.

68. Draper, *King's Mountain*, 193, 269, 470; Saye, *Memoirs of Major Joseph McJunkin*, 26.

69. Moss, *Patriots at the Cowpens*, 185, 234.

70. Solomon Abbott, pension, 1 Oct. 1835, M804, Roll 4; James Harden, pension, 21 Aug. 1832, M804, Roll 1186; Moss, *Patriots at the Cowpens*, 246 (entry for Benjamin West); Henry Pettit, pension, 24 Oct. 1832, M804, Roll 1920; Hugh Warren, pension, 16 June 1834, M804, Roll 2497. Tramell led his company with platoons under Lawson and Coulter. Some name Dickson and Coulter as lieutenants, Lawson and Dickson as captains.

71. Draper, *King's Mountain*, 74; Saye, *Memoirs of Major Joseph McJunkin*, 36.

72. James Collins, pension, 8 Apr. 1832, M804, Roll 613. A close reading of his pension suggests Collins called up the men of his company who were not already in the field on 16 January. This implies that his company was larger than twenty-four men at Cowpens.

73. Moss, *Roster of South Carolina Patriots*, 50. John Barry, his brother, apparently alternated command of this company because each served as a private under the other at different times.

74. Adam J. Files, pension, 3 Feb. 1834, M804, Roll 973; Jeremiah J. Files, pension, 4 Feb. 1833, M804, Roll 973; Moss, *Roster of South Carolina Patriots*, 305, 311–12.

75. Carroll, "Random Recollections," 43; Draper, *King's Mountain*, 467–68; Moss, *Patriots at the Cowpens*, 69; Samuel Park, pension, 14 Apr. 1834, M804, Roll 1869.

76. Draper, *King's Mountain*, 468; Robert Long, pension, 7 Oct. 1832, M804, Roll 1581. One platoon was commanded by James Dillard of Ninety Six District.

77. Moss, *Patriots at the Cowpens*, 200–201; Moss, *Roster of South Carolina Patriots*, 421. John Ridgeway was a platoon leader in Harris's company.

78. Moss, *Patriots at the Cowpens*, 69; O'Neall and Chapman, *Annals of Newberry*, 506.

79. John Irby, pension, 22 Jan. 1833, M804, Roll 1394; Samuel Sexton, pension, 17 Sept. 1833, M804, Roll 2154. As newly elected junior officers with new companies, Sexton and Irby had no seniority and were probably placed on the left flank of Hayes's Battalion.

80. Draper, *King's Mountain*, 74, 469; Joshua Palmer, pension, 3 Oct. 1832, M804, Roll 1865; see also Thomas Young's 12 June 1833 supporting statement in Palmer's pension file; Saye, *Memoirs of Major Joseph McJunkin*, 2.

81. O'Neall and Chapman, *Annals of Newberry*, 38; Saye, *Memoirs of Major Joseph McJunkin*, 33.

82. Moss, *Roster of South Carolina Patriots*, 20–21, 31–32, 379, 472, 690, 693, 744, 927.

83. Samuel Caldwell, pension, 30 Oct. 1832, M804, Roll 449; James Carlisle, pension, 28 Oct. 1835, M804, Roll 470; Draper, *King's Mountain*, 132, 285, 468; Aaron Guyton, pension, 1 Oct. 1833, M804, Roll 1149; Moss, *Roster of South Carolina Patriots*, 20–21, 94–95, 379, 692–93. Captains Samuel Caldwell and Francis Carlisle were Montgomery's platoon leaders. Grant's son, William Jr., was a lieutenant in his company. Lieutenant Joseph Hughes, an experienced combat veteran, commanded a company at Cowpens because Captain Benjamin Jolly volunteered for the cavalry. Hughes's "company" may have been a platoon under Captain William Grant since Hughes was a lieutenant and they both came from Pinckney-ville, S.C. In a typical company rotation, Grant may have led the duty, and the nonduty, halves of the company. In that case, Hughes led Jolly's company, as a platoon under Grant.

84. Draper, *King's Mountain*, 465; Moss, *Patriots at the Cowpens*, 1. He probably commanded a "company" of Fairfield County men with James Adair as their platoon leader.

85. Draper, *King's Mountain*, 285; Samuel Otterson, pension, 20 Sept. 1832, M804, Roll 1853.

86. James Jackson to Daniel Morgan, 20 Jan. 1795, Myers, *Cowpens Papers*, 45–46; M'Call, *History of Georgia*, 505.

87. He is not the same George Walton who signed the Declaration of Independence and served as governor of Georgia. That George Walton was in Philadelphia in December 1780 and January 1781. Charles C. Jones, *Biographic Sketches*, 186.

88. Davis, *Georgia Citizens and Soldiers*, 159, 163, 215.

89. A Georgian, Donnolly, remains unidentified but probably was a skirmisher with other Georgians. It is possible he took Hammond's Georgia company when Hammond was promoted. M'Call notes a "captain Beale's company of Georgia militia" on the main line, but Georgia units were all skirmishers. Jackson is particular about Georgians and makes no mention of Beale or Beatty. It is likely that Beale is William Beal of Ninety Six, S.C., who later moved to Georgia. If so, Beal belongs in the South Carolina State Troops under Joseph Pickens as a platoon

leader. See Samuel Hammond's "Account of the Battle of the Cowpens," and Hammond, "Notes," in Joseph Johnson, *Traditions and Reminiscences*, 526–30 (esp. p. 528); James Jackson to Daniel Morgan, 20 Jan. 1795, Myers, *Cowpens Papers*, 46; Logan, *History of the Upper Country*, 2:51–53; Robert Long, supporting statement, 10 May 1833, for Samuel Hammond, pension, 31 Oct. 1832, M804, Roll 1176; and M'Call, *History of Georgia*, 506. Beale/Beatty as a possible North Carolinian is discussed below.

90. Robert E. Lee, *American Revolution in the South*, 399–402.

91. Ibid., 400.

92. Griffin Fauntleroy to Nathanael Greene, 7 Jan. 1781, Showman, *Greene Papers*, 7:71.

93. Berg, *Encyclopedia*, 29–30; Thomas Gibson, pension, 25 Apr. 1822, M804, Roll 1067; Richard Porterfield, pension, 10 July 1820, M804, Roll 1956.

94. Moss, *Patriots at the Cowpens*, 172, reports three Murphey brothers, former Delaware Continentals "incorporated" in the Continental dragoons.

95. Berg, *Encyclopedia*, 28; James Martin, pension, 8 Mar. 1832, M804, Roll 1639.

96. Nathanael Greene to Thomas Jefferson, 14 Dec. 1780, and Greene to Clement Read, 14 Dec. 1780, Showman, *Greene Papers*, 6:573, 576; Edmund Keeling, pension, 14 Apr. 1834, M804, Roll 1459. Keeling served under Captain Edmund Reid and was wounded at Cowpens. North Carolinian William Rodgers claimed service under Captain John Reid, pension, 20 July 1827, M804, Roll 2074.

97. William Kerr, pension, 21 Feb. 1835, M804, Roll 1476; James Riggs, pension, 5 Aug. 1834, M804, Roll 2047; Peter Roberts, pension, 31 Mar. 1835, M804, Roll 2059; John Thompson, pension, 11 Oct. 1855, M804, Roll 2376 (rejected claim). These Cowpens men stand out because they specify longer-than-usual militia service, held cavalry ranks such as "coronet," or served under officers not assigned to William Washington, yet claimed Washington as a commander instead of being militia.

98. Samuel Hammond, pension, 31 Oct. 1832, M804, Roll 1176. Hammond stated South Carolina State Troops assigned to Washington were those with swords and pistols. Those without were skirmishers. McCall's men are different from forty-five "militia volunteers" equipped with swords the night before Cowpens.

99. Ibid.; Moss, *Roster of South Carolina Patriots*, 227, 586.

100. McCall joined Morgan after Kings Mountain. See John Harris, pension, 5 Mar. 1833, M804, Roll 1200, supplementary statement; Manuel McConnell, pension, 18 Sept. 1832, M804, Roll 1670. In his pension, 20 Oct. 1837, M804, Roll 1129, Georgian George Gresham specified that his commander at Cowpens was Major McCall, indicating he and his "company" were part of the South Carolina State Troops.

101. William Venable, pension, 8 Oct. 1832, M804, Roll 2456; Young, "Memoir," 84–88, 100–105. Those equipped with swords the night before the battle affect Washington's total strength. McCall's South Carolina State Troops with sabers served with Washington, as cavalry, after joining in early January. "Volunteer" dragoon militiamen on the night of 16–17 January included some with sabers; those without received the forty-five sabers issued by Morgan. Morgan earlier requested one hundred swords from Greene; he issued all he had. Samuel Hammond, pension, 31 Oct. 1832, M804, Roll 1176; Daniel Morgan to Nathanael Greene, 31 Dec. 1780,

Showman, *Greene Papers*, 7:30–31. The cavalrymen, McCall with 25, at least 45 militia volunteers, and perhaps 30 state troops from North Carolina and Virginia, more than doubled Washington's strength of 82 men noted by James Martin, pension, 8 Mar. 1832, M804, Roll 1639. At a minimum, Washington had 150 men and may have led as many as 200.

102. Bass, *Green Dragoon*, 11–12.

103. Ibid., 12–14; Raddall, "Tarleton's Legion," 4.

104. Bass, *Green Dragoon*, 15–18.

105. Ibid., 19, 46–47.

106. Ibid., 11, 47–49; Katcher, *Encyclopedia*, 83–84. A company that became part of the British Legion was the Caledonian Volunteers; another was possibly the Bucks County Dragoons under Captain Christian Huck.

107. Michael Dougherty, "Soldier of Fortune," in Ward, *Delaware Continentals*, 538; Henry Lee, *Memoirs of the War*, 154, 164–66, 170; Raddall, "Tarleton's Legion," 3, 14.

108. Garden, *Anecdotes of the American Revolution*, 284, 287–88; Raddall, "Tarleton's Legion," 2, 9, 12.

109. Katcher, *Encyclopedia*, 31–32.

110. Army, *List of All the Officers of the Army*, 75; "State of the Troops," in Reese, *Cornwallis Papers*, 221; Ford, *British Officers*, 136; Groves, *Historical Records of the 7th or Royal Regiment of Fusiliers*, 91–92, 95; MacKenzie, *Strictures on Lt. Col. Tarleton's History*, 88, 110; Tarleton, *Campaigns of 1780–81*, 212; Wheater, *Historical Record of the Seventh or Royal Regiment of Fusiliers*, 76.

111. Army, *List of All the Officers of the Army*, 146; Fetter, "Who Were the Foreign Mercenaries?," 508–13; Katcher, *Encyclopedia*, 67–68.

112. Campbell, *Expedition against the Rebels of Georgia*; Katcher, *Encyclopedia*, 67–69; MacKenzie, *Strictures on Lt. Col. Tarleton's History*, 111.

113. "State of the Troops," in Reese, *Cornwallis Papers*, 221; Samuel Graham, "An English Officer's Account," 241–49, 267–73, 241; MacKenzie, *Strictures on Lt. Col. Tarleton's History*, 111.

114. Katcher, *Encyclopedia*, 13–14.

115. Clark, *Loyalists in the Southern Campaign*, 1:242–43; MacKenzie, *Strictures on Lt. Col. Tarleton's History*, 117.

116. Army, *List of All the Officers of the Army*, 86; Clark, *Loyalists in the Southern Campaign*, 1:242–43; "State of the Troops," in Reese, *Cornwallis Papers*, 221; Katcher, *Encyclopedia*, 35; MacKenzie, *Strictures on Lt. Col. Tarleton's History*, 113. The officer commanding the 16th may have been Colin Graham but he does not appear in any list of prisoners.

117. Katcher, *Encyclopedia*, 84; Raddall, "Tarleton's Legion," 6.

118. Clark, *Loyalists in the Southern Campaign*, 2:214–16; Hanger, *Address to the Army*, 92–93n; Katcher, *Encyclopedia*, 83; Lambert, *South Carolina Loyalists*, 149; Hall et al., *Muster Rolls*, 578, 583–84; Raddall, "Tarleton's Legion," 6, 16–17.

119. Tarleton, *Campaigns of 1780–81*.

120. "State of the Troops," in Reese, *Cornwallis Papers*, 221; Clark, *Loyalists in the Southern Campaign*, 2:197–250. The British Legion infantry at Cowpens is usually considered to have had about 200–250 men, but returns for the 25 December 1780

muster show only 175. Totals obtained by Cornwallis, dated 15 January, show that the whole legion had 451 men, but approximately 250 were dragoons.

121. Army, *List of All the Officers of the Army*, 53; Fortescue, *History of the 17th Lancers*, 33, 58; Mackenzie, *Strictures on Lt. Col. Tarleton's History*, 113.

122. Fortescue, *History of the 17th Lancers*, 50, 53–55.

123. Ibid., 56–57; Tarleton, *Campaigns of 1780–81*, 184, 212, 216.

124. Army, *List of All the Officers of the Army*, 53; Clark, *Loyalists in the Southern Campaign*, 2:227; Fortescue, *History of the 17th Lancers*, 63.

125. Fortescue, *History of the 17th Lancers*, 63.

126. Raddall, "Tarleton's Legion," 6.

127. Caruana, *Grasshoppers and Butterflies*, 22, 25; Tarleton, *Campaigns of 1780–81*, 210.

128. William Johnson, *Sketches of Nathanael Greene*, 1:384–85; E. Alfred Jones, *Journal of Alexander Chesney*, 20–22. These militiamen are probably the "mounted infantry" Tarleton mentioned as bringing up the rear during his approach march. Tarleton, *Campaigns of 1780–81*, 215.

CHAPTER THREE

1. Greene instructed Morgan to "Employ [this force] against the enemy . . . either offensively or defensively as your own prudence and discretion may direct, acting with caution, and avoiding surprizes." Nathanael Greene to Daniel Morgan, 16 Dec. 1780, Showman, *Greene Papers*, 6:589–90. Cornwallis ordered Tarleton that, "if Morgan is . . . any where within your reach, I should wish you to push him to the utmost." Cornwallis to Tarleton, 2 Jan. 1781, Tarleton, *Campaigns of 1780–81*, 244–45.

2. Anderson, "Journal," 209; James Cook, "Map of the Province of South Carolina," n.p., London, 1773; Henry Mouzon, "An Accurate Map of North and South Carolina," N.C. Department of Cultural Resources; Long, "Statement of Robert Long"; Mills, *Atlas*; Seymour, *Journal of the Southern Expedition*, 11–13.

3. Bailey, *History of Grindal Shoals*, 19, 21; E. Alfred Jones, *Journal of Alexander Chesney*, 21–22, 128–29; Benjamin Martin, pension, 25 Mar. 1833, M804, Roll 1637.

4. Bailey, *History of Grindal Shoals*, 19; Long, "Statement of Robert Long," 5; Daniel Morgan to Nathanael Greene, 31 Dec. 1780 and 4 and 15 Jan. 1781, Showman, *Greene Papers*, 7:30–31, 50–51, 127–29.

5. Tarleton, *Campaigns of 1780–81*, 12, 184, 210–11.

6. Lord Cornwallis to Banastre Tarleton, 2 Jan. 1781, ibid., 211, 244–45; Fortescue, *History of the 17th Lancers*, 56–57; O'Neall and Chapman, *Annals of Newberry*, 37.

7. Banastre Tarleton to Lord Cornwallis, 4 Jan. 1781, Tarleton, *Campaigns of 1780–81*, 246.

8. Ibid.

9. Long, "Statement of Robert Long," 5.

10. Bailey, *Commanders at Kings Mountain*, 400; Draper, *King's Mountain*, 76; Long, "Statement of Robert Long," 5; Mills, *Atlas*.

11. Carroll, "Random Recollections," 40–47, 97–107 (esp. 45); O'Neall and Chapman, *Annals of Newberry*, 37; William Johnson, *Sketches of Nathanael Greene*, 2:385; E. Alfred Jones, *Journal of Alexander Chesney*, 21; McCrady, *History of South Carolina in the Revolution, 1780–1783*, 28; Tarleton, *Campaigns of 1780–81*, 212. The

11 January campsite is called "Tarleton's Tea Tables" by residents. Jonathan Hart, personal communication, 30 Mar. 1992; Newberry-Saluda Regional Library, personal communication, 7 Apr. 1992.

12. Feaster, *History of Union County*, 27–28; Samuel Hand, pension, 6 Oct. 1832, M804, Roll 1179; Long, "Statement of Robert Long," 5; Joseph McJunkin, pension, 25 Dec. 1833, M804, Roll 1688; Samuel Thompson, pension, 27 Aug. 1833, M804, Roll 2378.

13. Mills, *Atlas*; O'Neall and Chapman, *Annals of Newberry*, 37; Tarleton, *Campaigns of 1780–81*, 213.

14. Tarleton, *Campaigns of 1780–81*, 177–79.

15. Anderson, "Journal," 209; Landrum, *Upper South Carolina*, 242; Mills, *Atlas*; Seymour, *Journal of the Southern Expedition*, 13; Young, "Memoir," 84–88, 100–105.

16. Tarleton's route approximates modern-day Route 9, which crosses northern South Carolina and connects county-seat towns.

17. James Alexander, pension, 9 Oct. 1832, M804, Roll 28; Samuel Hand, pension, 6 Oct. 1832, M804, Roll 1179; Long, "Statement of Robert Long," 5; David Morton, pension, 9 Oct. 1832, M804, Roll 1778, supplementary statement, 23 Sept. 1834; Samuel Park, pension, 14 Apr. 1834, M804, Roll 1869, supplementary statement, 26 Aug. 1834.

18. Samuel Moore, pension, 11 Oct. 1832, M804, Roll 1759.

19. Aaron Guyton, pension, 1 Oct. 1833, M804, Roll 1149; Samuel Shaw, "Revolutionary War Letters to Captain Winthrop Sargent," 281–324 (esp. p. 320).

20. Draper, *King's Mountain*, 94; Pugh, "Cowpens Campaign and the American Revolution," 219; Tarleton, *Campaigns of 1780–81*, 213.

21. Landrum, *Upper South Carolina*, 272; MacKenzie, *Strictures on Lt. Col. Tarleton's History*, 96; Mills, *Atlas;* Tarleton, *Campaigns of 1780–81*, 213.

22. Josiah Martin, pension, 1 Oct. 1832, M804, Roll 1641.

23. James Dillard, supporting statement, 15 May 1833, in Samuel Hammond, pension, 31 Oct. 1832, M804, Roll 1176.

24. Three of Captain Kinlock's British Legion dragoons were noted as "taken 14 Jan 1781" or "deserted 14 Jan 1781." Kinlock commanded Tarleton's headquarters troop. The men Gresham captured may have been a patrol screening Tarleton's advance. Clark, *Loyalists in the Southern Campaign*, 2:213; George Gresham, pension, 20 Oct. 1837, M804, Roll 1129.

25. E. Alfred Jones, *Journal of Alexander Chesney*, 21–22; Tarleton, *Campaigns of 1780–81*, 213–14. Tarleton's men may have eaten their last rations on 15 January. Their growing food crisis seems confirmed by Tarleton sending Chesney to have local mills grind for the army.

26. Tarleton, *Campaigns of 1780–81*, 214. Tarleton's use of "Thickelle" Creek indicates he was using the Mouzon Map, the only contemporary map where this term appears. For contemporary maps, see John Collet's *Compleat Map of North-Carolina* and Henry Mouzon's *Accurate Map of North and South Carolina*, both in the N.C. State Archives, Department of Cultural Resources, Raleigh.

27. Dennis Tramell, pension, 10 Dec. 1833, M804, Roll 2408.

28. James Graham, *Life of General Daniel Morgan*, 290; M'Call *History of Georgia*, 505; Samuel Park, pension, 14 Apr. 1834, M804, Roll 1869; Seymour, *Journal of the*

Southern Expedition, 13. Seymour identifies militia accompanying the Continentals as McCall's South Carolina State Regiment (about 90 men) and three Georgia companies under Major James Jackson (about 55 men). The remainder were Hayes's Little River Battalion not on rear guard. McDowell's North Carolinians had not yet rejoined; they left Burr's Mill about noon. Pickens arrived some time after 9:00 P.M. and brought in about 150 men from the "north side of Broad River."

29. James Braden, pension, 1 July 1839, M804, Roll 314; William Lilly, pension, 19 Oct. 1833, M804, Roll 1563; Christian Peters, pension, 19 Sept. 1832, M804, Roll 1917; John Eager Howard, "Account of the Battle of Cowpens," in Robert E. Lee, *American Revolution in the South*, 226.

30. Dennis Tramell, pension, 10 Dec. 1833, M804, Roll 2408; Rockwell, "Battle of Cow-pens," 356–59; Samuel C. Williams, "General Richard Winn's Notes," 9.

31. Saye, *Memoirs of Major Joseph McJunkin*, 32–33; Young, "Memoir," 88. The quotes are from Young. Saye should be used with great caution as he embellished McJunkin's pension account.

32. Robert E. Lee, *American Revolution in the South*, 226; Daniel Morgan to William Snickers, Jan. 23, 1781, Horatio Gates Papers.

33. John Marshall, *Life of George Washington*, 303–4.

34. Rockwell, "Battle of Cow-pens," 356. Rockwell stated that he had this information from "a gentleman who has often heard the facts given stated by those who had been eye-witnesses and actors in what they described."

35. Joseph Johnson, *Traditions and Reminiscences*, 526–27; Benjamin Martin, pension, 25 Mar. 1833, M804, Roll 1637. Johnson cites from Samuel Hammond's "Notes" and provides an introduction to the order. "To show those concerned what would be their stations, the author drew out a rough sketch of the disposition set forth in the general order." As Hammond recalled them, his own orders concerned only the troops who would form the skirmish line. Hammond provided little information about the Virginians, Continentals, and cavalry. Hammond's notes reflect the situation about 9:00 P.M. on 16 January, before final plans were worked up and a decision to engage at the Cowpens was made. The quote about camping ready for battle is from Martin.

36. Draper, *King's Mountain*, 270; Long, "Statement of Robert Long," 6. The sign and countersign may be an error in recollection, as they were also used at Kings Mountain.

37. Henry Wells, pension, 29 Jan. 1834, M804, Roll 2529.

38. William Jewell, pension, 28 Aug. 1832, M804, Roll 1415; William Shaw, pension, 12 Sept. 1818, M804, Roll 2161.

39. John Eager Howard, "Account of the Battle of Cowpens," in Robert E. Lee, *American Revolution in the South*, 96; Young, "Memoir," 88. The first quote is Howard's; the second Young's.

40. Bartholomees, "Fight or Flee," 130–33.

41. Moss, *Patriots at the Cowpens*, 141, 236. It may be a well-worn cliché that an army travels on its stomach, but contrasting British and American performances at Cowpens, Guilford Courthouse, Hobkirk's Hill, and Eutaw Springs show it is correct. In all four cases, Americans were fed before fighting and the British were not. It would not have taken many beeves to feed the men in the Flying Army.

Twenty beeves, each providing 300 pounds of meat, or 60 hogs, providing 100 pounds each, would be enough to give 2,000 men three pounds of meat each.

42. Samuel Hammond, "Notes," in Joseph Johnson, *Traditions and Reminiscences*, 527.
43. See Von Steuben's instructions on ammunition; Riling, *Regulations*, 117–21. Riling reprinted Von Stueben's regulations drawn up during the Valley Forge encampment in 1778. This is an ideal supported by orderly books with references to maintaining forty rounds as well as three flints per man.
44. E. Alfred Jones, *Journal of Alexander Chesney*, 21–22.
45. Tarleton, *Campaigns of 1780–81*, 214. Given the timeframe, these may have been Pickens's men coming from north of the Broad River. It is possible they were North Carolina militia from northwest of Cowpens. Since they were from Green River, it is unlikely the report refers to David Campbell's Virginia militiamen, who reached Morgan just as fighting began.
46. MacKenzie, *Strictures on Lt. Col. Tarleton's History*, 96; Charles Stedman, *American War*, 320; Tarleton, *Campaigns of 1780–81*, 214.
47. Tarleton, *Campaigns of 1780–81*, 214–15.
48. MacKenzie, *Strictures on Lt. Col. Tarleton's History*, 97; Stedman, *American War*, 320; Tarleton, *Campaigns of 1780–81*, 214–15.
49. Henry Lee, *Memoirs of the War*, 253; Long, "Statement of Robert Long," 5–6; MacKenzie, *Strictures on Lt. Col. Tarleton's History*, 85; Stedman, *American War*, 320.
50. Tarleton, *Campaigns of 1780–81*, 215. The dragoons were probably Hovenden's British Legion troop because their "quartermaster Wade" captured Sergeant Everheart of the Third Continental Light Dragoons in a running clash 3 to 5 miles from the battlefield.
51. The British infantry followed a route cleared of ambushes and obstructions by the advance party which left at 2:00 A.M. If they moved at a pace of 2.5 miles per hour (one mile every 24 minutes), they reached Macedonia Creek by 6:00 A.M. This is only 5 miles from Cowpens, and, given the difficulty of the march, the rate is fairly quick.
52. Rockwell, "Battle of Cow-pens," 358.
53. Daniel Morgan to Nathanael Greene, 19 Jan. 1781, Showman, *Greene Papers*, 7:152–55.
54. Tarleton, *Campaigns of 1780–81*, 215. Today, technical distinctions are made between first light and sunrise. First light occurs when the sky starts to lighten and is called Beginning Morning Nautical Twilight. Sunrise is about a half hour later when the sun actually comes up.
55. Anderson, "Journal," 209; Collins, *Autobiography*, 56; Seymour, *Journal of the Southern Expedition*, 13. Others reporting rapid deployment include militiamen William Neel, pension, 29 Oct. 1832, M804, Roll 1804, and Christian Peters, pension, 19 Sept. 1832, M804, Roll 1917.
56. James Simons to William Washington, 3 Nov. 1803, Balch, *Papers*, 45–47; Young, "Memoir," 88.
57. Joseph Johnson, *Traditions and Reminiscences*, 529; James Jackson to Daniel Morgan, 20 Jan. 1795, Myers, *Cowpens Papers*, 45–46. Moss, *Patriots at the Cowpens*, 122; Saye, *Memoirs of Major Joseph McJunkin*, 33.

58. Tarleton, *Campaigns of 1780–81*, 215; Young, "Memoir," 88, 102.

59. James Simons to William Washington, 3 Nov. 1803, Balch, *Papers*, 45–47.

60. Balch, *Papers*, 47–48; Lawrence Everheart, pension, 7 Apr. 1834; Simons to Washington, 3 Nov. 1803, ibid.; Tarleton, *Campaigns of 1780–81*, 103. The distance given in Everheart's pension shows that Tarleton was near the old American vidette location when the interview took place.

61. MacKenzie, *Strictures on Lt. Col. Tarleton's History*, 97; Stedman, *American War*, 320; Tarleton, *Campaigns of 1780–81*, 215. The two videttes were Everheart and Deshasure.

62. Lawrence Everheart, pension, 7 Apr. 1834.

63. MacKenzie, *Strictures on Lt. Col. Tarleton's History*, 96–97; Tarleton, *Campaigns of 1780–81*, 215.

64. Carroll, "Random Recollections," 100.

65. Robert E. Lee, *American Revolution in the South*, 226; McCall, *History of Georgia*, 507. MacKenzie implies there was more light when the British arrived than American accounts do. The difference may be because Americans marked the British arrival when the horsemen appeared rather than when MacKenzie arrived thirty minutes later with the light infantry.

66. Christian Peters, pension, 19 Sept. 1832, M804, Roll 1917.

67. William Johnson, *Sketches of Nathanael Greene*, 1:372; Henry Lee, *Memoirs of the War*, 255; Saye, *Memoirs of Major Joseph McJunkin*, 33.

68. Saye, *Memoirs of Major Joseph McJunkin*, 33.

CHAPTER FOUR

1. Uzal Johnson, "Manuscript Diary Kept by a Loyalist Military Surgeon," Princeton University Library, Princeton, N.J. See pages 69–71 for description of halt at "Buck Creek" on 6 September 1780. A similar entry can be found in the "Diary of Lieut. Anthony Allaire of Ferguson's Corps," in Draper, *King's Mountain*, 506–7. Earlier American camps at Cowpens occurred during the pursuit of Ferguson in early October 1780. See Draper, *King's Mountain*, 222–23.

2. Spartanburg County road standards were not set until 1825, when roads were to be "at least 18 feet wide." Commissions of the Roads Journal, Spartanburg District, 1825–1840, S.C. Department of Archives and History, Columbia, cited in Bearss, *Historic Grounds and Resource Study*, 107.

3. Draper, *King's Mountain*, 222–23; Robert S. Hoskins, pension, 15 May 1835, M804, Roll 1331.

4. Dennis Tramell, pension, 10 Dec. 1833, M804, Roll 2408. Little Buck Creek is the old name of modern-day Cudd's Creek.

5. Bearss, *Historic Grounds and Resource Study*, 195; Perry, "Revolutionary Incidents, Number 7, The Cowpens," Benjamin Franklin Perry Papers, University of North Carolina, Chapel Hill. The veteran who accompanied Perry was probably Captain Thomas Farrow.

6. Hammond, "Notes," in Joseph Johnson, *Traditions and Reminiscences*, 526; George Wilson, pension, 19 Nov. 1832, M804, Roll 2605.

7. James McCroskey, pension, 20 Aug. 1832, M804, Roll 1673; William Seymour,

Journal of the Southern Expedition, 13; Samuel C. Williams, "General Richard Winn's Notes," 9.

8. Landrum, *Upper South Carolina*, 276–77.

9. E. Alfred Jones, *Journal of Alexander Chesney*, 22.

10. Perry, "Revolutionary Incidents No. 7, The Cowpens," Perry Papers; Young, "Memoir," 84–88, 100–105.

11. Young, "Memoir," 100.

12. *Gaffney Ledger*, 3 Mar. 1898, cited in Bearss, *Historic Grounds and Resource Study*, 146.

13. William Gordon, *Independence of the United States of America*, 4:34; O'Neall, "Revolutionary Incidents," 38; MacKenzie, *Strictures on Lt. Col. Tarleton's History*, 97; Young, "Memoir," 100.

14. *Gaffney Ledger*, 3 Mar. 1898, cited in Bearss, *Historic Grounds and Resource Study*, 146.

15. This observation received little credibility because it dated from 1898. However, Benjamin F. Perry toured the battlefield circa 1834 with Captain Farrow and "had the pleasure of spending a night with this worthy and venerable soldier. . . . The order & position of the American Army in the battle of the Cowpens was related with a particularity which was really remarkable." Perry "also had . . . the entire Battle Ground pointed out to him by one of the few surviving gallant officers who commanded in the Battle. . . . Gen. Morgan drew up his little army on a slight ridge, *extending from the head of one of these spring branches to the other*. The road . . . passes immediately between these two branches; which at that time, were *pretty well lined with cane & small reeds* [emphasis added]." A similar statement was published in 1843 when J. B. O'Neall wrote of "the ground between the two reedy branches the heads of Suck Creek." The presence of cane can also be deduced from the name "Cowpens," as well. Agricultural historians have long known the importance of cane as winter cattle forage in backcountry South Carolina. By 1802, overgrazing reduced the cane stands. Perry, Revolutionary Incidents No. 7, "The Cowpens," and No. 10, Benjamin Franklin Perry Papers, University of North Carolina, Chapel Hill; Anonymous, "Revolutionary Incidents—The Cowpens," *Magnolia* 1 (1842), 42 (this article may have been written by Perry); O'Neall, "Revolutionary Incidents," 38; Dunbar, "Colonial Carolina Cowpens," 126–27.

16. As will be shown, the actual militia position was about 40 to 50 yards north and downslope from the crest.

17. This term was not used by participants. During maneuvering before infantry fighting commenced, Joseph Hayes moved his Little River battalion to this point, halfway between the militia line and the skirmishers.

18. "Pigree Map," National Archives.

19. William Johnson, *Sketches of Nathanael Greene*, 1:377. The southern edge of the swale is shown on the Pigree Map as a series of lines, or hatching, where the Continentals were posted. It appears on the Hammond Map as a "Valley or ravine"; Joseph Johnson, *Traditions and Reminiscences*, 529. Both maps will be discussed in detail during identification of the American positions.

20. Hardwoods do not grow well in wet soil of the type in the swale. See Bishop et al., *Soil Survey of Cherokee County*, 1–14, 27, 64.

21. The "clump of pines" and the "slope" were first brought to my attention in 1988 by Kenneth R. Haynes of Reidsville, N.C. Both terms were used in Christopher Brandon's "Account" in Draper, *King's Mountain*, 285–86.

22. Henry Connelly, pension, 1 Aug. 1833, M804, Roll 627. Connelly's initial position on the main-line right flank indicates horses were tied east of Morgan Hill about 175 yards northeast of Marker no. 9. In this area, the ground rises north and west, creating a slope north of Suck Creek no. 2. Soil conditions in this area tend to suggest that pines, rather than hardwoods, were the typical growth. See Bishop et al., *Soil Survey of Cherokee County*, 1–14, 27, 64.

23. Anderson, "Journal," 209; Hanger, *Address to the Army*, 104; E. Alfred Jones, *Journal of Alexander Chesney*, 21; James Kelly, pension, 28 Apr. 1835, M804, Roll 1466; Josiah Martin, pension, 2 Oct. 1832, M804, Roll 1641; John R. Shaw, *Narrative*, 54; John Thomas, pension, 9 Aug. 1832, M804, Roll 2370. The quote is from Hanger.

24. James I. Kochan, then a staff member at Morristown National Historical Park, located two maps in the quartermaster general's documents in the National Archives. His recognition of the battle of Cowpens on a document otherwise associated with New York is comment enough on his knowledge of the Revolutionary War.

    The Cowpens maps, their associated texts, and other accounts are often confusing in their use of right and left. Does the person, mean *his* left, or *military* left? That is, does the term *left* mean as the observer sees it from where he is facing, or from the perspective of a military man talking about the flank of a unit? At Cowpens, the British right and American left were east of the Green River Road; the British left and American right were west of the road. The orientation has obvious implications and will be discussed as appropriate.

25. Hammond, "Notes," 526, in Joseph Johnson, *Traditions and Reminiscences*, 526–30.

26. Ibid., 528. These locations agree with Perry, "Revolutionary Incidents No. 7, The Cowpens," Perry Papers, and George Wilson, pension, 19 Nov. 1832, M804, Roll 2605.

27. The "Clove Map" and the "Pigree Map" are in the National Archives. Both maps follow Morgan's report closely in showing the American positions. It is possible these were drawn by Major Edward Giles, as the handwriting on both maps is quite similar to that in letters written by Giles and he went north to carry the news of the victory to Philadelphia and General Washington.

28. Morgan detailed the distinction in his 23 Jan. 1781 letter to William Snickers, Horatio Gates Papers. The same distinction was made by Nathanael Greene in orders issued before the battle of Eutaw Springs, 8 Sept. 1781. See Showman, *Greene Papers*, 9:302, 305.

29. John Collins, pension, 8 Apr. 1832, M804, Roll 613; James Henry, pension, 10 Dec. 1832, M804, Roll 1252; John Eager Howard to John Marshall, 1804, Bayard Papers; Long, "Statement of Robert Long," 6; John Powell, pension, 25 July 1820, M804, Roll 1962; Samuel Sexton, pension, 17 Sept. 1833, M804, Roll 2154; William Slone,

pension, 9 Feb. 1835, M804, Roll 2200; Augustin Webb, pension, 15 Oct. 1832, M804, Roll 2514.

30. James Jackson to Daniel Morgan, 20 Jan. 1795, Myers, *Cowpens Papers*, 46; Young, "Memoir," 88. The videttes were stationed near modern-day Daniel Morgan School, where several routes from Union County converge before passing through the Cowpens crossroads as the Green River Road.

31. This is suggested by William Johnson, who reported they had been told to fight in groups of three with two reserving their fire. William Johnson, *Sketches of Nathanael Greene*, 1:378.

32. Samuel Hammond, pension, 31 Oct. 1832; Hammond, "Notes," in Joseph Johnson, *Traditions and Reminiscences*, 528; Daniel Morgan to Nathanael Greene, 19 Jan. 1781, Showman, *Greene Papers*, 7:152–55.

33. Richard Crabtree, pension, 2 Aug. 1834, M804, Roll 674.

34. Admittedly, this alignment is subjective. Casualties to the Surry/Wilkes and Burke men show they were on the right. The other three North Carolina companies were closer to the road. Specific references to alignment have not been confirmed, but comments and asides in pension documents tend to support this interpretation.

35. Hammond, "Account of the Battle of Cowpens," in Joseph Johnson, *Traditions and Reminiscences*, 526–30 (see esp. 528); James Jackson to Daniel Morgan, 20 Jan. 1795, Myers, *Cowpens Papers*, 46; Robert Long, 10 May 1833, supporting statement for Samuel Hammond, pension, 31 Oct. 1832, M804, Roll 1176. Beale/Beatty as a North Carolinian is discussed below.

36. Long, "Statement of Robert Long," 6. Locating McDowell to their front shows Hayes's Battalion extended beyond both sides of the Green River Road. Locating Triplett in their rear is correct since the Virginia militia had their right flank in the road.

37. A reverse slope defense places defenders behind the military crest.

38. Daniel Morgan to Nathanael Greene, 19 Jan. 1781, Showman, *Greene Papers*, 7:152–55.

39. Young, "Memoir," 100.

40. Long, "Statement of Robert Long," 6; Long, supporting statement for Samuel Hammond, pension, 31 Oct. 1832, M804, Roll 1176.

41. Robert Long, pension, 7 Oct. 1832, M804, Roll 1581.

42. Ewing served as a Continental but was commissioned as a militia captain "after the fall of Charleston." Dillard was a captain about 1 August 1780. Harris was a captain-lieutenant during 1780. Sexton was commissioned a captain under Hayes during 1780. Irby raised a volunteer company and was commissioned in November 1780. Both Sexton and Irby brought in their men just before the battle. Irby actually says his men were assigned to Hayes's Battalion rather than being part of it. Moss, *Roster of South Carolina Patriots*, 57, 256, 300, 421, 484, 855.

    Identifying company commanders is not a genealogical exercise. Men reported commanders in their pension records. If the location of the unit is known, it is possible to use that pensioner's recollection of what he saw, or how he was wounded, to locate other observers on the field and to generate accurate details about the battle.

Hayes's companies were in the center and gave way when the British infantry charged. Wounds suffered by these men provided insights when placed in their correct location.

43. Moss, *Roster of South Carolina Patriots*, 20–21, 427, 508, 692–93, 927. Hughes replaced Benjamin Jolly as company commander; Joseph Hughes, pension, 20 Sept. 1832, M804, Roll 1360. One company was out scouting when the battle began and was not in the battle itself. This company participated in the pursuit and harassed Tarleton's retreat. Samuel Otterson, pension, 20 Sept. 1832, M804, Roll 1853.

44. Moss, *Roster of South Carolina Patriots*, 50, 189, 305, 311–12. Files's company is a problem. He could be placed under Captain Parson with Roebuck, under Major Noble of Hayes's Battalion, or with the South Carolina State Troops under Hammond. Pension records suggest he was with Thomas.

45. Long, "Statement of Robert Long," 6.

46. James Kelly, pension, 28 Apr. 1835, M804, Roll 1466.

47. John Baldwin, pension, 28 Aug. 1832, M804, Roll 123.

48. Daniel Morgan to Nathanael Greene, 19 Jan. 1781, Showman, *Greene Papers*, 7:152–55; Pigree Map, National Archives. The slope shown on the Pigree Map rises southward into the first terrace above the swale. It is the lower rear slope of militia ridge. In 1990, this position was four to six feet lower than the militia-line position.

49. Long, "Statement of Robert Long," 6; Young, "Memoir," 100.

50. Hammond noted Tate and Buchanan were on the right on 16 January. Hammond is correct only if Tate is Edmund Tate, not James Tate, who led a company on the left. The right-flank Tate is Edmund, often confused with James, who led an Augusta County company on the left flank under Triplett. Howard was very specific, "I am positive that Triplett and Tate were on *my left*." Here Howard is referring to James, not Edmund. Hammond, "Notes," in Joseph Johnson, *Traditions and Reminiscences*, 528; John Eager Howard to John Marshall, 1804, Bayard Papers; Daniel Morgan to Nathanael Greene, 19 Jan. 1781, Showman, *Greene Papers*, 7:152–55. See also John Eager Howard, "Account of the Battle of Cowpens," in Henry Lee Jr., *Campaign of 1781 in the Carolinas*.

51. There were few North Carolina Continentals when Cowpens occurred. Morgan reported the main-line flanks were covered by North Carolinians and Captain Connelly stated, "I was a volunteer . . . called the State Troops or Malitia [*sic*], a part of the men under my command was drafted men for eighteen months. A part . . . was for six months and about forty was volunteers for and during the war." These men may not have been Continentals. Since they were mounted and their commander is not listed in Heitman, they do not seem to have been Continentals. Whatever the affiliation, Connelly stated he was "under" Howard on the right flank. The word distinguishes his account from other militiamen who only mention Howard as present. Henry Connelly, pension, 1 Aug. 1833, M804, Roll 627. Coupled with Mordecai Clark's old company on the left, Morgan's statement that the flanks were covered by North Carolinians makes sense.

52. Buchanan and Lawson seem to have been reinforced by two companies of David Campbell's Virginia Militia, one of which joined Morgan on 16 January. The other arrived just as the battle began. It is possible these 100 militiamen were

placed behind Brandon and Hayes, but this position is suggested only by Long's cryptic comment about Virginians breaking, which might more accurately refer to their opening ranks to let the militia through. James Braden, pension, 1 July 1839, M804, Roll 314; Christian Peters, pension, 19 Sept. 1832, M804, Roll 1917.

53. Gibbon, *Artillerist's Manual*, 54; Riling, *Regulations*, 6–9, 31, and Plate 1; Long, "Statement of Robert Long," 6; William Neel, supplementary statement to pension, 19 Mar. 1836, M804, Roll 1804. Gibbon is used only to show width of a man in ranks (two feet) because Von Steuben does not give this figure.

54. James Tate's Augusta Riflemen were between Combs and Gilmore's Rockbridge Rifles on the left. Hammond's statement that "Capts. Tate and Buchanan, with the Augusta Riflemen, were to support the right of the line" has proven very confusing. Hammond is correct about Tate and Buchanan on the right flank. (See n. 50 above.)

55. Two authors mention a captain named either Beatty or Beale stationed on the far-right flank. Morgan stated that the flanks were covered by North Carolinians; it is likely Beatty was from *North* Carolina and commanded Burke County men after Mordecai Clark volunteered as a dragoon. The North Carolina company is detailed in pension documents. William Capps, pension, 27 Mar. 1845, M804, Roll 466; Hammond, "Notes," in Joseph Johnson, *Traditions and Reminiscences*, 528; M'Call, *History of Georgia*, 506; Daniel Morgan to Nathanael Greene, 19 Jan. 1781, Showman, *Greene Papers*, 7:152–55; Adam Rainbault, pension, 3 Oct. 1832, M804, Roll 1994.

56. Benjamin Martin, pension, 23 Mar. 1833, M804, Roll 1637.

57. Hammond, "Notes," in Joseph Johnson, *Traditions and Reminiscences*, 528. The relevant terminology is: "A third line, will be formed, advancing its left wing toward the enemy, so as to bring it nearly parallel with the left of the continental troops, . . . will form to the right of the second line, the left nearly opposite to the right of the second line, one hundred yards in its rear; the right extending towards the enemy, so as to be opposite to or parallel with the second line."

58. John R. Shaw, *Narrative*, 54; Stewart, *Highlanders of Scotland*, 2:70–71; John Thomas, pension, 9 Aug. 1832, M804, Roll 2370. Shaw was not at Cowpens. The same wording is in the 1781 *Annual Register* account cited by MacKenzie in *Strictures on Lt. Col. Tarleton's History*, 94. A similar account is in Keltie, *History of the Scottish Highlands*, 2, 462: "The second line . . . immediately faced to the right and inclined backwards, and by this skilful manoeuvre opened a space by which the front line retreated." The similarity of wording to Stewart's account suggests Keltie used Stewart as his source.

59. John Eager Howard, "Account of the Battle of Cowpens," in Robert E. Lee, *American Revolution in the South*, 96. Richard Swearingen, pension, 13 Nov. 1832, M804, Roll 2329, suggests this when he notes the "regulars came up."

60. It would be pointless to list every historian of the battle. They *all* omit these two aspects of Morgan's tactical arrangements.

61. William Johnson, *Sketches of Nathanael Greene*, 1:379. Johnson seems to be writing with hindsight in this statement. Morgan was initially quite upset with Howard when the main line withdrew.

62. James Kelly, pension, 28 Apr. 1835, M804, Roll 1466.

63. M'Call, *History of Georgia*, 506. The hollow way is the swale behind the Continentals; the eminence is Morgan Hill.

64. Daniel Morgan to Nathanael Greene, 19 Jan. 1781, Showman, *Greene Papers*, 7:152–55; Young, "Memoir," 100. The Green River Road curves to the northeast after passing through the main-line area, so Young's observation fits both the terrain and the infantry deployment with Washington's dragoons all posted west of the road.

65. Young, "Memoir," 100.

66. Collins, *Autobiography*, 56; Henry Connelly, pension, 15 Aug. 1833, M804, Roll 628; John Eager Howard to John Marshall, 1804, Bayard Papers.

67. Several pensioners noted they were with the baggage guard. Thomas Berry, pension, 7 June 1832, M804, Roll 228; Robert Carithers, pension, 3 Sept. 1832, M804, Roll 469; George Wiginton, pension, 11 Dec. 1833, M804, Roll 2572.

68. Nathanael Greene to George Washington, 1 May 1781, in Sparks, *Correspondence of the American Revolution*, 3: 229.

69. Stewart, *Sketches of Highlanders*, 2:70–73.

70. Henry Connelly, pension, 15 Aug. 1833, M804, Roll 628; William Neel, pension, 29 Oct. 1832, M804, Roll 1804; Young, "Memoir," 100.

71. Moss, *Patriots at the Cowpens*, 5.

72. Young, "Memoir," 100.

73. William Johnson, *Sketches of Nathanael Greene*, 1:379.

74. Ibid., 1:373.

CHAPTER FIVE

1. Morgan described the battle's start twice. "Majors McDowell and Cunningham gave them a heavy and galling fire"; "They formed into one Line Raisd a prodjious Yell, and came Running at us as if they Intended to eat us up." Daniel Morgan to Nathanael Greene, 19 Jan. 1781, Showman, *Greene Papers*, 7:152–55; Daniel Morgan to William Snickers, 23 Jan. 1781, Horatio Gates Papers. The first quote is Morgan to Greene, the second, Morgan to Snickers.

2. Collins, *Autobiography*, 56; Tarleton, *Campaigns of 1780–81*, 215.

3. John Baldwin, pension, 28 Aug. 1832, M804, Roll 123; Richard Crabtree, pension, 2 Aug. 1834, M804, Roll 674; Henry Lee, *Memoirs of the War*, 254; James McDonald, pension, 31 May 1834, M804, Roll 1677.

4. William Johnson, *Sketches of Nathanael Greene*, 1:378; M'Call, *History of Georgia*, 506.

5. Tarleton, *Campaigns of 1780–81*, 215. The question of swamps at Cowpens appears to be moot unless Tarleton meant there were no swamps in the woods, which is correct. There was boggy ground around every creek head on both sides of the Green River Road.

6. This assessment was made after an early-morning battlefield walk in intermittent rain. From Hayes Rise, it is possible to see lighter background down the road. At the height of a mounted man at the rivulet's head, it is not possible to see uproad beyond the ridge. If Tarleton moved off the road to his right, he could not see much due to the tree-covered, mottled background, nor could he approach closely due to skirmish fire. Using terrain and the dark, Morgan effectively, if temporarily, concealed most of his force.

7. Anderson, "Journal," 209; Collins, *Autobiography*, 56; Long, "Statement of Robert Long," 5–6.

With heavier tree cover on the main line, sunrise was slightly later than in the open areas where militia stood. Damp, cloudy weather conditions made visibility difficult. Available light at daybreak was unsuited for either observation or aiming. Poor light under the trees where the Continentals were posted may have totally obscured them when the British arrived.

The interval between lightening sky at dawn and actual sunrise is a period when even a vague outline is difficult to see. The interval of poor light lasts about thirty minutes in damp, cloudy weather at Cowpens. Tarleton used this time to deploy his troops and learn more of American dispositions. "Tarleton did halt the troops for near half an hour, and made them throw off their knapsacks and blankets to render them light for action." Feaster, *History of Union County*, 79; Hanger, *Address to the Army*, 99.

8. William Johnson, *Sketches of Nathanael Greene*, 1:379–80; Tarleton, *Campaigns of 1780–81*, 215.

9. Some attribute this reconnaissance to Ogilvie or the 17th Light Dragoons. In fact, Hovenden's British Legion troop—which encountered the American patrol, discovered the pickets, and drove them in—did this. Ogilvie's British Legion troop and the 17th Light Dragoons backed up Hovenden. Next in line of march, they were stationed on the British flanks during the battle. Hovenden's troop lost seventeen killed in action between the end of December 1780 and 23 February 1781. It is probable some fell in this reconnaissance by fire. Some authors claim fifteen dragoons were shot down, a specific incident that actually occurred later in the battle. Clark, *Loyalists in the Southern Campaign*, 2:203–4; Lawrence Everheart, pension, 7 Apr. 1834, M804, Roll 944; Fleming, *Cowpens*, 63; Roberts, *Battle of Cowpens*, 86; Schenk, *North Carolina*, 213; James Simons to William Washington, 3 Nov. 1803, Balch, *Papers*, 45–47.

10. Skirmishers "behind a rivulet" were protected from attack by boggy ground created by springs and rain. See E. Alfred Jones, *Journal of Alexander Chesney*, 22.

11. M'Call, *History of Georgia*, 506.

12. Ibid.

13. William Johnson, *Sketches of Nathanael Greene*, 2:379–80; M'Call, *History of Georgia*, 507.

14. Tarleton, *Campaigns of 1780–81*, 216. The British right is located by a combination of factors. Cunningham and Hammond had at least 115 men along rising ground east of the road. Shoulder to shoulder in one line, they occupied about 250 feet. At open order, the British infantry covered approximately five feet per man in two ranks. Given the numbers of light infantrymen (about 150) and the British Legion infantry (about 200), the British extended about 120 yards east of the road. The British deployment shows the skirmish line was heavy, but well spread out, averaging perhaps three feet per man.

American numbers are derived from Showman, *Greene Papers*, 7:157–58 (nn. 4–6); and James Jackson to Daniel Morgan, 20 Jan. 1795, Myers, *Cowpens Papers*, 46. The Georgians had about 55, South Carolina State Troops, about 60. Skirmishers were probably in groups, within loosely formed companies. See, for example,

M'Call, *History of Georgia*, 506. British numbers are from "Strength Report, 15 Jan. 1781," Reese, *Cornwallis Papers*. Open-order spacing for the British is based on Tarleton's comment about the "loose manner of forming in the south," and Abner Nash's report of British infantry at Camden deployed at five-foot intervals in a single line. Tarleton, *Campaigns of 1780–81*, 221; Nash to Delegates in Congress, 23 Aug. 1780, *State Records of North Carolina*, 15, 60.

15. Tarleton, *Campaigns of 1780–81*, 214.

16. Ibid., 216.

17. Ibid. Tarleton said they closed within 300 yards, but this is incorrect and seems due to unfamiliar terrain and poor light. If Tarleton's distances were correct, the 7th would have been deployed in the bog around the rivulet; at about 200 yards, the 7th was beyond the rivulet. Few Americans noted Tarleton's two-stage deployment, indicating how smoothly the British went from column to line.

18. Hanger, *Address to the Army*, 104; William Johnson, *Sketches of Nathanael Greene*, 1:379. There *was* constriction on the British left. The 71st was supposed to be posted between Ogilvie's British Legion dragoons and the 7th Fusiliers. There was no room to deploy between the two units because the dragoons could not move farther west, perhaps because of the ravine that borders the field today. Mixing the 7th and 71st flanks provides clear evidence that the western edge of the battlefield constricted troop movements.

The 169 men in the 7th Regiment required about 70 yards if men were shoulder to shoulder in two ranks with a cannon located in the regiment's center. An additional 22 yards must be added for Ogilvie's troop. Forty dragoons occupied a space of 22 yards (3.3 feet per horseman) if deployed in two ranks; if in one rank, they required 44 yards.

The distance between the Green River Road and the ravine on the west side of the battlefield is about 130 yards. The 71st had 240 men who required a minimum of 80 yards if in two ranks with no space between companies. After deducting space for dragoons and 7th Fusiliers, between 26 and 42 yards remained for the 71st. This was approximately half of the width they required. A nineteenth-century source provides information on space taken by mounted men in different formations. See Gorgas, *Ordnance Manual*, 438. Gorgas is cited only to provide information about space required by horsemen, data not found in Von Steuben.

19. Hanger, *Address to the Army*, 101–2, 104–5; MacKenzie, *Strictures on Lt. Col. Tarleton's History*, 97; Tarleton, *Campaigns of 1780–81*, 216.

20. M'Call, *History of Georgia*, 507.

21. William Lorance, pension, 3 Dec. 1832, M804, Roll 1584.

22. William Johnson, *Sketches of Nathanael Greene*, 1:378; Henry Lee, *Memoirs of the War*, 256; Lorance, pension, 1832.

23. John Baldwin, pension, 28 Aug. 1832, M804, Roll 123; James Jackson to Daniel Morgan, 20 Jan. 1795, Myers, *Cowpens Papers*, 46; Henry Lee, *Memoirs of the War*, 253; Daniel Morgan to Nathanael Greene, 19 Jan. 1781, Showman, *Greene Papers*, 7:152–55. Morgan's comment about a "heavy and galling fire" is telling. A rifleman himself, Morgan undoubtedly watched with a practiced eye, and his praise is a valuable comment on their performance. The quotes are, in order, from Morgan, Jackson, Lee, and Baldwin.

1. Views of the second-line action are often misplaced chronologically. According to MacKenzie, "Two-thirds of the British infantry officers, had already fallen, and nearly the same proportion of privates" (*Strictures on Lt. Col. Tarleton's History*, 99).

2. Feaster, *History of Union County*, 79. Feaster is quoting one of Joseph McJunkin's postwar addresses on the Cowpens battlefield.

3. Stedman, *American War*, 321; Tarleton, *Campaigns of 1780–81*, 216.

4. Haggis, "Firesides Revisiting." This observation is supported by Anderson, "Journal," 209. The three-pounders are discussed by Caruana, *Grasshoppers and Butterflies*, and Muller, *Treatise of Artillery*.

5. Caruana, *Grasshoppers and Butterflies*, 31–32.

6. Young, "Memoir," 100.

7. Anderson, "Journal," 207; Jeremiah Dial, pension, 15 Aug. 1832, M804, Roll 808.

8. Collins, *Autobiography*, 56–57; Gordon, *Independence of the United States of America*, 4:34; John Eager Howard to John Marshall, 1804, Bayard Papers; William Johnson, *Sketches of Nathanael Greene*, 1:380; Henry Lee, *Memoirs of the War*, 256; Stedman, *American War*, 321; Stewart, *Highlanders of Scotland*, 1:71; Young, "Memoir," 100.

9. Ramsay, *History of the Revolution in South Carolina*, 233; John Thomas, pension, 9 Aug. 1832, M804, Roll 2370; Young, "Memoir," 100.

10. Samuel Shaw, "Revolutionary War Letters to Captain Winthrop Sargent," 321; Stedman, *American War*, 321; Stewart, *Highlanders of Scotland*, 2:71; Young, "Memoir," 100.

11. Tarleton, *Campaigns of 1780–81*, 216. Tarleton seems reasonably correct, but his figure may be low. Hayes, Brandon, Thomas, and Roebuck each had between 150 and 200 men. Hammond had at least 115 men on the left flank. North Carolinians under McDowell numbered more than 200 men. The totals suggest there were at least 900 men on line, a very conservative figure well over Morgan's 800. If Continental infantry and dragoons (380) and Virginians (200+) are subtracted, the entire militia contingent is 220, which is simply not credible.

12. William Johnson, *Sketches of Nathanael Greene*, 1:380; M'Call, *History of Georgia*, 507.

13. Daniel Morgan to Nathanael Greene, 19 Jan. 1781, Showman, *Greene Papers*, 7:152–55. The quote is from p. 154.

14. Feaster, *History of Union County*, 79.

15. Carroll, "Random Recollections," 101; O'Neall and Chapman, *Annals of Newberry*, 36. The small parties may have been designed to tempt the British into firing early. It was not a new tactic; some of the same Americans did it against Tarleton at Blackstock's.

16. Clark, *Loyalists in the Southern Campaign*, 2:234; Raddall, "Tarleton's Legion," 43; Saye, *Memoirs of Major Joseph McJunkin*, 33.

17. O'Neall and Chapman, *Annals of Newberry*, 36; Young, "Memoir," 100. The firing pattern differs from the Von Steuben manual, but there were obvious reasons to do so. Riling, *Regulations*, 65.

18. Gordon, *Independence of the United States of America*, 4, 34; Richard Swearingen, pension, 13 Nov. 1832, M804, Roll 2329; John Thomas, pension, 9 Aug. 1832,

M804, Roll 2370. British accounts suggest the distance was half that reported by the Americans and claim they were within 20 or 25 yards when the first volley was discharged. See Stewart, *Highlanders of Scotland*, 2:71.

19. Henry Lee, *Memoirs of the War*, 257; Stewart, *Highlanders of Scotland*, 2:71.

20. Daniel Morgan to Nathanael Greene, 19 Jan. 1781, Showman, *Greene Papers*, 7:154. According to Von Steuben's manual, fire is by alternate units. If Brandon fired first, Thomas was next, then Hayes, and finally Roebuck. Given delays in the 7th Regiment's advance, Thomas and Roebuck were under little pressure because the fusiliers took longer to reach the killing distance.

21. Hanger, *Sportsmen*, 199–200.

22. Henry Lee, *Memoirs of the War*, 257; Stewart, *Highlanders of Scotland*, 2:71.

23. Collins, *Autobiography*, 57; John Eager Howard to John Marshall, 1804, Bayard Papers; John Thomas, pension, 9 Aug. 1832, M804, Roll 2370.

24. MacKenzie, *Strictures on Lt. Col. Tarleton's History*, 99; Stewart, *Highlanders of Scotland*, 2:71. MacKenzie's precise quote is, "Fatigue, however, enfeebled the pursuit, much more than loss of blood."

25. Perry, "Revolutionary Incidents, Number 7, The Cowpens," Benjamin Franklin Perry Papers, University of North Carolina, Chapel Hill. One of Perry's informants was Captain Thomas Farrow, a Cowpens veteran who served with the Spartanburg militia.

26. Feaster, *History of Union County*, 79.

27. Henry Pettit, pension, 24 Oct. 1832, M804, Roll 1920; Hugh Warren, pension, 16 June 1834, M804, Roll 2497, supplementary statement.

28. James Dillard, pension, 7 July 1833, M804, Roll 817; Richard Griffin, pension, 28 Nov. 1832, M804, Roll 1132; Samuel Smith, pension, 11 Sept. 1843, M804, Roll 2231; Henry Stewart, 7 Jan. 1846, supporting statement in Samuel Hogg, pension, 15 Sept. 1836, M804, Roll 1300.

29. Long, "Statement of Robert Long," 6; MacKenzie, *Strictures on Lt. Col. Tarleton's History*, 97–98; John R. Shaw, *Narrative*, 53–55; Stedman, *American War*, 320–24; Stewart, *Highlanders of Scotland*, 2:71; John Thomas, pension, 9 Aug. 1832, M804, Roll 2370; Tarleton, *Campaigns of 1780–81*, 216.

30. In 1983, a re-created unit fired battalion volleys with forty-one seconds between first and second fire without haste. Reloading and a new firing sequence are included in this time. The demonstrations show four battalions could fire a five-volley sequence in less than a minute with full expectation that the first unit could reload and be ready to fire when ordered.

31. While distance (90 feet, or 36 paces) and time (20 to less than 18 seconds) decrease, military reloading is measured at the pace of the slowest, not the fastest, rifleman.

32. John Eager Howard to John Marshall, 1804, Bayard Papers.

33. Collins, *Autobiography*, 57.

34. Richard Griffin, pension, 28 Nov. 1832, M804, Roll 1132.

35. Gordon, *Independence of the United States of America*, 4:34; William Johnson, *Sketches of Nathanael Greene*, 1:380; Henry Lee, *Memoirs of the War*, 257; MacKenzie, *Strictures on Lt. Col. Tarleton's History*, 97–98; M'Call, *History of Georgia*, 507.

36. John R. Shaw, *Narrative*, 55.

37. William Johnson, *Sketches of Nathanael Greene*, 1:380, is the earliest account de-

scribing withdrawal around the left flank. Johnson formalized the myth of South Carolina militia moving across the field from right to left. Those continuing the "rout tradition" include James Graham, *Life of General Daniel Morgan*, 300–301; Schenck, *North Carolina*, 214–15; McCrady, *South Carolina in the Revolution, 1780–1783*, 45–46; Higginbotham, *Daniel Morgan*, 137; Rankin, *North Carolina Continentals*, 271; Treacy, *Prelude to Yorktown*, 102–3; Roberts, *Cowpens*, 89–90; Lumpkin, *From Savannah to Yorktown*, 129; Fleming, *Cowpens*, 67; Black, *War for America*, 210; and Morrill, *Southern Campaigns*, 130.

Authors earlier than, or contemporary with, Johnson did not claim a militia retreat around the left flank. They include Gordon, *Independence of the United States of America*; M'Call, *History of Georgia*; John Marshall, *Life of George Washington*, 305–6, 507; Mills, *Statistics of South Carolina*, 270; Moultrie, *Memoirs of the American Revolution*; Ramsay, *History of the Revolution in South Carolina*, 233.

38. Anderson, "Journal," 209; Seymour, *Journal of the Southern Expedition*, 13. Both Anderson and Seymour were with the Delaware company in the center of the main line. They saw the retreating militia immediately to their front, a good indicator that there was no underbrush.

39. The traditional account is patently erroneous. Tarleton, no friend of South Carolina militiamen, reported nothing of the sort, and American participants confirm Tarleton's observations.

40. Hammond, "Account of the Battle of Cowpens," in Joseph Johnson, *Traditions and Reminiscences*, 528; John R. Shaw, *Narrative*, 55; Stewart, *Highlanders of Scotland*, 2:71. Morgan initially placed his Virginia companies *en échelon* to the rear center rather than moving them backward during the battle or leaving them in place to be disrupted by fleeing militia. The openings might be what Robert Long meant by his cryptic comment that the "Virginians broke before we reached them." Long, "Statement of Robert Long," 6.

41. Anderson, "Journal," 209; John Eager Howard to John Marshall, 1804, Bayard Papers; M'Call, *History of Georgia*, 507.

42. Pindell, "A Militant Surgeon of the Revolution," 309–23.

43. John R. Shaw, *Narrative*, 55.

44. Daniel Morgan to Nathanael Greene, 19 Jan. 1781, Showman, *Greene Papers*, 7:152–55; Tarleton, *Campaigns of 1780–81*, 216.

45. Jeremiah Dial, pension, 15 Aug. 1832, M804, Roll 808; Charles Holland, pension, 10 Oct. 1832, M804, Roll 1308. At no other time were Hammond's men closely engaged with sword-carrying British.

46. Collins, *Autobiography*, 57; Long, "Statement of Robert Long," 6; MacKenzie, *Strictures on Lt. Col. Tarleton's History*, 98.

47. James Kelly, pension, 28 Apr. 1835, M804, Roll 1466; Joshua Palmer, 9 Oct. 1820, supporting statement in John Whelchel, pension, 9 Oct. 1823, M804, Roll 2547; see also Whelchel's supplementary statement.

48. Brandon, "Account," in Draper, *King's Mountain*, 285–86; Joseph Hughes, pension, 20 Sept. 1832, M804, Roll 1360; M'Call, *History of Georgia*, 507.

49. Draper, *King's Mountain*, 326, 469; Moss, *Patriots at the Cowpens*, 213.

50. James Carlisle, pension, 28 Oct. 1835, M804, Roll 470; Adam J. Files, pension, 3 Feb. 1834, M804, Roll 973; Jeremiah Files, pension, 4 Feb. 1833, M804, Roll 973.

51. Brandon, "Account," in Draper, *King's Mountain*, 285–86; Long, "Statement of Robert Long," 6; Pindell, "Militant Surgeon of the Revolution," 317–18.

52. Brandon, "Account," in Draper, *King's Mountain*, 286; Henry Connelly, pension, 1 Aug. 1833, M804, Roll 627; Collins, *Autobiography*, 57.

53. Collins, *Autobiography*, 57; William Johnson, *Sketches of Nathanael Greene*, 1:380.

CHAPTER SEVEN

1. Henry Lee, *Memoirs of the War*, 255–56; John R. Shaw, *Narrative*, 54.

2. William Bivins, pension, 22 Sept. 1834, M804, Roll 249.

3. Henry Wells, pension, 29 Jan. 1834, M804, Roll 2529.

4. Stedman, *American War*, 321.

5. Anderson, "Journal," 209; Stedman, *American War*, 321–22; Young, "Memoir," 84–88, 100–102.

6. M'Call, *History of Georgia*, 507. The men who fired first were Hammond's skirmishers on the far-left flank, the small Burke County, N.C., company, and James Gilmore's "Rockbridge Rifles."

7. William Johnson, *Sketches of Nathanael Greene*, 1:380; John Thomas, pension, 9 Aug. 1832, M804, Roll 2370.

8. Once the Virginians moved forward, the main line temporarily took the shape of "a kind of pincer" described by an unknown Virginia rifleman. Chastellux, *Travels in North America*, 2:399. A similar formation is described by J. B. O'Neall in his "Revolutionary Incidents," 38: "The whole militia command, when overpowered, were directed to form on the right and left of the regulars. This formation could not be in line, but must have been at right angles with the regulars . . . the regulars in the centre, the militia the right and left wings thrown forward, on the right and left of the road, and making the exact form of the letter E, which, from infancy, has always been represented to the writer as the form of Morgan's line of battle." O'Neall pointed out that the "ground between the heads of 'Suck Creek,' is not more than sufficient for the formation of Howard's regulars." Both accounts describe the line after the Virginians closed up and Hammond and McDowell placed their skirmishers forward of the flanks.

9. Daniel Morgan to Nathanael Greene, 19 Jan. 1781, Showman, *Greene Papers*, 7:154; Richard Swearingen, pension, 13 Nov. 1832, M804, Roll 2329.

10. Anderson, "Journal," 209; John Eager Howard to John Marshall, 1804, Bayard Papers; William Johnson, *Sketches of Nathanael Greene*, 1:380; Morgan to Greene, 19 Jan. 1781, Showman, *Greene Papers*, 7:152–55.

11. Young, "Memoir," 100.

12. Henry Lee, *Memoirs of the War*, 257; Tarleton, *Campaigns of 1780–81*, 216. The difference in sound between musket and rifle is readily apparent. The higher-pitched crack of a rifle is due to the smaller ball being patched. The patch acts as a gas seal, giving the ball a higher velocity. Musket balls travel slower and are not sealed in the barrel.

13. MacKenzie, *Strictures on Lt. Col. Tarleton's History*, 98; Seymour, *Journal of the Southern Expedition*, 15; Stedman, *American War*, 321–22.

14. Henry Lee, *Memoirs of the War*, 257; Jeremiah Preston, pension, 20 Dec. 1843,

M804, Roll 1972; Andrew Rock, pension, 14 Nov. 1850, M804, Roll 2069; Henry Wells, pension, 29 Jan. 1834, M804, Roll 2529.

15. Preston, pension, 1843.

16. William Johnson, *Sketches of Nathanael Greene*, 1:380. Seventeen shots in 30 minutes is about a shot every 2 minutes. This is very slow, even for a rifle. If Preston fired 14 shots in the firefight, one in the volley after the withdrawal and two in the counterattack and mopping up, the remaining 14 shots could be fired in less than 10 minutes. With no shots in the counterattack, 16 shots were possible in a 10-minute firefight. Time/space/march rates for the British advance, 71st advance, and main-line retreat confirm a short fight. Morgan's aide told an American officer that "the enemy came up to this line[;] they received such severe and well directed fires for 15 minutes." Samuel Shaw, "Revolutionary War Letters to Captain Winthrop Sargent," 321. Even this may be too long. Preston's ammunition expenditure is one shot a minute, if Shaw meant only the firefight.

17. Benjamin Martin, pension, 25 Mar. 1833, M804, Roll 1637; George Rogers, pension, 24 Sept. 1832, M804, Roll 2074; see supplementary statement; John Thomas, pension, 9 Aug. 1832, M804, Roll 2370.

18. William McCoy, pension, 7 Oct. 1832, M804, Roll 1672.

19. Heavy losses fighting the militia shortened the British line, alleviating constriction on the right flank caused by marshy ground. Reducing the front by closing intervals between men east of the road allowed space for the 17th Light Dragoons to charge without going over wet ground. More space was available to maneuver on the British left as they advanced. Casualties in the right Maryland Continental company and Buchanan's militia company suggest the 7th Regiment did not extend past the Continental center.

20. Peterson, *Continental Soldier*, 60–61.

21. "Return of the Men Killed and Wounded in Capt. Kirkwood's Company at the Cowpens, 17th Jan'ry 1781," in Delaware, *Delaware Archives* 1:254.

22. In the British manual, the command "fire" was preceded by "present," when muskets were supposed to be leveled. Americans were told to "aim." The difference may reflect basic assumptions about musketry skills, weapons accuracy, or a fundamental approach to inflicting casualties versus the shock effect of a massed volley. Peterkin, *Exercise of Arms*, 17, 77.

23. Gordon, *Independence of the United States of America*, 4:34; Tarleton, *Campaigns of 1780–81*, 217; Young, "Memoir," 100. The quote is Tarleton's. Howard took pride in noting, "When my regiment fell back at the battle of the Cowpens . . . it was not occasioned by the fire of the enemy." John Eager Howard to John Marshall, 1804, Bayard Papers.

24. William Johnson, *Sketches of Nathanael Greene*, 1:380; Henry Lee, *Memoirs of the War*, 257; Tarleton, *Campaigns of 1780–81*, 217. The quote is from Tarleton.

25. Seymour, *Journal of the Southern Expedition*, 13.

26. Clark, *Loyalists in the Southern Campaign*, 2:227–28; Gordon, *Independence of the United States of America*, 4:34; E. Alfred Jones, *Journal of Alexander Chesney*, 22; MacKenzie, *Strictures on Lt. Col. Tarleton's History*, 98, 109; M'Call, *History of Georgia*, 507; Tarleton, *Campaigns of 1780–81*, 217.

27. E. Alfred Jones, *Journal of Alexander Chesney*, 22. If Chesney meant that only part of the 71st ("a detachment") broke McDowell's men, it is likely that the High-landers advanced with one company on line and the remainder in column, trotting up the slope. This formation is very useful for providing a battle line to obliquely flank the Americans. A greater distance between lines when the volley was fired allows more time for the Americans to withdraw *en échelon* to their new positions.

28. Stewart, *Highlanders of Scotland*, 2:71.

29. MacKenzie, *Strictures on Lt. Col. Tarleton's History*, 98.

30. Connelly's state troops and Burke County men on the third-line flanks did not report sword injuries.

31. Joseph James, pension, 17 Nov. 1836, M804, Roll 1405; James Patterson, pension, 7 June 1832, M804, Roll 1887.

32. John Fields, pension, 25 Mar. 1850, M804, Roll 971; William Meade, pension, 26 Dec. 1833, M804, Roll 1703.

33. John Eager Howard, "Account of the Battle of Cowpens," in Robert E. Lee, *American Revolution in the South*, 98. "We were ordered to take no prisoners, except a few Continentals." *The Pennsylvania Packets*, Saturday, 17 Feb. 1781. "Giv-ing no quarter" meant that any attempts by their opponents to surrender would be disregarded by the Highlanders.

34. Anderson, "Journal," 209; John Eager Howard to John Marshall, 1804; Daniel Morgan to Nathanael Greene, 19 Jan. 1781, Showman, *Greene Papers*, 7:152–55. The quotes are in the following order: Howard, Anderson, and Morgan. Howard's numbers are not correct because he had five, 60-man Continental companies, Trip-lett more than 150 Virginians, and Edmund Tate another 100 or more Virginians.

35. Henry Lee, *Memoirs of the War*, 257; Tarleton, *Campaigns of 1780–81*, 217. The quotes are by Tarleton and Lee, respectively.

36. John Eager Howard, "Account of the Battle of Cowpens," in Robert E. Lee, *American Revolution in the South*, 97; William Johnson, *Sketches of Nathanael Greene*, 1:300–301; Henry Lee, *Memoirs of the War*, 257.

37. M'Call, *History of Georgia*, 507.

38. John Eager Howard to John Marshall, 1804, Bayard Papers.

39. Riling, *Regulations*, 12, 29–30.

40. Young, "Memoir," 100.

41. John Eager Howard to John Marshall, 1804, Bayard Papers.

42. Abraham Hamman, pension, 13 Nov. 1832, M804, Roll 1174.

43. Either Morgan or Howard placed Oldham under arrest during the battle. Ibid.

44. John Brownlee, pension, 29 May 1818, M804, Roll 383; William Warren, pension, 19 Nov. 1832, M804, Roll 2499.

45. A 1757 manual for Scottish Highlanders emphasized taking aim: "as you Present, clap your Head to your Piece, and Right-eye along the barrel; make sure of your Aim, for one Shot well pointed is worth a Dozen thrown away. This is my Reason of making Present a single Word of Command, by not crowding it amongst the other Motions, the Soldier has Time to point well at his Enemy." Grant, *New Highland Military Discipline*, 17.

46. Thomas Crowell, pension, 8 June 1833, M804, Roll 703; James Braden, pension, 1 July 1839, supplementary statement, M804, Roll 314.

47. Hill, "Killiecrankie," 126–28. Hill does not discuss the period after 1746, but the highland charge best explains the 71st action. Instead of throwing down muskets and wielding swords, at Cowpens the Scots went in with the bayonet, showing a change in weapons technology and tactics since 1746.

48. John Eager Howard to John Marshall, 1804, Bayard Papers; John Eager Howard, "Account of the Battle of Cowpens," in Robert E. Lee, *American Revolution in the South*, 97; William Johnson, *Sketches of Nathanael Greene*, 1:300–301.

49. John Eager Howard to John Marshall, 1804, Bayard Papers.

50. Seymour, *Journal of the Southern Expedition*, 13–14; John Thomas, pension, 9 Aug. 1832, M804, Roll 2370.

51. William Johnson, *Sketches of Nathanael Greene*, 1:381. Von Steuben explains firing and retrograde movements. See Riling, *Regulations*, 64–66.

52. John Eager Howard, "Account of the Battle of Cowpens," in Robert E. Lee, *American Revolution in the South*, 97; William Johnson, *Sketches of Nathanael Greene*, 1:381; M'Call, *History of Georgia*, 507–8.

53. John Eager Howard, "Account of the Battle of Cowpens," in Robert E. Lee, *American Revolution in the South*, 97; M'Call, *History of Georgia*, 507–8.

54. Henry Lee, *Memoirs of the War*, 257.

55. William Johnson, *Sketches of Nathanael Greene*, 1:381.

56. Anderson, "Journal," 209; Daniel Morgan to Nathanael Greene, 19 Jan. 1781, Showman, *Greene Papers*, 7:152–55; John Thomas, pension, 9 Aug. 1832, M804, Roll 2370.

57. Stedman, *American War*, 322; Tarleton, *Campaigns of 1780–81*, 217.

58. Tarleton, *Campaigns of 1780–81*, 217.

59. Anderson, "Journal," 209.

60. MacKenzie, *Strictures on Lt. Col. Tarleton's History*, 99–100; M'Call, *History of Georgia*, 507–8.

61. George Smith, *Universal Military Dictionary*, 224. The highland charge had a devastating effect even on well-trained men due to its physical and psychological impacts. See Hill, "Killiecrankie," 131, 133.

62. William Johnson, *Sketches of Nathanael Greene*, 1:381; MacKenzie, *Strictures on Lt. Col. Tarleton's History*, 99–100; Stedman, *American War*, 322.

63. John Eager Howard to John Marshall, 1804, Bayard Papers.

64. Harvey, *Manual Exercise*, 13; Pickering, *Easy Plan of Discipline*, 41; Riling, *Regulations*, 13; George Smith, *Universal Military Dictionary*, 198.

65. Harvey, *Manual Exercise*, 13; Pickering, *Easy Plan of Discipline*, 41; Riling, *Regulations*, 13, 56–57; George Smith, *Universal Military Dictionary*, 198.

66. Firing was by platoon, company, or divisions (two companies). If they fired and withdrew by platoon, the timeframe is twice as long as for company withdrawal. If they withdrew by division, the timeframe is half as much. It is most likely that the Maryland and Delaware Continentals fired and withdrew by company, although they could have done so by division.

67. This distance is well within the traditional range for firing before initiating the charge. Hill, "Killiecrankie," 133.

68. John Thomas, pension, 9 Aug. 1832, M804, Roll 2370.

69. William Johnson, *Sketches of Nathanael Greene*, 1:381–82; Peterkin, *Exercise of Arms*, 79, 98, 124, 135, 168.

70. Riling, *Regulations*, 66.

71. John Eager Howard to John Marshall, 1804, Bayard Papers; John Eager Howard, "Account of the Battle of Cowpens," in Robert E. Lee, *American Revolution in the South*, 97–98; Daniel Morgan to Nathanael Greene, 19 Jan. 1781, Showman, *Greene Papers*, 7:152–55. The quotes are in order.

72. Stewart, *Highlanders of Scotland*, 1:73. Emphasis added.

73. William Johnson, *Sketches of Nathanael Greene*, 1:381–82.

74. Ibid., 381.

75. Anderson, "Journal," 209; William Johnson, *Sketches of Nathanael Greene*, 1:381–82; Henry Lee, *Memoirs of the War*, 257; M'Call, *History of Georgia*, 507–8; John R. Shaw, *Narrative*, 54–55; Stewart, *Highlanders of Scotland*, 2:71; John Thomas, pension, 9 Aug. 1832, M804, Roll 2370; Tarleton, *Campaigns of 1780–81*, 217.

76. John Eager Howard to John Marshall, 1804, Bayard Papers; John Eager Howard, "Account of the Battle of Cowpens," in Robert E. Lee, *American Revolution in the South*, 97–98; MacKenzie, *Strictures on Lt. Col. Tarleton's History*, 99.

77. Anderson, "Journal," 209; M'Call, *History of Georgia*, 508; Daniel Morgan to Nathanael Greene, 19 Jan. 1781, *Greene Papers*, 7:152–55; Tarleton, *Campaigns of 1780–81*, 217.

78. Gordon, *Independence of the United States of America*, 4:34–35.

79. Stewart, *Highlanders of Scotland*, 2:71.

80. Anderson, "Journal," 209.

81. Seymour, *Journal of the Southern Expedition*, 15.

82. Jacob Taylor, pension, 21 May 1833, supplementary statement, M804, Roll 2347.

83. John Bantham, pension, 2 Apr. 1818, M804, Roll 136.

84. Henry Lee, *Memoirs of the War*, 228; M'Call, *History of Georgia*, 508; Stewart, *Highlanders of Scotland*, 2:72. Most militia fighting on the American right during the counterattack were from the Spartanburg Regiment. Howard noted in his 1804 letter to John Marshall that "a part of them fell into the rear of my right flank where they afterwards renewed the action."

85. Gordon, *Independence of the United States of America*, 4:35; William Johnson, *Sketches of Nathanael Greene*, 1:381; Stewart, *Highlanders of Scotland*, 2:72.

86. Henry Lee, *Memoirs of the War*, 257; Daniel Morgan to Nathanael Greene, 19 Jan. 1781, *Greene Papers*, 7:152–55; John R. Shaw, *Narrative*, 55; Stedman, *American War*, 322; Tarleton, *Campaigns of 1780–81*, 217.

87. Hill, "Killicrankie," 139.

88. Gordon, *Independence of the United States of America*, 4:34–35; Stedman, *American War*, 322–23.

89. John Eager Howard, "Account of the Battle of Cowpens," in Robert E. Lee, *American Revolution in the South*, 98. In Howard to Marshall, Howard says the counterattack began when the British were "within 30 yards of us with two field pieces" (John Eager Howard to John Marshall, 1804, Bayard Papers).

90. Scottish sources allude to a lack of support. Stewart, *Highlanders of Scotland*, 2:72.

91. John Eager Howard, "Account of the Battle of Cowpens," in Robert E. Lee, *American Revolution in the South*, 97.

92. Anonymous, "Account of Richard Anderson," 200.

93. Ibid.

94. John Eager Howard to John Marshall, 1804, Bayard Papers; Howard, "Account of the Battle of Cowpens," in Robert E. Lee, *American Revolution in the South*, 98.

95. Gordon, *Independence of the United States of America*, 4:35; John R. Shaw, *Narrative*, 55: Stedman, *American War*, 323; Tarleton, *Campaigns of 1780–81*, 217.

96. Tarleton, *Campaigns of 1780–81*, 217.

97. Andrew Rock, pension, 14 Nov. 1850, M804, Roll 2069; Henry Wells, pension, 29 Jan. 1834, M804, Roll 2529.

98. James Braden, pension, 1 July 1839, supplementary statement, M804, Roll 314; Isaac Way, pension, 26 Aug. 1832, M804, Roll 2510.

99. Gordon, *Independence of the United States of America*, 4:35; John Eager Howard, "Account of the Battle of Cowpens," in Robert E. Lee, *American Revolution in the South*, 98; William Johnson, *Sketches of Nathanael Greene*, 1:382; M'Call, *History of Georgia*, 508; Stewart, *Highlanders of Scotland*, 2:72. The Americans gave quarter, but there is a hint of regret about it. See anecdote in *The Pennsylvania Packets*, 17 Feb. 1781: "the Highlanders of the 71st . . . plucked the feathers from their caps . . . cryed, 'dear, good Americans, have mercy upon us! . . . We were ordered to take no prisoners, except a few continentals.' We wish, it was replied, that this had been known a little sooner."

100. James Jackson to Daniel Morgan, 20 Jan. 1795, Myers, *Cowpens Papers*, 46. Jackson's statement about the colors of the 71st is not correct. The Scots did not lose their colors. It is possible a 7th Regiment color ensign withdrew and took refuge with the reforming Highlanders. Given earlier examples of Jackson's bravery, the attempt to capture the colors rings true, even if they were not from the 71st.

101. Andrew Pickens to Henry Lee, 28 Aug. 1811, Draper Papers. Jackson introduced McArthur to Morgan. See Jackson to Morgan, 20 Jan. 1795, Myers, *Cowpens Papers*.

102. Collins, *Autobiography*, 57; Gordon, *Independence of the United States of America*, 4:35; Seymour, *Journal of the Southern Expedition*, 14; Samuel Shaw, "Revolutionary War Letters to Captain Winthrop Sargent," 321. The two light infantry companies were probably from the 16th Regiment and the Prince of Wales American Regiment. The other two companies, from the 71st, seemed to have moved across the field, where they formed a rallying point after their regiment's reversal.

    A lack of references to the 7th Fusiliers suggests they did not wear distinctive headgear and were indistinguishable from other British line infantry. This also suggests British Legion infantry wore red coats. Highlanders were wearing bonnets, but not kilts.

103. Hugh McNary, pension, 5 Sept. 1832, M804, Roll 1698. The officer was probably not a dragoon, as McNary made no reference to his saber which would have been a practical trophy for any mounted American. The incident probably occurred behind the British right, where McNary could have ridden straight forward after remounting. McNary's victim was either an aide to Tarleton or an officer from the British Legion because he was on horseback.

104. William Johnson, *Sketches of Nathanael Greene*, 1:381–82; Tarleton, *Campaigns of 1780–81*, 217–18; Young, "Memoir," 101.

CHAPTER EIGHT

1. British and American cavalry performed differently at Cowpens. "We made a most furious charge, and cutting through the British cavalry, wheeled and charged them in the rear." "An order was dispatched to the cavalry to charge. . . . The cavalry did not comply with the order." The title is taken from Young, but it could apply to the British at certain phases of the battle. Tarleton, *Campaigns of 1780–81*, 217; Young, "Memoir," 84–88, 100. The first quote is Young's, the second Tarleton's.

2. Economy of force means having the power necessary to accomplish a goal. This is as true for a small-unit action within a larger battle as it is with an army. Mass means having superior power at the critical time and place. Matlof, *American Military History*, 6–7. The two principles of war were not articulated as such in the eighteenth century.

3. Daniel Morgan to Nathanael Greene, 19 Jan. 1781, Showman, *Greene Papers*, 7:152–55. The particular quote is on page 153.

4. John Eager Howard to John Marshall, 1804, Bayard Papers; Robert E. Lee, *American Revolution in the South*, 588; Morgan to Greene, 19 Jan. 1781, Showman, *Greene Papers*, 7:153.

5. MacKenzie, *Strictures on Lt. Col. Tarleton's History*, 98, 113; James Simons to William Washington, 3 Nov. 1803, Balch, *Papers*, 46; Tarleton, *Campaigns of 1780–81*, 216.

6. Young, "Memoir," 100.

7. Jeremiah Dial, pension, 15 Aug. 1832, M804, Roll 808.

8. Tarleton, *Campaigns of 1780–81*, 216; Brandon, "Account," in Draper, *King's Mountain*, 285–86.

9. Tarleton, *Campaigns of 1780–81*, 217.

10. Anderson, "Journal," 209; Jeremiah Dial, pension, 15 Aug. 1832, M804, Roll 808.

11. James Simons to William Washington, 3 Nov. 1803, Balch, *Papers*, 46.

12. Collins, *Autobiography*, 57.

13. Young, "Memoir," 100.

14. John Eager Howard, "Account of the Battle of Cowpens," in Henry Lee Jr., *Campaign of 1781 in the Carolinas*, 96.

15. John Eager Howard to John Marshall, 1804, Bayard Papers.

16. James Simons to William Washington, 3 Nov. 1803, Balch, *Papers*, 46.

17. Tarleton, *Campaigns of 1780–81*, 217. Tarleton's order was to his reserve cavalry. Both flank troops were already engaged. This is the first of two attempts by Tarleton to get his reserve to advance.

18. Stedman, *American War*, 322.

19. Young, "Memoir," 100. Tarleton's dragoons were reportedly mounted on the finest horses in the Carolinas. Young, seeing a riderless horse, changed mounts.

20. MacKenzie, *Strictures on Lt. Col. Tarleton's History*, 98.

21. E. Alfred Jones, *Journal of Alexander Chesney*, 22. Ogilvie's troop, which did charge, enlisted at least twelve men soon after Camden. The men were probably American prisoners. Clark, *Loyalists in the Southern Campaign*, 2:228–29. The legion's lack of will may explain why they were in reserve.

22. William Johnson, *Sketches of Nathanael Greene*, 2:381.

23. Stedman, *American War*, 323; Young, "Memoir," 100–101. The first quote is Stedman's, the second, Young's.

24. Anderson, "Journal," 209; John Eager Howard to John Marshall, 1804, Bayard Papers. Similar statements are found in E. Alfred Jones, *Journal of Alexander Chesney*, 22; James Kelly, pension, 28 Apr. 1835, M804, Roll 1466; Long, "Statement of Robert Long," 6; and Stedman, *American War*, 323.

25. James Simons to William Washington, 3 Nov. 1803, Balch, *Papers*, 46. Simons's statement that the legion infantry was mixed with the 71st implies that the 7th Fusiliers and British Legion infantry were not wearing fusilier caps and green coats, respectively.

26. Ibid.

27. John Eager Howard, "Account of the Battle of Cowpens," in Robert E. Lee, *American Revolution in the South*, 98; Stedman, *American War*, 323.

28. Balch, *Papers*, 50. Balch quoted Sergeant Lawrence Everheart, a prisoner in the British rear. "Buford's Play" is akin to "Remember Waxhaws," referring to a 1780 Tarleton atrocity.

29. William Johnson, *Sketches of Nathanael Greene*, 1:382.

30. Tarleton, *Campaigns of 1780–81*, 217.

31. Stedman, *American War*, 322–23.

32. Hanger, *Address to the Army*, 109–10; Tarleton, *Campaigns of 1780–81*, 217–18.

33. Tarleton, *Campaigns of 1780–81*, 218.

34. William Johnson, *Sketches of Nathanael Greene*, 1:382.

35. John Eager Howard to John Marshall, 1804, Bayard Papers, marginal note.

36. James Simons to William Washington, 3 Nov. 1803, Balch, *Papers*, 46.

37. James Busby, pension, 2 Mar. 1835, M804, Roll 431, statement of A. Smith, 2 June 1835.

38. Clark, *Loyalists in the Southern Campaign*, 2:245; Ward, *Delaware Continentals*, 536–38.

39. William Johnson, *Sketches of Nathanael Greene*, 1:382.

40. John Eager Howard to John Marshall, 1804, Bayard Papers; M'Call, *History of Georgia*, 508.

41. A recent sample of historians who mention the fight between Tarleton and Washington includes Fleming, *Cowpens*, 76, 78–79; Morrill, *Southern Campaigns*, 132; and Treacy, *Prelude to Yorktown*, 108–9.

42. Samuel Shaw, "Revolutionary War Letters to Captain Winthrop Sargent," 321.

43. John Eager Howard to John Marshall, 1804, Bayard Papers. Similar statements can be found in Balch, *Papers*, 49, and M'Call, *History of Georgia*, 508–9.

44. John R. Shaw, *Narrative*, 55. Pensioners report Tarleton lost fingers. See James Kelly, pension, 28 Apr. 1835, M804, Roll 1466: "Washington made a hack at Tarlton & disabled Tarltons fingers & glanced his head with his sword." There *were* fingers on the battlefield. American dragoon Joseph Croes reported, "he lost two of his fingers at the Battle of Cowpens." Croes, pension, 14 Mar. 1832, M804, Roll 694.

45. Stewart, *Highlanders of Scotland*, 2:72.

46. John Eager Howard to John Marshall, 1804, Bayard Papers; William Johnson, *Sketches of Nathanael Greene*, 1:382–83; McCall, *History of Georgia*, 508.

47. John Eager Howard to John Marshall, 1804, Bayard Papers; William Johnson, *Sketches of Nathanael Greene*, 1:383; McCall, *History of Georgia*, 508–9. Lee claimed Washington was wounded by the shot that felled his horse. Henry Lee, *Memoirs of the War*, 258.

48. Moss, drawing from the pension application by Shope's widow, reported this incident in *Patriots at the Cowpens*, 211.

49. William Johnson, *Sketches of Nathanael Greene*, 1:382.

50. Collins, *Autobiography*, 56–57.

51. Ibid.

52. Gordon, *Independence of the United States of America*, 4:35.

53. James Simons to William Washington, 3 Nov. 1803, Balch, *Papers*, 46. Details vary, but an incident did occur. Everheart's horse was given to Surgeon Pindell, who was "well mounted on a Horse taken by Sargt Everhart from a British Officer at the Cow Penns, after having been cruelly wounded & taken Prisoner by Picking up & presenting one of their own Muskets at the Officer as he was retreating by the spot Tarleton had left him." Pindell to Frisby Tilghman et al., 8 Dec. 1816, in Pindell, "Militant Surgeon of the Revolution," 317–18.

54. E. Alfred Jones, *Journal of Alexander Chesney*, 22; Young, "Memoirs," 101.

55. John Eager Howard to John Marshall, 1804, Bayard Papers.

56. William Johnson, *Sketches of Nathanael Greene*, 2:385.

57. Gordon, *Independence of the United States of America*, 4:35; Samuel Graham, "English Officer's Account," 248; Daniel Morgan to Nathanael Greene, 19 Jan. 1781, Showman, *Greene Papers*, 7:152–55; James Simons to William Washington, 3 Nov. 1803, Balch, *Papers*, 46; Stedman, *American War*, 323.

58. Young, "Memoir," 101.

59. Ibid. The armorers wagon refers to the traveling forge Morgan captured.

60. Tarleton, *Campaigns of 1780–81*, 218.

61. John Eager Howard to John Marshall, 1804, Bayard Papers; Lamb, *Original and Authentic Journal*, 342; Tarleton, *Campaigns of 1780–81*, 218.

62. Young, "Memoir," 101–2.

63. Ibid.

64. Tarleton, *Campaigns of 1780–81*, 218.

65. Andrew Pickens to Henry Lee, 28 Aug. 1811, Draper Papers.

66. William Goodlet, pension, 4 Mar. 1831, M804, Roll 1090; John Rainey, pension, 16 Aug. 1832, M804, Roll 1995.

67. Andrew Pickens to Henry Lee, 28 Aug. 1811, Draper Papers.

68. Anderson, "Journal," 209; Seymour, *Journal of the Southern Expedition*, 14–15; Samuel Shaw, "Revolutionary War Letters to Captain Winthrop Sargent," 321; Young, "Memoir," 101–2.

69. O'Neall and Chapman, *Annals of Newberry*, 162.

70. Samuel Hammond, pension, 31 Oct. 1832, M804, Roll 1176.

71. Benjamin Copeland, pension, 2 Sept. 1834, M804, Roll 650; E. Alfred Jones, *Journal of Alexander Chesney*, 22; O'Neall and Chapman, *Annals of Newberry*, 39. The quote is from O'Neall and Chapman. Pursuit details also can be found in William Hodge, pension, 20 Apr. 1832, M804, Roll 1295; William Johnson,

Sketches of Nathanael Greene, 2:383; and James Kelly, pension, 28 Apr. 1835, M804, Roll 1466. The road network is in Mills, *Atlas*.

72. O'Neall and Chapman, *Annals of Newberry*, 39.

73. William Johnson, *Sketches of Nathanael Greene* 2:383.

74. Josiah Martin, pension, 1 Oct. 1832, M804, Roll 1641.

75. Mills, *Atlas*; Stedman, *American War*, 323; Tarleton, *Campaigns of 1780–81*, 218.

76. Young, "Memoir," 102.

77. Samuel Otterson, pension, 20 Sept. 1832, M804, Roll 1853; Saye, *Memoirs of Major Joseph McJunkin*, 41.

78. Young, "Memoir," 102. Deshasure was a volunteer dragoon captured with Everheart as Tarleton advanced toward Cowpens. A fellow Union County militiaman, Samuel Clowney, escaped. Henry W. Deshasure, pension, 3 Sept. 1832, M804, Roll 801; James Simons to William Washington, 3 Nov. 1803, Balch, *Papers*, 46. Captain Grant was probably William Grant Sr.

79. Tarleton, *Campaigns of 1780–81*, 222.

80. Samuel Graham, "English Officer's Account," 241–49, 267–73; Stedman, *American War*, 323.

81. Young, "Memoir," 102.

CHAPTER NINE

1. Cary Howard, "John Eager Howard," 303. The grim exchange between two very brave, battle-hardened officers was not entirely jocular. The third line's right-flank withdrawal might have been a disaster. British historian Stedman took a longer view: "Cowpens formed a very principal link in the chain of circumstances which led to the independence of America" (*American War*, 325).

2. Samuel Shaw, "Revolutionary War Letters to Captain Winthrop Sargent," 321. Three weeks later, Morgan's soldiers and Salisbury evacuees wore so much British clothing that Greene's officers commented on many men in scarlet and green coats. Garden, *Anecdotes of the American Revolution*, 3:193.

3. Logan, *History of the Upper Country*, 2:103.

4. James Jackson to Daniel Morgan, 9 Feb. 1795, Myers, *Cowpens Papers*, 47–48.

5. The flags were sent to Congress. The 7th lost their colors twice during the Revolution—once at Chambly, Canada, and the other time at Cowpens. Daniel Morgan to Nathanael Greene, 11 Apr. 1781, in Showman, *Greene Papers*, 8:84–85; John R. Shaw, *Narrative*, 53–55; Tarleton, *Campaigns of 1780–81*, 218. The light infantry and legion had no colors. The 71st Regiment had no colors at Cowpens; Morgan to Greene, 19 Jan. 1781, Showman, *Greene Papers*, 7:152–55. Cowpens mythology has the two cannon being captured by the British at Camden in August 1780, recaptured at Guilford Courthouse in March 1781, and surrendered at Yorktown in October. Attempts to identify the guns as prizes taken at Saratoga were unsuccessful. Strack, "Three Pound Verbruggen Gun." The subsequent recapture at Guilford Courthouse is untrue, as the Americans lost only four six-pounders there. Donald Long, personal communication, 22 Sept. 1996; Nathanael Greene to Samuel Huntington, 16 Mar. 1781, Showman, *Greene Papers*, 7:433–35.

6. Militiamen remembered the forge but not the cannon. Patrick Norris, pension, 22 Sept. 1833, M804, Roll 1826.

7. Collins, *Autobiography*, 57–58. Since they were not in the regular service, the militiamen relied on receiving ammunition when they turned out for duty; otherwise, they had to capture their military supplies from the enemy.

8. Cary Howard, "John Eager Howard," 303.

9. Carroll, "Random Recollections," 102–3; Moss, *Patriots at the Cowpens*, 69. In some accounts, Dugan's trophy was used to kill him.

10. Tarleton, *Campaigns of 1780–81*, 219.

11. John Jones, *Treatment of Wounds and Fractures*, 17.

12. Ibid., 14.

13. Ibid.

14. Jeremiah Files, pension, 4 Feb. 1833, M804, Roll 973; William Meade, pension, 26 Dec. 1833, M804, Roll 1703.

15. Lawrence Everheart, pension, 7 Apr. 1834, M804, Roll 944; Dennis Tramell, pension, 10 Dec. 1833, M804, Roll 2408.

16. William Warren, pension, 19 Nov. 1832, M804, Roll 2499.

17. Joseph James, pension, 17 Nov. 1836, M804, Roll 1405.

18. John Pindell to Frisby Tilghman et al., 8 Dec. 1816, in Pindell, "Militant Surgeon of the Revolution," 317–18.

19. William Bivins, pension, 22 Sept. 1834, M804, Roll 249; John Brownlee, pension, 29 May 1818, M804, Roll 383; Nathaniel Dickenson, pension, 23 June 1835, M804, Roll 814; Henry Hayman, pension, 6 July 1835, M804, Roll 1234; William Venable, pension, 8 Oct. 1832, M804, Roll 2456. The critically wounded Whelchel was on duty in "about forty days." See John Whelchel, pension, 9 Oct. 1823, M804, Roll 2547, supplementary statement, 29 Aug. 1833.

20. Joseph Croes, pension, 14 Mar. 1832, M804, Roll 694; A. Smith, supporting statement, 2 June 1835, in James Busby, pension, 2 Mar. 1835, M804, Roll 431; Benjamin Trusloe, pension, 11 Oct. 1841, M804, Roll 2417.

21. William Bivins, pension, 22 September 1834, M804, Roll 249; John Brownlee, pension, 29 May 1818, M804, Roll 383; Henry Hayman, pension, 6 July 1835, M804, Roll 1234.

22. Nathaniel Dickison, pension, 23 June 1835, M804, Roll 814; William McCoy, pension, 7 Oct. 1832, M804, Roll 1672; William Isaac Simmons, pension, 12 Jan. 1846, M804, Roll 2187; Jacob Taylor, pension, 18 May 1849, supplementary statement, 21 May 1833, M804, Roll 2347.

23. Duffy, *Military Experience*, 247; John Gunnell, pension, 3 Aug. 1818, M804, Roll 1146.

24. Andre Corvisier, cited in Duffy, *Military Experience*, 245–47. These observations might shift dramatically if British wounds were documented.

25. Donald Henderson, "Smallpox," in Wyngaardem and Smith, *Textbook of Medicine*, 1791.

26. Robert Long, pension, 7 Oct. 1832, M804, Roll 1581; James Neill, pension, 17 Dec. 1832, M804, Roll 1805; John Verner, pension, 11 Mar. 1853, M804, Roll 2457.

27. Joseph Brown, pension, 16 June 1834, M804, Roll 372; Donald Henderson, "Smallpox," in Wyngaardem and Smith, *Textbook of Medicine*, 1791–92.

28. James Dawson, pension, 28 Apr. 1818, M804, Roll 771; Henderson, "Smallpox," 1791; Robert Long, pension, 7 Oct. 1832, M804, Roll 1581; Moss, *Patriots at the Cowpens*, 594; James Neill, pension, 17 Dec. 1832, M804, Roll 1805; John Verner, pension, 11 Mar. 1853, M804, Roll 2457; Saye, *Memoirs of Major Joseph McJunkin*, 37.
29. Dawson, pension, 1818; Henderson, "Smallpox," 1791.
30. Collins, *Autobiography*, 57–58; Dennis Tramell, pension, 10 Dec. 1833, M804, Roll 2408. The first quote is from Tramell, the second from Collins.
31. George Gresham, pension, 20 Oct. 1837, M804, Roll 1129; Aaron Guyton, pension, 1 Oct. 1833, M804, Roll 1149. The first quote is from Gresham, the second, Guyton.
32. Manuel McConnell, pension, 18 Sept. 1832, M804, Roll 1670; Adam Rainboult, pension, 3 Oct. 1832, M804, Roll 1994.
33. Phillip Evans, pension, 20 Mar. 1833, M804, Roll 941; Richard Swearingen, pension, 13 Nov. 1832, M804, Roll 2329.
34. Prisoner counts are found in the pension applications of Benjamin Arnold, pension, 31 Jan. 1833, M804, Roll 77; John Baldwin, pension, 28 Aug. 1832, M804, Roll 123; Joseph Brown, pension, 16 June 1834, M804, Roll 372; Henry Connelly, pension, 1 Aug. 1833, M804, Roll 627; Benjamin Copeland, pension, 2 Sept. 1834, M804, Roll 650; Richard Jones, pension, 24 Sept. 1832, M804, Roll 1444; Christopher McVany, pension, 3 Aug. 1832, M804, Roll 1701; Jeremiah Preston, pension, 20 Dec. 1843, M804, Roll 1972; and Henry Wells, pension, 29 Jan. 1834, M804, Roll 2529.
35. Daniel Morgan to Nathanael Greene, 19 Jan. 1781, Showman, *Greene Papers*, 7:152–55; Seymour, *Journal of the Southern Expedition*, 14. Edward Stevens, a Virginia general, reported totals similar to Seymour's in Stevens to Thomas Jefferson, 24 Jan. 1781, Boyd, *Jefferson Papers*, 4:440–41.
36. Morgan to Greene, 19 Jan. 1781; Stevens to Jefferson, 24 Jan. 1781. Musket totals do not seem to include carbines captured from dragoons. Any carbines and swords were probably kept by mounted men who had an immediate need for them.
37. Morgan to Greene, 23 Jan. 1781, Showman, *Greene Papers*, 7:178.
38. John Pindell to Frisby Tilghman et al., 8 Dec. 1816, Pindell, "Militant Surgeon of the Revolution," 317–18.
39. The POWs started north about noon. William Johnson, *Sketches of Nathanael Greene*, 1:385.
40. O'Neall, "Revolutionary Incidents," 39.
41. Adam J. Files, pension, 3 Feb. 1834, M804, Roll 973; Jeremiah Files, pension, 4 Feb. 1833, M804, Roll 973; George Hillen, pension, 15 Mar. 1834, M804, Roll 1280; William Neel, pension, 29 Oct. 1832, and 1836 supplementary statement, M804, Roll 1804. Adam Files stayed with his wounded brother and uncle at McDowell's. The quote is by Jeremiah Files.
42. Josiah Martin, pension, 1 Oct. 1832, M804, Roll 1641.
43. James McCleskey, pension, 3 Sept. 1832 (see also 1833 supplementary statement), M804, Roll 1668; Reuben Nail, pension, 6 May 1834, M804, Roll 1800.
44. Virginia militia accounts detailing post-battle movement include John Gilmore, pension, 3 Sept. 1832, M804, Roll 1077; Abner Hamilton, pension, 21 Sept. 1832, M804, Roll 1170; John Thomas, pension, 9 Aug. 1832, M804, Roll 2370; and James Wright, pension, 16 July 1834, M804, Roll 2649.

45. Typical accounts can be found in pension applications of Benjamin Arnold, pension, 31 Jan. 1833, M804, Roll 77; James Carlisle, pension, 28 Oct. 1835, M804, Roll 470; Joseph McPeters, pension, 15 Oct. 1832, M804, Roll 1699; and James Neill, pension, 17 Dec. 1832, M804, Roll 1805.

46. Thomas Jefferson to Nathanael Greene, 10 Feb. 1781, Showman, *Greene Papers*, 7:273–74.

47. Clark, *Loyalists in the Southern Campaign*, 3:254.

48. Simcoe, *Military Journal*, 127.

49. Nathanael Greene to William L. Davidson, 19 Jan. 1781, Showman, *Greene Papers*, 7:144; Daniel Morgan to Greene, 23 Jan. 1781, Showman, *Greene Papers*, 7:178.

50. Richard Crabtree, pension, 2 Aug. 1834, M804, Roll 674.

51. James Carlisle, pension, 28 Oct. 1835, M804, Roll 470.

52. William Neel, pension, 29 Oct. 1832, M804, Roll 1804; Seymour, *Journal of the Southern Expedition*, 15. The first quote is Neel's; the second is Seymour's.

53. Davidson, *Piedmont Partisan*, 118.

54. Nathanael Greene to Militia Officers, 31 Jan. 1781 and 1 Feb. 1781, Showman, *Greene Papers*, 7:227–28, 231.

55. John Gunby to Greene, 28 Jan. 1781, Showman, *Greene Papers*, 7:210–11; Lewis Morris to Gunby, 2 Feb. 1781, Showman, *Greene Papers*, 7:234.

56. John Moore, pension, 13 Aug. 1832, M804, Roll 1756.

57. Nathanael Greene to John Lop, 3 Feb. 1781, Showman, *Greene Papers*, 7:240–41.

58. Greene to Daniel Morgan, 10 Feb. 1781, Showman, *Greene Papers*, 7:271.

59. Robert E. Lee, *American Revolution in the South*, 247.

60. Ibid.

61. Nathanael Greene to Daniel Morgan, 10 Feb. 1781, Showman, *Greene Papers*, 7:271.

62. Lord Cornwallis to Greene, 2 Feb. 1781, Showman, *Greene Papers*, 7:250–51.

63. Baker, *Another Such Victory*, 75–76.

64. Frederick J. Turner, "Western State-Making."

65. Hartz, *Liberal Tradition in America*, 95.

66. Moss, *Patriots at the Cowpens*.

67. Ibid.

68. Catron, "Go West, Young Veteran," 3, 12.

69. Ibid., 4, 8.

70. Ibid., 4, 5, 13.

71. Ibid., 6; Papenfuse and Stiverson, "General Smallwood's Recruits," 131.

72. Catron, "Go West, Young Veteran," 10.

73. Clark, *Loyalists in the Southern Campaign*, 2:239; Raddall, "Tarleton's Legion," 36.

74. Clark, *Loyalists in the Southern Campaign*, 2:239; Raddall, "Tarleton's Legion," 36.

75. Raddall, "Tarleton's Legion," 37.

76. Clark, *Loyalists in the Southern Campaign*; Raddall, "Tarleton's Legion," 36–38.

77. Clark, *Loyalists in the Southern Campaign*, 3:242–44, 248; Samuel Moore, pension, 11 Oct. 1832, M804, Roll 1759.

EPILOGUE

1. Higginbotham, *George Washington*, 12, 14–15, 22, 32–33, 69–70, 104.

2. Seymour, *Journal of the Southern Expedition*, 14.

3. "Return of the Men Killed and Wounded in Capt. Kirkwood's Company at the Cowpens, 17th Jan'ry 1781," Delaware, *Delaware Archives*, 1:254, lists fourteen casualties but omits Ensign William Bivins and Private Henry Wells. Bivins was crippled for life, but Wells was not badly wounded. William Bivins, pension, 22 Sept. 1834, M804, Roll 24; Henry Wells, pension, 29 Jan. 1834, M804, Roll 2529. The omission of Bivins may be an oversight, but Wells was still with the company and thus not reported as wounded.

4. Jethro Sumner, "Americans Killed and Wounded at Cowpens," in Walter Clark, *State Records of North Carolina*, 419–20.

5. See, for example, Henry Lee, *Memoirs of the War*, 254.

6. Samuel Hammond, "Notes," in Joseph Johnson, *Traditions and Reminiscences*, 526–30; John Eager Howard to John Marshall, 1804, Bayard Papers.

7. Most British accounts reflect a traditional three-line formation by referring to militia and Continentals as two lines with American dragoons as reserve. While they recognized Morgan's deployment, they did not recognize its subtleties. The error was fatal.

8. John Eager Howard, "Account of the Battle of Cowpens," in Robert E. Lee, *American Revolution in the South*, 98; Tarleton, *Campaigns of 1780–81*, 214.

9. William Johnson, *Sketches of Nathanael Greene*, 1:376.

10. In the drum manual, "right wheel" is beaten as two rolls, a single stroke, and a flam. "Forward march" is the start of the drum beat following the command ("Forward" or "To the Front. March!") and is beaten as a strong double flam. See Hauley, Bub, and Frueh, *Standardized Fife Tunes and Drum Accompanyment*; Riling, *Regulations*, 13, 91. These two drum commands cannot be mistaken.

11. Tarleton, *Campaigns of 1780–81*, 217, 221.

12. Ibid., 245.

13. In discussing these conditions, veterans of the 1st Battalion, 75th Infantry (Ranger), used the term "droning," referring to "driving on" while semi-conscious due to sleep deprivation. I am indebted to Kevin Quarles, Michael Matt, and Frank Walker for their help. In a recent study, Richard A. Fox pointed out other impacts of fatigue. See Fox, *Archaeology, History, and Custer's Last Battle*, 267–69.

14. Curtis, *Organization of the British Army*, 90.

15. Babits, "Military Documents and Archaeological Sites," 59–62, applies to Americans. Similar behavior by the British during their maneuvering in the Carolinas seems almost universal in foot armies. See, for example, Engles, *Alexander the Great*, 14–22 (carriage of rations), 123–30 (rations), 153–56 (march rates).

16. Unlike the Cowpens advance, Tarleton plundered farms of cattle and provisions during the 1780 Blackstock's campaign. See Saye, *Memoirs of Major Joseph McJunkin*, 29, and Tarleton, *Campaigns of 1780–81*, 213–14.

17. S. L. A. Marshall, *Soldier's Load*, 46. Something similar can be documented for American soldiers at Guilford Courthouse on 15 March 1781. See Babits, "'Fifth' Maryland at Guilford Courthouse," 370–78.

18. Dinter, *Hero or Coward*, 13, 15.

19. Feaster, *History of Union County*, 79; Saye, *Memoirs of Major Joseph McJunkin*, 33.

20. Gordon, *Independence of the United States of America*, 4:34; Stewart, *Highlanders of*

Scotland, 2:70–73; Richard Swearingen, pension, 13 Nov. 1832, M804, Roll 2329; John Thomas, pension, 9 Aug. 1832, M804, Roll 2370.

21. MacKenzie, *Strictures on Lt. Col. Tarleton's History*, 99.

22. Ibid., 95; Stedman, *American War*, 320; Tarleton, *Campaigns of 1780–81*, 214–15.

23. Gabriel, *No More Heroes*, 84.

24. Stedman, *American War*, 322; Tarleton, *Campaigns of 1780–81*, 217, 221. Tarleton used the word "terror" to describe his "most disciplined soldiers" and their rout.

25. John Eager Howard, "Account of the Battle of Cowpens," in Robert E. Lee, *American Revolution in the South*, 98.

26. Du Picq, *Battle Studies*, 149; Fox, *Custer*, 46–49; S. L. A. Marshall, *Men Against Fire*, 144–45.

27. Fox, *Archaeology, History, and Custer's Last Battle*, 49.

28. Dollard and Horton, *Fear in Battle*, 28; MacKenzie, *Strictures on Lt. Col. Tarleton's History*, 99. The 71st light infantry companies apparently moved across the field and were with their regiment at the surrender. No militia reported encountering Highlanders on the American left, and the Pigree Map shows light infantry outside the 71st, so these Scots rejoined their comrades and may be those mentioned as being in compact order.

29. John Eager Howard, "Account of the Battle of Cowpens," in Robert E. Lee, *American Revolution in the South*, 98.

30. Gabriel, *No More Heroes*, 52.

31. Stewart, *Highlanders of Scotland*, 2:72.

32. MacKenzie, *Strictures on Lt. Col. Tarleton's History*, 99.

33. Gabriel, *No More Heroes*, 84.

34. Dinter, *Hero or Coward*, 30.

35. Ibid., 42–43; Dollard and Horton, *Fear in Battle*, 46.

Bibliography

A NOTE ON THE SOURCES

Documentary sources used in preparing this Cowpens study range from official reports composed within a day or two of the battle to recollections of elderly veterans applying for pensions fifty years later. The two extremes are not unbiased. Commanders had equally valid reasons for both providing what information they did and excluding other material. In a similar vein, veterans wanted a pension and used their best recollection to validate claims when written proof of their service was missing. As with all written material by and about Cowpens participants, there is truth and distortion in these extremes. Considering, in addition, other written materials produced while the veterans were alive, we can discover numerous alternative explanations for what happened.

A case in point is MacKenzie's attack on Tarleton. After the war, Tarleton published his memoirs of the southern campaign. MacKenzie, who was wounded at Cowpens, then attacked Tarleton whom he, and other Scots, loathed. Hanger defended Tarleton and pointed out errors in MacKenzie's attack. The bitter exchange contains much incidental information explaining many minor details of the Cowpens fighting. This information is useful and valid not because it was part of the postwar controversy, but because it presents more general knowledge or explanation of the Cowpens battle.

I evaluated authors for accuracy by cross-checking with all other sources and resolving apparent conflicts in the accounts. What eventually emerged was a clearer picture because the battle was based on a sequence of base-line episodes. Patterns that crosscut rank, position, and loyalty to a cause provided a framework and means of evaluating testimony about when and where something occurred.

Once episodes were identified spatially and chronologically, various document classes provided additional details. Pension documents were especially revealing. Battle information in a pension file was often minimal and disjointed, but when placed within the context of a specific episode, details recalled long after the event expand what little is known two hundred years later. These details are particularly important because they were never intended for explicating the Cowpens fighting.

As an example, understanding what North Carolina skirmishers did on the right flank came from pension records that mentioned saber wounds. In the absence of any known encounter between dragoons and North Carolina militia, a search was made for an event in which militiamen were assaulted by the dragoons. A Tory provided the key when he noted that provincials were broken by a charge of Ogilvie and the 71st. Once an encounter was confirmed, it was possible to attribute other accounts to the flank fighting based on recollections by men in the same units.

For a Cowpens campaign overview, the best primary sources are Tarleton's *Campaigns*, Stedman's *American War*, and Williams's "Narrative of the Campaign of 1780."

Secondary overviews are Ward's *Delaware Continentals*, Dederer's *Making Bricks without Straw*, Johnson's *Sketches of the Life and Correspondence of Nathanael Greene*, Lambert's *South Carolina Loyalists*, Myers's *Cowpens Papers*, Pancake's *Destructive War*, Schenk's *North Carolina*, and Weigley's *Partisan War*. Several dissertations were used, including Bartholomees's analysis of militia combat, Conrad's work on Nathanael Greene and the Southern Campaign, Ferguson's dissertation on Andrew Pickens, Pugh's study of the Cowpens Campaign, and Treacy's published version of her dissertation, *Prelude to Yorktown*.

For the armies, an overview is available in Duffy's *Military Experience in the Age of Reason*. The American military is outlined in Berg's *Encyclopedia of Continental Army Units*, but more details are found in Peterson's *Book of the Continental Soldier*. Detailed presentations on specific American units are in Diehl's "Rockbridge Men at War," Papenfuse and Stiverson's "General Smallwood's Recruits," Sanchez-Saavedra's *Guide to Virginia Militia*, Steuart's *Maryland Line*, and Ward's *Delaware Continentals*. Katcher's *Encyclopedia of British, Provincial and German Army Units* and Kemp's *British Army* were useful short overviews of the British army. Specific units were covered by Clark's *Loyalists in the Southern Campaign*, Fortescue's *History of the 17th Lancers*, Groves's *Historical Records of the 7th*, Keltie's *History of the Scottish Highlands*, Raddall's "Tarleton's Legion," Stewart's *Sketches of . . . the Highlanders*, and Wheater's *Historical Record of the Seventh or Royal Regiment*.

Tactics and weaponry are discussed in a variety of sources. Minutiae are well covered, though scattered, in *The Military Collector and Historian* and Calver and Bolton's *History Written with Pick and Shovel*. Artillery is presented in Caruana's study of three-pounders and Gooding's *Introduction to British Artillery*. Individual weapons are well covered by Darling's *Red Coat and Brown Bess*, Neumann's *Swords and Blades* and *Weapons*, and Peterson's *Arms and Armor* and *The Book of the Continental Soldier*.

How weapons were employed comes from contemporary manuals. The 1764 *Manual Exercise* is a starting point for understanding British battlefield movements. Grant's *New Highland Military Discipline* shows differences between English and Scottish approaches. For the Americans, Riling's republication of the Von Steuben *Regulations* is essential, but the best analysis of Von Steuben, by far, is Peterkin's *Exercise of Arms*. Many authors have written on the battle. The most useful are contemporaries Henry Lee, William Johnson, and John Marshall. Secondary authors include Kenneth Roberts, M. F. Treacy, and Thomas J. Fleming.

The battle can be subdivided into episodes including prebattle skirmishing, skirmish line, militia line, main line, flank fighting, cavalry actions, and pursuit. Each episode contributed to the battle's outcome but not everyone saw these events in the same way, much less wrote about them. Accordingly, discussion of sources has relied on different accounts for each event.

For the prebattle skirmishing, Tarleton's *Campaigns* provides a framework, but some skirmishing is detailed in Everheart's pension application and James Simons's supporting letter. The three accounts provide a matrix for pension documents and later, though still contemporary, accounts from local historians.

The best sources on the skirmish line are Hammond, Hanger, McJunkin, and Morgan, including some later writings based on statements Hammond and McJunkin made after the battle. William Johnson is fairly useful in providing details about the skirmish line. His known associates include William Washington, and Johnson himself probably visited the battlefield. However, his quotations should be questioned.

To understand the militia-line organization and its short fight, the best sources are Christopher Brandon, James Collins, Robert Long, and Roderick MacKenzie. Details are in Howard's various writings and in the Seymour and Anderson journals. While Johnson provides details, his version of the militia withdrawal misled historians, even though it was not supported by contemporaries or participants. Saye's "Memoir of McJunkin" should be treated with caution in many places. It is based on earlier writings by McJunkin and can be compared with his pension for accuracy.

Main-line fighting was best detailed by Howard in several accounts, including a letter to John Marshall that addresses specific questions about his actions. Other sources are Anderson, Seymour, and Benjamin Martin of Combs's Virginians. Tarleton, Hanger, MacKenzie, Kelty, and Stewart provide British viewpoints.

The flank fighting is a melange of cryptic commentary. The pension records mention saber wounds that must be explained. Chesney provided a setting for a dragoon–North Carolina encounter by reporting a contest between McDowell, the dragoons, and 71st.

Cavalry actions are best described by Young and Simons. When their accounts are combined with Tarleton, a different sequence of mounted activity emerges than that in traditional versions. Lee is a secondary source with considerable detail. He had many opportunities to discuss the engagement with Washington during their later campaigns in 1781.

Pursuit is covered by Young; Tarleton and Otterson provide support. Details are found in Seymour, Howard, and pension documents. Johnson misled historians by saying Tarleton's baggage was plundered by Tories. Local historians provided information about Tarleton's retreat in terms of the early nineteenth century.

Sites can be identified in Mills's *Atlas* and then tentatively marked on modern county road maps. Cartographic overviews which proved useful were the 1775 Mouzon Map and the 1773 Cook Map. (Tarleton's use of "Thickelle" Creek suggests he was using the Mouzon map.) Faden's map illustrating Tarleton's *Campaigns* was helpful. Some background material was obtained by working with Collet's 1770 map. Of particular utility were modern topographic and county road maps of the operations area. These detailed maps show the modern road network, streams, and ridges in detail. Comparing them to eighteenth-century maps, Mills's, and written material helped pinpoint prebattle movements as well as the pursuit. The best battlefield maps are the Hammond, Pigree, and Clove maps, as well as a two-foot contour survey of the park.

There are many minor details from varied sources which make the battle come alive, especially in the pension files. Too numerous to mention in detail, they are cited in the text. Three pension accounts serve as examples. Tramell provides key elements of the militia line's right flank and command structure, as well as a revealing comment by Morgan. Wells comments on the movements of the Delaware Company and mentions he was wearing coat, vest, and shirt when wounded. Martin details Virginia militia units and places his company in the Green River Road while naming the Maryland officers next to him.

MANUSCRIPT SOURCES
Baltimore, Maryland
Maryland Historical Society
  Bayard Papers
    John Eager Howard Papers, MS 109
  Mordecai Gist Papers
    Orderly Book, Vol. 3, 26 July–15 August 1780, MS 390
  Otho Holland Williams Papers
    "Calendar of the General Otho Holland Williams Papers in the Maryland
      Historical Society," compiled and edited by Elizabeth Merritt. Works
      Project Administration, Baltimore, 1940
    Orderly Book, 1780–81, MS 768
Chapel Hill, North Carolina
Wilson Library, University of North Carolina
  Southern Historical Collection
    Benjamin Franklin Perry Papers
Cleveland, Ohio
Case Western Reserve Historical Society
  Draper Papers, VV
Dallas, Texas
Dallas Historical Society
  Henry C. Coit Collection
London, England
  Cook, James. "Map of the Province of South Carolina, with All Rivers, Creeks,
    Bays, Inletts" (N.p., 1773)
New York, New York
New-York Historical Society
  Horatio Gates Papers
Princeton, New Jersey
Princeton University
  Thorne Boudinot Collection
    Uzal Johnson, "Manuscript Diary Kept by a Loyalist Military Surgeon"
Raleigh, North Carolina
Division of Archives and History, North Carolina Department of Cultural Resources
  Treasurer and Comptroller Papers
    British Soldier's Account Book
    Military Papers
  Collet, John. "A Compleat Map of North-Carolina from an Actual Survey"
    (London, 1770)
  Mouzon, Henry. "An Accurate Map of North and South Carolina" (London, 1770)
Washington, D.C.
Library of Congress
  Otho H. Williams, "Orderly Book of the 6th Maryland Regiment, 4 April–11
    August 1780"
National Archives
  "The Clove Map," RG 93, "Miscellaneous Numbered Records of the
    Revolutionary War, Microcopy 859, Roll 82, document no. 23813

"The Pigree Map," RG 93, "Miscellaneous Numbered Records of the Revolutionary War," Microcopy 859, Roll 97, document no. 28475

Revolutionary War Pension Applications and Bounty-Land-Warrant Application Files, RG 15, Microcopy 804

NEWSPAPERS
Gaffney Ledger
Newberry Conservatist
Niles Weekly Register
Pennsylvania Packet

BOOKS AND ARTICLES

Alexander, Arthur J. "How Maryland Tried to Raise Her Continental Quotas." *Maryland Historical Magazine* 42 (1942): 184–96.

Alexander, J. B. *The History of Mecklenburg County from 1740 to 1900*. Charlotte, N.C., 1982.

Anderson, Thomas. "Journal of Lieutenant Thomas Anderson of the Delaware Regiment, 1780–1782." *Historical Magazine* 1 (1867): 207–11.

Anonymous. "Account of Richard Anderson." *Niles Weekly Register* 32 (Mar.–Sept. 1827): 200.

Anonymous. "Revolutionary Incidents." *Magnolia* 1 (1842): 42.

Army, British. *A List of All the Officers of the Army: Viz. the General and Field Officers; the Officers of the Several Troops, Regiments, Independent Companies, and Garrisons: With an Alphabetical Index to the Whole*. London, 1780.

——. *A List of All the Officers of the Army: Viz. the General and Field Officers; the Officers of the Several Troops, Regiments, Independent Companies, and Garrisons: With an Alphabetical Index to the Whole*. London, 1781.

Babits, Lawrence E. "The 'Fifth' Maryland at Guilford Courthouse: An Exercise in Historical Accuracy." *Maryland Historical Magazine* 84 (1989): 370–78.

Bailey, J. D. *Commanders at Kings Mountain*. Greenville, S.C., 1980.

——. *History of Grindal Shoals and Some Early Adjacent Families*. Greenville, S.C., 1981.

Baker, Thomas E. *Another Such Victory*. New York, 1981.

Balch, Thomas, ed. *Papers Relating Chiefly to the Maryland Line during the Revolution*. Philadelphia, 1857.

Bass, Robert D. *The Green Dragoon*. Columbia, S.C., 1973.

Bearss, Edwin C. *The Battle of Cowpens*. Washington, D.C., 1967.

——. *Historic Grounds and Resources Study: Cowpens National Battlefield, South Carolina*. Denver, 1975.

Beatty, William. "Journal of Capt. William Beatty, 1776–1781." *Maryland Historical Magazine* 3 (1908): 104–19.

Berg, Fred A. *Encyclopedia of Continental Army Units*. Harrisburg, Pa., 1972.

Bishop, R. L., S. B. Rochester, W. E. Jones, and W. A. Davis. *Soil Survey of Cherokee County, South Carolina*. Washington, D.C., 1962.

Black, Jeremy. *War for America*. New York, 1991.

Boyd, Julian P., ed. *The Papers of Thomas Jefferson*. Vols. 4–5. Princeton, N.J., 1951–52.

Brawley, James S. *The Rowan Story, 1753–1953*. Salisbury, N.C., 1953.

Brown, Tarleton. *Memoirs of Tarleton Brown, a Captain in the Revolutionary Army, Written by Himself.* Barnwell, S.C., 1894.

Calderhead, William L. "Thomas Carney: Unsung Soldier of the American Revolution." *Maryland Historical Magazine* 84 (1989): 319–27.

Calver, W. L., and R. P. Bolton. *History Written with Pick and Shovel.* New York, 1966.

Campbell, Colin, ed. *Journal of an Expedition against the Rebels of Georgia in North America under the Orders of Archibald Campbell.* Darien, Ga., 1981.

Carroll, B. R. "Random Recollections of Revolutionary Characters and Incidents." *Southern Literary Journal and Magazine of Arts* 4 (1838): 40–47, 97–107.

Caruana, Adrian B. *Grasshoppers and Butterflies: The Light 3-Pounders of Pattison and Townshend.* Bloomfield, Ontario, 1980.

———. *The Light 6-Pdr. Battalion Gun of 1776.* Bloomfield, Ontario, 1977.

Chalkley, Lyman. *Chronicles of the Scotch-Irish Settlement in Virginia.* Baltimore, 1966.

Chastellux, Marquis de. *Travels in North America in the Years 1780, 1781 and 1782.* Vol. 2, edited by Howard C. Rice Jr. Chapel Hill, N.C., 1963.

Clark, Murtie June. *Loyalists in the Southern Campaign.* 3 vols. Baltimore, 1981.

Clark, Walter, ed. *The State Records of North Carolina.* Vol. 15. Raleigh, 1898. Reprint. New York, 1970.

Collins, James P. *Autobiography of a Revolutionary Soldier.* 1859. Reprint. New York, 1979.

Commager, Henry S., and Richard B. Morris. *The Spirit of 'Seventy-Six.* New York, 1958.

Crow, Jeffrey J., and Larry E. Tise, eds. *The Southern Experience in the American Revolution.* Chapel Hill, N.C., 1978.

Cuneo, John R. *Robert Rogers of the Rangers.* Ticonderoga, N.Y., 1988.

Curtis, E. E. *The Organization of the British Army in the American Revolution.* New Haven, Conn., 1926.

Dann, John C. *The Revolution Remembered.* Chicago, 1980.

Darling, Anthony D. *Red Coat and Brown Bess.* Ottawa, Ontario, 1970.

Davidson, Chalmers G. *Piedmont Partisan.* Davidson, N.C., 1968.

Davis, Robert S., Jr. *Georgia Citizens and Soldiers of the American Revolution.* Easley, S.C., 1983.

Dederer, John M. *Making Bricks without Straw: Nathanael Greene's Southern Campaign and Mao Tse-Tung's Mobile War.* Manhattan, Kans., 1983.

Delaware, State of. *Delaware Archives: Military.* 3 vols. Wilmington, Del., 1911–19.

Delbruck, Hans. *History of the Art of War.* Vol. 1. Westport, Conn., 1980.

Diehl, George W. "Rockbridge Men at War, 1760–1782." *Daughters of the American Revolution Magazine* (March 1968): 261–65, 360.

Dinter, Elmar. *Hero or Coward.* London, 1985.

Dollard, John, and Donald Horton. *Fear in Battle.* New York, 1976.

Draper, Lyman C. *King's Mountain and Its Heroes.* Baltimore, 1974.

Duffy, Christopher. *The Military Experience in the Age of Reason.* New York, 1987.

Dunbar, Gary S. "Colonial Carolina Cowpens." *Agricultural History* 35 (1961): 125–30.

Duncan, Louis C. *Medical Men in the American Revolution, 1775–1783.* Carlisle Barracks, Pa., 1931.

du Picq, Ardent. *Battle Studies.* Harrisburg, Pa., 1946.

Dupuy, Trevor N., Curt Johnson, and Grace P. Hayes. *Dictionary of Military Terms.* New York, 1986.

Elting, John R. *The Era of the American Revolution.* San Rafael, Calif., 1974.

Engles, Donald W. *Alexander the Great and the Logistics of the Macedonian Army.* Berkeley, Calif., 1978.

Ervin, Samuel J. *A Colonial History of Rowan County, North Carolina.* James Sprunt Historical Publications, vol. 16, no. 1. Chapel Hill, N.C., 1917.

Faden, William. "The Marches of Lord Cornwallis in the Southern Provinces." Frontispiece map in Banastre Tarleton, *The Campaigns of 1780 and 1781 in the Southern Provinces of North America.* Dublin, 1786. Reprint. Spartanburg, S.C., 1967.

Feaster, William R., ed. *A History of Union County, South Carolina.* Greenville, S.C., 1977.

Fetter, Frank W. "Who Were the Foreign Mercenaries of the Declaration of Independence?" *Pennsylvania Magazine of History and Biography* 104 (1980): 508–13.

Fleming, Thomas J. *Cowpens.* Washington, D.C., 1988.

———. *Now We Are Enemies.* New York, 1960.

Ford, Worthington C. *British Officers Serving in the American Revolution, 1774–1783.* Brooklyn, N.Y., 1897.

Fortescue, J. W. *A History of the 17th Lancers.* London, 1895.

Fox, Richard A., Jr. *Archaeology, History, and Custer's Last Battle.* Norman, Okla., 1993.

Gabriel, Richard A. *No More Heroes: Madness and Psychiatry in War.* New York, 1987.

Galvin, John R. *The Minute Men.* Washington, D.C., 1989.

Garden, Alexander, ed. *Anecdotes of the Revolutionary War in America.* Charleston, S.C., 1822.

Georgia, State of. *The Counties of the State of Georgia.* Savannah, 1981.

Gibbon, John. *The Artillerist's Manual.* New York, 1860. Reprint. Westport, Conn., 1970.

Gooding, S. James. *An Introduction to British Artillery in North America.* Ottawa, Ontario, 1972.

Gordon, William. *The History of the Rise, Progress, and Establishment of the Independence of the United States of America.* 4 vols. London, 1788.

Gorgas, Josiah. *The Ordnance Manual for the Use of the Officers of the Confederate States Army.* Richmond, Va., 1863. Reprint. Dayton, Ohio, 1976.

Graham, James. *The Life of General Daniel Morgan.* New York, 1859.

Graham, Joshua. "General Joseph Graham's Narrative of the Revolutionary War in North Carolina in 1780 and 1781." In *The Papers of Archibald D. Murphey*, edited by William H. Hoyt, 2:212–311. Raleigh, 1914.

Graham, Samuel. "An English Officer's Account of His Services in America, 1779–1781." *Historical Magazine* 9 (1865): 241–49, 267–73.

Grant, George. *The New Highland Military Discipline.* Ottawa, Ontario, 1967.

Griffen, Clarence W. *History of Old Tryon and Rutherford Counties, North Carolina, 1730–1936.* Asheville, N.C., 1937.

Groves, Percy. *Historical Records of the 7th or Royal Regiment of Fusiliers.* Guernsey, England, 1903.

Haggis, Obadiah. "Firesides Revisiting." *Newberry Conservatist,* 11 May 1858.

Hall, Clayton C., Henry Stockbridge, and Bernard C. Steiner, eds. *Muster Rolls and Other Records of the Service of Maryland Troops in the American Revolution*. Vol. 18 of *Maryland Archives*. Baltimore, 1900. Reprint. Baltimore, 1972.

Hanger, George (Lord Coleraine). *An Address to the Army in Reply to Strictures by Roderick M'Kenzie (Late Lieut. in the 71st Regmt.) on Tarleton's History of the Campaigns of 1780 and 1781*. London, 1789.

———. *Colonel George Hanger to All Sportsmen*. Richmond, Surrey, England, 1814.

———. *The Life, Adventures, and Opinions of Col. George Hanger*. London, 1801.

Hartz, Louis. *The Liberal Tradition in America*. New York, 1983.

Harvey, Edward. *The Manual Exercise as Ordered by His Majesty, in 1764*. New York, 1775.

Hatch, Charles E., Jr. *The Battle of Guilford Courthouse*. Washington, D.C., 1971.

Hauley, R., W. Bub, and W. Frueh, eds. *A Collection of Standardized Fife Tunes and Drum Accompanyment from the Period 1775–1783*. Albany, N.Y., 1989.

Hay, Gertrude S. *Roster of Soldiers from North Carolina in the Revolution*. Baltimore, 1972.

Heitman, Francis B. *Historical Register of Officers of the Continental Army*. Baltimore, 1982.

Higginbotham, Don. *Daniel Morgan, Revolutionary Rifleman*. Chapel Hill, N.C., 1961.

———. *The War of American Independence*. Bloomington, Ind., 1971.

———. *George Washington and the American Military Tradition*. Athens, Ga., 1985.

Hill, J. Michael. "Killiecrankie and the Evolution of Highland Warfare." *War in History* 1 (1994): 125–39.

Hoffman, Ronald, et al., eds. *An Uncivil War: The Southern Backcountry during the American Revolution*. Charlottesville, Va., 1985.

Hollingsworth, J. G. *History of Surry County*. N.p., 1935.

Holschlag, Stephanie L., and Michael J. Rodeffer. *Ninety Six: Siege Works Opposite Star Redoubt*. Ninety Six, S.C., 1976.

Holschlag, Stephanie, Michael J. Rodeffer, and Marvin L. Cann. *Ninety Six: The Jail*. Ninety Six, S.C., 1978.

Howard, Cary. "John Eager Howard: Patriot and Public Servant." *Maryland Historical Magazine* 62 (1967): 300–317.

Hoyt, William H., ed. *The Papers of Archibald D. Murphey*. Raleigh, N.C., 1914.

Hunter, C. L. *Sketches of Western North Carolina Historical and Biographical*. Raleigh, N.C., 1877.

Johnson, Joseph. *Traditions and Reminiscences Chiefly of the American Revolution in the South*. Charleston, S.C., 1851.

Johnson, William. *Sketches of the Life and Correspondence of Nathanael Greene*. 2 vols. Charleston, S.C., 1822.

Jones, Charles C. *Biographical Sketches of the Delegates from Georgia to the Continental Congress*. Spartanburg, S.C., 1972.

Jones, E. Alfred, ed. *The Journal of Alexander Chesney*. London, 1921. Reprint. Easley, S.C., n.d.

Jones, John. *Plain, Concise Practical Remarks on the Treatment of Wounds and Fractures*. Philadelphia, 1776. Reprint. New York, 1971.

Katcher, Phillip R. N. *Encyclopedia of British, Provincial and German Army Units, 1775–1783*. Harrisburg, Pa., 1973.

———. *Uniforms of the Continental Army*. York, Pa., 1981.

Keegan, John. *The Face of Battle*. New York, 1977.

Kelly, James C., and William C. Baker. *The Sword of the Lord and Gideon: A Catalogue of Historical Objects Related to the Battle of King's Mountain*. Boone, N.C., 1980.

Keltie, John S. *A History of the Scottish Highlands, Highland Clans and Highland Regiments*. Edinburgh, 1877.

Kemp, Alan. *The British Army in the American Revolution*. London, 1973.

Lamb, Roger. *An Original and Authentic Journal of Occurrences during the Late American War from Its Commencement to the Year 1783*. 1809. Reprint. New York, 1968.

Lambert, Robert S. *South Carolina Loyalists in the American Revolution*. Columbia, S.C., 1987.

Lancaster, Bruce. *The American Revolution*. New York, 1985.

Landers, H. L. *Historical Statements Concerning the Battle of Kings Mountain and the Battle of the Cowpens, South Carolina*. Washington, D.C., 1928.

Landrum, J. B. O. *Colonial and Revolutionary History of Upper South Carolina*. Greenville, S.C., 1897.

———. *History of Spartanburg County*. Atlanta, 1900.

Lawrence, Alexander A. *Storm over Savannah*. Athens, Ga., 1951.

Lawson, Cecil C. P. *A History of the Uniforms of the British Army*. London, 1961.

Lee, Henry. *Memoirs of the War in the Southern Department of the United States*. 2 vols. New York, 1812. Reprint. New York, 1970.

Lee, Henry, Jr. *The Campaign of 1781 in the Carolinas; With Remarks Historical and Critical on Johnson's "Life of Greene"*. Philadelphia, 1824. Reprint. Spartanburg, S.C., 1975.

Lee, Robert E., ed. *The American Revolution in the South*. New York, 1869. Reprint. New York, 1969.

Lees, William. "When the Shooting Stopped, the War Began." In *Look to the Earth*, edited by Clarence Geier and Susan Frye, 39–59. Knoxville, Tenn., 1994.

Lesser, Charles H. *The Sinews of Independence*. Chicago, 1976.

Logan, John H., ed. *A History of the Upper Country of South Carolina*. 2 vols. Charleston, S.C., 1859. Reprint. Easley, S.C., 1980.

Long, Robert. "Statement of Robert Long." In *A History of the Upper Country of South Carolina*, edited by John H. Logan, 2:1–12. 1859. Reprint. Easley, S.C., 1980.

Lumpkin, Henry. *From Savannah to Yorktown*. Columbia, S.C., 1981.

McAllister, J. T. *Virginia Militia in the Revolutionary War*. Hot Springs, Va., 1913.

McCall, Mrs. Howard H. *Roster of Revolutionary Soldiers of Georgia*. Baltimore, 1969.

M'Call, Hugh. *The History of Georgia*. 2 vols. 1811, 1816. Reprint. Atlanta, 1981.

McConkey, Rebecca. *The Hero of Cowpens*. New York, 1881.

McConnell, David. *British Smooth-Bore Artillery: A Technological Study*. Ottawa, Ontario, 1988.

McCrady, Edward. *The History of South Carolina in the Revolution, 1775–1780*. New York, 1969.

———. *The History of South Carolina in the Revolution, 1780–1783*. New York, 1902.

MacKenzie, Roderick. *Strictures on Lt. Col. Tarleton's History "of the Campaign of 1780 and 1781, in the Southern Provinces of North America."* London, 1987.

Marshall, John. *The Life of George Washington.* 2 vols. New York, 1804–7. Reprint. 4 vols. Fredricksburg, Va., 1926.

Marshall, S. L. A. *Men Against Fire.* New York, 1947.

——. *The Soldier's Load and the Mobility of a Nation.* Quantico, Va., 1980.

Matlof, Maurice. *American Military History.* Washington, D.C., 1969.

Mills, Robert. 1825. Reprint. *Mills' Atlas of the State of South Carolina.* Easley, S.C., 1980.

——. *Statistics of South Carolina.* Charleston, S.C., 1826.

Moon, John C. *An Instructor for the Drum.* Williamsburg, Va., 1981.

Morrill, Dan L. *Southern Campaigns of the American Revolution.* Baltimore, 1992.

Moss, Bobby G. *The Patriots at the Cowpens.* Greenville, S.C., 1985.

——. *Roster of South Carolina Patriots in the American Revolution.* Baltimore, 1985.

Moultrie, William. *Memoirs of the American Revolution, So Far as It Related to the States of North and South Carolina, and Georgia.* 2 vols. New York, 1802.

Muller, John. *A Treatise of Artillery, 1780.* London, 1780. Reprint. Ottawa, Ontario, 1977.

Myers, Theodorus B. *Cowpens Papers.* Charleston, S.C., 1881.

Neumann, George C. *The History of Weapons of the American Revolution.* New York, 1967.

——. *Swords and Blades of the American Revolution.* Harrisburg, Pa., 1973.

O'Neall, J. B. "Revolutionary Incidents—Memoir of Joseph M'Junkin, of Union." *Magnolia* 2 (1843): 30–40.

O'Neall, John B., and John A. Chapman. *The Annals of Newberry.* Baltimore, 1974.

Palmer, William P., et al., eds. *Calendar of Virginia State Papers.* 11 vols. Richmond, Va., 1875–93.

Pancake, John S. *This Destructive War: The British Campaign in the Carolinas, 1780–1781.* University, Ala., 1985.

Papenfuse, Edward C., and Gregory A. Stiverson. "General Smallwood's Recruits: The Peacetime Career of the Revolutionary War Private." *William and Mary Quarterly* 30 (1973): 117–32.

Peterkin, Ernest W. *The Exercise of Arms in the Continental Infantry.* Alexandria Bay, N.Y., 1989.

Peterson, Harold L. *Arms and Armor in Colonial America.* Harrisburg, Pa., 1956.

——. *The Book of the Continental Soldier.* Harrisburg, Pa., 1968.

Phifer, Edward W. *Burke: The History of a North Carolina County, 1770–1920.* Morganton, N.C., 1977.

Pickens, A. L. *Skyagunsta, the Border Wizard Owl: Major General Andrew Pickens (1739–1817).* Greenville, S.C., 1934.

Pickering, Timothy. *An Easy Plan of Discipline for a Militia.* Salem, Mass., 1775.

Pindell, Richard. "A Militant Surgeon of the Revolution: Some Letters of Richard Pindell." *Maryland Historical Magazine* 18 (1923): 309–23.

Pope, Thomas H. *The History of Newberry County, South Carolina.* Columbia, S.C., 1973.

Posey, John T. *General Thomas Posey, Son of the American Revolution.* East Lansing, Mich., 1992.

Powell, William S. *The North Carolina Gazetteer.* Chapel Hill, N.C., 1968.

Raddall, Thomas H. "Tarleton's Legion." *Collections of the Nova Scotia Historical Society* 28 (1949): 1–50.

Ramsay, David. *The History of the American Revolution.* London, 1793.

———. *Ramsay's History of the Revolution in South Carolina.* Trenton, N.J., 1785. Reprint. Spartanburg, S.C., 1968.

Rankin, Hugh F. "Cowpens: Prelude to Yorktown." *North Carolina Historical Review* 31 (1954): 336–69.

———. *Greene and Cornwallis: The Campaign in the Carolinas.* Raleigh, N.C., 1976.

———. *The North Carolina Continentals.* Chapel Hill, N.C., 1971.

Read, Elizabeth. "John Eager Howard." *Magazine of American History* 7 (1881): 276–82.

"A Recollection of the American Revolutionary War by a British Officer." *Virginia Historical Register* 6 (1853): 204–11.

Reese, George H., comp. *The Cornwallis Papers.* Charlottesville, Va., 1969.

Riling, Joseph R. *Baron Von Steuben and His Regulations.* Philadelphia, 1966.

Roberts, Kenneth. *The Battle of Cowpens.* Garden City, N.Y., 1976.

Rockwell, J. R. "The Battle of Cow-pens." *Historical Magazine* 2 (1867): 356–59.

Rumple, Jethro. *A History of Rowan County, North Carolina.* Edited by Edith M. Clark. Baltimore, 1974.

Russell, T. Triplett, and John K. Gott. *Fauquier County in the Revolution.* Warrenton, Va., 1976.

Salley, A. S., Jr., ed. *Colonel William Hill's Memoirs of the Revolution.* Columbia, S.C., 1921.

Sanchez-Saavedra, E. M., comp. *A Guide to Virginia Militia Organizations in the American Revolution.* Richmond, Va., 1978.

Saye, James H. *Memoirs of Major Joseph McJunkin.* 1847. Reprint. Greenville, S.C., 1981.

Schenk, David. *North Carolina, 1780–1781: Being a History of the Invasion of the Carolinas.* Raleigh, N.C., 1887.

Scott, Douglas D., and Richard A. Fox Jr. *Archaeological Insights into the Custer Battle.* Norman, Okla., 1987.

Scott, Douglas D., Richard A. Fox Jr., Melissa A. Connor, and Dick Harmon. *Archaeological Perspectives on the Battle of the Little Bighorn.* Norman, Okla., 1989.

Scott, Douglas D., and William B. Hunt Jr. "The Civil War Battle of Monroe's Crossroads, Fort Bragg, North Carolina: An Historical Archaeological Perspective." National Park Service, Lincoln, Nebr., 1998.

Seymour, William. *A Journal of the Southern Expedition, 1780–1783.* Wilmington, Del., 1896.

Shaw, John R. *A Narrative of the Life and Travels of John Robert Shaw, the Well Digger.* 1807. Reprint. Lexington, Ky., 1931.

Shaw, Samuel. "Captain Samuel Shaw's Revolutionary War Letters to Captain Winthrop Sargent." *Pennsylvania Magazine of History and Biography* 70 (1946): 281–324.

Shea, William L. *The Virginia Militia in the Seventeenth Century.* Baton Rouge, La., 1983.

Showman, Richard K., et al., eds. *The Papers of General Nathanael Greene.* 10 vols. to date. Chapel Hill, N.C., 1980–98.

Shy, John. *A People Numerous and Armed: Reflections on the Military Struggle for American Independence.* New York, 1976.

Simcoe, John Graves. *Simcoe's Military Journal.* 1784. Reprint. Toronto, Ontario, 1962.

Smith, George. *An Universal Military Dictionary.* 1779. Reprint. Ottawa, Ontario, 1969.

Smith, Samuel S., and John R. Elting. "British Light Infantry, 1775–1800." *Military Collector and Historian* 27 (1975): 87–89.

Smoler, Frederic. "The Secret of the Soldiers Who Didn't Shoot." *American Heritage* 40, no. 2 (1989): 37–45.

Sons of the American Revolution. *Mecklenburg in the Revolution.* Charlotte, N.C., 1931.

Sparks, Jarod, ed. *Correspondence of the American Revolution: Being Letters of Eminent Men to George Washington, from the Time of His Taking Command of the Army to the End of His Presidency.* 12 vols. Boston, 1853.

Stedman, Charles. *The History of the Origin, Progress, and Termination of the American War.* 1794. Reprint. New York, 1969.

Stember, Sol. *The Bicentennial Guide to the American Revolution.* New York, 1974.

Steuart, Rieman. *A History of the Maryland Line in the Revolutionary War, 1775–1783.* Towson, Md., 1969.

Stevens, William. *A System for the Discipline of the Artillery of the United States of America.* New York, 1797.

Stevenson, W. F. *Wounds in War.* New York, 1898.

Stewart, David. *Sketches of the Character, Manners, and Present State of the Highlanders of Scotland.* 2 vols. Edinburgh, 1822.

Tarleton, Banastre. *A History of the Campaigns of 1780–1781 in Southern America.* 1787. Reprint. Spartanburg, S.C., 1967.

Tilden, G. "The Accoutrements of the British Infantryman, 1640–1940." *Journal of the Society for Army Historical Research* 47 (1969): 4–22.

Treacy, M. F. *Prelude to Yorktown.* Chapel Hill, N.C., 1963.

Turner, Frederick J. "Western State-Making in the Revolutionary Era." *American Historical Review* 1 (October 1895–July 1896): 70–87, 251–69.

Turner, Joseph B., ed. *The Journal and Order Book of Captain Robert Kirkwood of the Delaware Regiment of the Continental Line.* Wilmington, Del., 1910.

Uhlendorf, Bernard, ed. *The Siege of Charleston with an Account of the Province of South Carolina.* Ann Arbor, Mich., 1938.

Ultee, Maarten, ed. *Adapting to Conditions: War and Society in the Eighteenth Century.* University, Ala., 1986.

U.S. Bureau of the Census. *A Census of Pensioners for Revolutionary or Military Service.* Washington, D.C., 1841.

U.S. Geological Survey. *Cowpens Quadrangle,* 15-minute series (map). Washington, D.C., 1959.

Urwin, Gregory J. W. *The United States Infantry.* New York, 1988.

Ward, Christopher L. *The Delaware Continentals.* Wilmington, Del., 1941.

Weigley, Russell F. *The Partisan War: The South Carolina Campaign of 1780–1782*. Columbia, S.C., 1970.

Wheater, W. *Historical Record of the Seventh or Royal Regiment of Fusiliers*. Leeds, England, 1875.

White, Emmett R. *Revolutionary War Soldiers of Western North Carolina: Burke County*. Easley, S.C., 1984.

White, George. *Historical Collections of Georgia*. 1855. Reprint. Baltimore, 1969.

Wickwire, Francis, and Mary Wickwire. *Cornwallis: The American Adventure*. Boston, 1970.

Williams, Otho H. "A Narrative of the Campaign of 1780." In *Sketches of the Life and Correspondence of Nathanael Greene*, edited by William Johnson, 485–510. Charleston, S.C., 1822.

Williams, Samuel C., ed. "General Richard Winn's Notes, 1780." *The South Carolina Historical and Genealogical Magazine* 44 (1943): 1–10.

Wilson, Howard M. *Great Valley Patriots: Western Virginia in the Struggle for Liberty*. Verone, Va., 1976.

Winham, William. *A Plan of Discipline, Composed for the Use of the Militia of the County of Norfolk*. 1759. Reprint. Ottawa, Ontario, 1969.

Wood, W. J. *Battles of the Revolutionary War*. Chapel Hill, N.C., 1990.

Wyngaarden, James B., and Lloyd H. Smith Jr., eds. *Textbook of Medicine*. Philadelphia, 1988.

Young, Thomas. "Memoir of Major Thomas Young." *Orion* 3 (1843): 84–88, 100–105.

DISSERTATIONS, THESES, AND UNPUBLISHED PAPERS

Babits, Lawrence E. "Military Documents and Archaeological Sites: Methodological Contributions to Historical Archaeology." Ph.D. diss., Brown University, Providence, R.I., 1981.

Bartholomees, James B. "Fight or Flee: The Combat Performance of the North Carolina Militia in the Cowpens–Guilford Courthouse Campaign, January to March 1781." Ph.D. diss., University of North Carolina, Chapel Hill, N.C., 1978.

Catron, Lisa. "Go West, Young Veteran: Testing the Turner Hypothesis with the Patriots of Cowpens." Ms. on file, Department of History, Armstrong State College, Savannah, Ga., 1989.

Conrad, Dennis M. "Nathanael Greene and the Southern Campaigns, 1780–1783." Ph.D. diss., Duke University, Durham, N.C., 1979.

Ferguson, Clyde R. "General Andrew Pickens." Ph.D. diss., Duke University, Durham, N.C., 1960.

Pugh, R. C. "The Cowpens Campaign and the American Revolution." Ph.D. diss., University of Illinois, Urbana, Ill., 1951.

Strack, Stephen G. "History of the Three Pound Verbruggen Gun and Its Use in North America." Ms. on file, Cowpens National Battlefield, Chesnee, S.C., n.d.

Index

Cornwallis, Charles, Lord, 1, 3, 7, 10, 48, 133, 136, 147; invasion of North Carolina, 9; pursuit of Morgan and Greene, 143, 145, 146
Coulter, Lieutenant, 172 (n. 70)
Coulter's Ford Road, 62
Countersign, 54
Coventry, R.I., 5
Cowans Ford, N.C., 145
Crabtree, Richard, 81
Croes, Joseph, 139
Crowell, Thomas, 111
Cruger, John Harris, 4
Cudd's Creek. *See* Little Buck Creek
Cunningham, Major, 40, 72, 75, 82, 83
Cunningham, William, 39

Dan River, 145
Davidson, William L., 34, 144, 145
Dawson, James, 141
Dearing, William, 104, 171 (n. 45)
"Delaware Blues," 27
Deshasure (Deshaser), Henry W., 58, 135, 136, 201 (n. 78)
Dickison, Nathaniel, 139
Dickson (Dixon), Jeremiah, 38, 93, 172 (n. 70)
Dillard, James, 52, 75, 93, 183 (n. 42)
Dinning Creek, 49
Dobson, Henry, 28, 77
Donnolly, Captain, 173 (n. 89)
Dougherty, Michael, 129, 148
Draft/draftees, 30
Dragoons, 65, 66; tactics of, 20, 153. *See also* Army, British; Army, Continental
Draper, Lyman, 15, 149
Drum signals/beats, 1, 81, 117, 154–55
Dugan, James, 39, 138
Dugan, Robert, 39, 138
Duncan's Creek, 50
Duncanson, Captain, 122
Dunlap, Robert, 38
Duration. *See* Time frame
Dyer, Walter, 27

Easterwood Ford, S.C., 52
Elsbury, Lieutenant, 30
Enoree River, 51, 141
Erwin, Alexander, 171 (n. 58)
Eutaw Springs, S.C., 25, 39, 178 (n. 41)
Everheart, Lawrence, 58, 59, 127, 131, 138, 179 (n. 50), 200 (n. 53)
Ewing, James (lt., Md.), 28, 77, 120
Ewing, James (capt., S.C.), 39, 183 (n. 42)

Fair Forest Creek, 48, 49, 51
Fair Forest Meeting House, 49
Fair Forest Regiment. *See* Militia: South Carolina
Fair Forest Shoal, S.C., 49
Farr, William, 40, 75, 90
Farrow, Thomas, 39, 76, 93, 180 (n. 5), 181 (n. 15), 190 (n. 25)
Fatigue, 93, 101, 106, 113, 119, 155–59
Fauntleroy, Griffin, 41
Fauquier County, Va., 33
Ferguson, Patrick, 3
Files, Adam, 39
Files, Jeremiah, 39, 98
Files, John, Jr., 39
Files, John, Sr., 39, 76, 184 (n. 44)
First Delaware Regiment. *See* Army, Continental: Delaware
Fishdam Ford, S.C.: battle of, 44
Fishing Creek: battle of, 22, 40, 46
Flags (colors), 122, 137, 197 (n. 100), 201 (n. 5)
Fletchall, Thomas, 49
Fletcher's Mill, S.C., 141
Florida, 2
Flying Army. *See* Army, Flying
Food: American, 5, 7, 29, 52, 55, 145, 178 (n. 41); British, 9, 49, 145, 156–57, 177 (n. 25)
Forage, 5, 49, 51
Fort Granby, S.C., 5, 8
Fort Watson, S.C., 5
Fort Williams, S.C., 8, 49
Fox, Richard, 158
Fraser, Ensign, 45, 132

Frederick County, Va., 24, 168 (n. 13)
French and Indian War, 23, 40
Friday's Ferry, S.C., 5
Fusiliers. *See* Army, British: 7th Fusiliers

Gates, Horatio, 3, 24
Georgetown, S.C., 5, 8
Georgia Legion, 38
Georgia militia. *See* Militia: Georgia
Georgia refugees, 38, 58
Germain, George, Lord, 1
Gilbert Town, N.C., 138, 144
Giles, Edward, 25, 182 (n. 27)
Gilmore, James, 31, 33, 76, 101
Gist, Mordecai, 168
Glaubeck, Baron, 25, 132
Goudelock, William, 134–35
Graham, Colin, 175 (n. 116)
Graham, Joseph, 15
Grant, William, Jr., 173 (n. 83)
Grant, William, Sr., 40, 75, 136, 173
    (n. 83)
Granville County, N.C., 35
Grasse, Compte de, 147
Greene, Nathanael, 5, 24, 79, 102, 136,
    145
Green River, 56, 153, 179 (n. 45)
Green River Road, 51, 58, 60, 83, 134,
    153; road junction, 61, 62, 183 (n. 30);
    landscape feature, 63, 65, 66, 124, 186
    (n. 64); troops align on, 69–71, 78, 85,
    125
Greer, John, 52
Gresham, George, 52, 174 (n. 100)
Grindal Shoals, S.C., 49, 51, 52, 135;
    Morgan camps at, 7, 48
Guides. *See* Scouts
Guilford County, N.C., 35
Guilford Court House, N.C., 145; battle
    of, 15, 25, 41, 47, 141, 144, 146, 147, 178
    (n. 41), 201 (n. 5)
Gunnell, John, 139
Guyton, Aaron, 31, 52

Hailey, John, 149
Hamilton's Ford, S.C., 132–36

Hammett, George, 149
Hammond, Samuel: on skirmish line,
    28, 60, 65, 72, 73, 174 (n. 98), 208;
    orders to, 54, 66, 69, 72, 178 (n. 35);
    map, 66–69, 72, 77, 178 (n. 35); on
    militia line, 86, 97; on main line, 101,
    122, 125, 154
Hammond's Store, S.C., 41, 49, 141
Hampton, Captain, 30
Hampton, Samuel, 30, 36
Hanger, George (Lord Colraine), 46,
    154, 208, 209; on muskets, 13, 165
    (nn. 5, 6); on rifles, 14, 18, 165 (n. 6);
    on tactics, 18, 94; on South Carolina
    "crackers," 19; on Cowpens, 84, 128
Hanging Rock, S.C., 3
Harden, James, 38
Harris, William, 39, 75, 183 (n. 42)
Harriss, John, 106
Harvin, Edward, 166 (n. 24)
Hayes, Joseph, 31, 36, 39, 49, 73, 74, 75,
    86, 90
Hayes, Michael, 149
Hayes Rise, 63, 65, 80, 86
Hayes's Battalion. *See* Militia: South
    Carolina
Heard, Richard, 40
Hicks, Kit, 139
Hick's Creek, S.C. *See* Cheraws
Highlanders. *See* Army, British: 71st
    Regiment
Hillsborough, N.C., 3, 8, 33
Hobkirk's Hill, S.C., 16, 25, 41, 166
    (n. 24), 178 (n. 41)
Hogg, Samuel, 93
Holland, Charles, 97
Horse Creek, 62
Hovenden, Richard, 44, 81, 179 (n. 50)
Howard, John Eager, 25–26, 53, 70, 92,
    94, 130, 131, 209; and main line, 76,
    100, 102, 109; misunderstood order,
    109–12, 113; counterattack, 114, 116–17,
    120, 122, 127
Howe, Richard, 2
Howe, William, 2
Huck, Christian, 3, 175 (n. 106)

Maple Swamp, 65, 73, 74, 76, 77, 109, 120, 122

Marion, Francis, 8, 28

Marshall, John, 54, 209

Martin, Benjamin, 77, 209

Martin, Josiah, 143

Maryland and Delaware Division, 26, 45

Maryland Continental troops. *See* Army, Continental: Maryland

Maryland Regiment Extraordinary, 25

Maryland Regiment(s). *See* Army, Continental: Maryland

Matt, Michael, 205 (n. 13)

Meade, William, 107, 138

Mecklenburg County, N.C., 35

Militia, 29

—Georgia, 25, 40, 52, 58, 65, 72, 75, 82, 83, 97, 101, 125, 177 (n. 28), 187 (n. 14)

—North Carolina: Lincoln/Rutherford, 30, 35, 36, 73; Surry/Wilkes, 30, 35, 36, 73, 76, 107, 126, 144, 183 (n. 34); Rowan, 30, 35, 36, 73, 144, 145; Clark's Burke County Company, 33, 35, 76, 77; northern counties, 35; McDowell's Battalion, 35, 52, 63, 65, 72, 74, 76, 82, 83, 105, 107, 120, 122, 123, 177 (n. 23); Burke, 35, 73, 76, 81, 107, 126; in flank fight, 106, 126, 154; postwar movements, 147–48

—South Carolina, 36, 49, 52, 54, 63, 73, 77, 78, 79, 86, 89, 95, 96, 97, 98, 99, 122, 154, 157; Pickens's Long Cane Regiment, 28, 49, 177 (n. 28); Thomas's Spartanburg Regiment, 30, 36, 49, 51, 73–76, 86, 92, 95, 99, 105, 119, 120, 196 (n. 84); Hayes's Little River Regiment, 32, 39, 48, 49, 73–76, 86, 92, 93, 94, 95, 98, 99, 122, 177 (n. 28); Roebuck's Battalion (Spartanburg), 38, 49, 74–75, 92, 93, 105, 120; Tramell's Company, 38, 52, 93; Brandon's Fair Forest Regiment, 40, 73–75, 86, 90, 92, 94, 95, 98, 99, 122, 157; Pickens's Brigade,

48, 49, 51, 62, 71, 89, 119, 122; volunteer dragoons, 78, 124; smallpox in, 140–41; in North Carolina, 144; postwar movements, 147–48

—Virginia, 52, 71, 76; Gilmore's Company (Rockbridge Rifles), 31, 32, 33, 77, 101, 103; David Campbell's Regiment, 33, 34; Buchanan's Company (Augusta County), 33, 76, 101, 104; Combs's Company (Fauquier County), 33, 77, 92, 102, 104, 105, 112; Tate's (Tait) Company (Augusta County), 33, 77, 101; formation, 33–34; positioning at Cowpens, 62–63, 67, 69, 73; on third line, 76–78, 101, 115, 152, 154; in counterattack, 122, 142; in pursuit, 134–35; in North Carolina, 144; Triplett's Battalion, 151

Militia, Loyalist (Tory), 29

Militia ridge, 65, 86, 87, 123, 126

Mitchell, John, 106

Moffett, John, 40

Monck's Corner, S.C., 5, 22, 41, 44

Monmouth, N.J., 3

Montgomery, Robert, 40, 75

Morgan, Daniel, 1, 7, 10, 25, 60, 80, 100, 136; tactics of, 22, 61, 72, 73, 77–79, 86, 90, 93, 96, 124, 151–55, 208; biography, 23–24; organizes battlefield, 52, 72; decision to fight, 59, 70, 73; at militia line, 87, 89, 90, 96, 99, 100; at main line, 100, 102, 112, 113; on prisoners, 143; in North Carolina, 144, 145; on American strength, 150–52

Morgan Hill, 63, 65, 76, 78, 79, 99, 114, 119, 124, 125, 127, 186 (n. 63)

Moore, John, 168 (n. 13)

Moore, Samuel, 51, 149

Morris, Jesse, 30

Mud Lick, S.C., 38

Muller, John, 21

Musgrove's Mill, S.C., 3, 15

Musicians. *See* Drum signals/beats

Muskets, 11–14, 90, 95, 100, 103, 104, 111, 164 (n. 4), 165 (nn. 5, 6), 166 (n. 28),

192 (n. 12), 193 (nn. 16, 22), 194 (n. 45);
accuracy of, 13, 165 (nn. 6, 7), 194
(n. 45); firing of, 103, 166 (n. 28), 193
(n. 16); captured, 143

Uniforms, 47; American, 20, 101, 125, 126, 209; caps, dragoon, 20, 167 (n. 41); British, 20, 197 (n. 99), 199 (n. 25)
Union County, S.C., 39, 58, 75
Union Crossroads, S.C., 49, 51

Vance, David, 35
Verner, John, 140
Vernon, Nathaniel, 129
Videttes (pickets), 58, 59, 72, 180 (n. 60), 183 (n. 30)
Virginia Continentals. *See* Army, Continental: Virginia
Virginia militia. *See* Militia: Virginia
Virginia State Troops. *See* State troops: Virginia
Von Steuben, Frederick Wilhelm (baron), 12; manual of, 17, 31, 116, 166 (n. 28)

Wade (quartermaster), 59, 179 (n. 50)
Walker, Frank, 205 (n. 13)
Walker, Thomas, 106
Wallace, Andrew, 28, 76, 103, 115, 126, 151; "misunderstood order," 109–12, 154–55
Walton, George, 40, 173 (n. 87)
Warren, Hugh, 93
Warren, William, 111, 139
Warren County, N.C., 35
Washington, George, 5, 7, 25, 147, 150
Washington, William, 25, 27, 40, 42, 49, 54, 59, 78, 89, 124, 134, 209; at Rugeley's Mill, 6; raids Hammond's Store, 8; right flank, 109, 117; on Morgan Hill, 125; "duel" with Tarleton, 130; pursuit, 133–34; withdrawal, 144
Watkins, Gassaway, 28

Waxhaws, S.C., 2, 22, 28, 42, 44, 46, 55, 169 (n. 25), 199 (n. 28)
Way, Isaac, 122
Weather, 79, 156–57, 187 (n. 7)
Weitzell's Mill, N.C., 14
Wells, Henry, 55, 100, 121, 205 (n. 3), 209
West Indies, 2, 42, 146
Whelchel, John, 98, 138
Whiskey Rebellion, 24
White, Anthony, 41
White, Henry, 31, 38
White, Joseph, 36
White County, Tenn., 149
White Hall, S.C., 38
Whiteside, Captain, 51–52
Wilkes County, Ga., 40
Willett, Samuel, 149
Willett, Walter, 149
Williams, Otho H., 145, 168 (n. 13)
Williams's Regiment, 39
Wilmington, N.C., 146
Wilmot, Nova Scotia, 149
Wilson, George, 62
Wilson, William, 35
Winchester, Va., 24, 144
Winn, James, 33
Winn, Richard, 22, 62
Winnsboro, S.C., 3, 7; British garrison at, 5, 6; supplies at, 8
Wofford's Iron Works, 48, 51, 52
Work, John, 170 (n. 38)
Wounded. *See* Casualties, American

Yadkin River, 145
Yarborough, Captain, 170 (n. 27)
Yorktown, Va., 1, 3, 6, 144, 147
Young, Thomas, 53, 78, 103, 155, 209; on left flank, 89; counterattack, 123, 124, 126, 127; in pursuit, 132, 133, 135, 159